Also by Adrian Incledon-Webber

DVD:

Intuition – Your Hidden Treasure

Courses:

Introduction to Dowsing
Dowsing for Health I and II
Earth Energies I
Dowsing for Health and Healing I, II and III
Healing Your Home I and II
Healing with Sacred Symbols

HEAL

YOUR

HOME

TO HEAL YOURSELF

Adrian Incledon-Webber

First published in Great Britain in 2013 by Dowsing Spirits
Second Publishing in 2018 by Dowsing Spirits

Copyright © 2018. Adrian Incledon-Webber
Cover Design © 2018 Huw Lloyd-Jones

ISBN: 978-0-9957555-1-2

The moral right of the author has been asserted.

Heal Your Home is intended to complement and support, not replace, normal allopathic medicine or medical treatment. If you suffer from any acute or chronic disease you should always seek medical attention from a qualified doctor immediately. The author and publisher accept no liability for damage of any nature resulting directly or indirectly from the application or use of any information contained within this book. Any application of this method is at the reader's sole discretion and risk.

Some of the names, identities and places have been changed in the case studies used. Where real names have been used, permission has been obtained.

Second Edition

Acknowledgements

I would like to thank the following people who have made this book possible:

Andy Roberts, who opened the door that finally got me onto my correct pathway. His unique form of mentoring, his humour and patience made me see the light, literally!

My two boys, Alistair and Charles, who both thought that I was going mad at one stage but they humoured me and hey guys, look what I am doing now!

My surrogate parents, Sean and Helen O'Geary for their unconditional love, support and interesting late-night debates, on so many different subjects.

David Lockwood, for his friendship and beautiful outlook on life, and Nigel Twinn for his advice and gentle cajoling which gave me the confidence to carry on and finish the book.

Tim Walter of Knights Rose for believing that I would be good in front of his camera. The resulting DVD is one that I am proud of; it shows what modern dowsing is all about.

Tash Deacon, a gifted young artist, who created the images for this book.

The late great Hamish Miller, Neil Wood, Janita Goodwin, Billy Gawn, Linda Monjack, Stuart Gordon, The British Society of Dowsers including Helen, Sally and Leisa, John and Jill Moss, all of the committee and members of The Earth Energies Group. Tony and Marguerite Talmage and the people of Guernsey, now my spiritual home.

Sally, Craig and Emily, for just being there.

Stephen Russell (aka The Barefoot Doctor) for offering to write the foreword to this book. Thank you for your support and kind words.

My clients, this book is part of all our journeys, thank you for believing in what I do, we got there in the end!

And finally, I can't forget Michelle Gordon who brought this book to print. Her knowledge and enthusiasm got me over the last and biggest hurdle, publishing my work. Thank you from the bottom of my heart.

This book is dedicated to a cottage in Leckhampton, Cheltenham, and the beautiful woman who lived there. A haven from the outside world that gave me the opportunity to start writing this book.

Allyson, you are always in my heart. Thank you for believing in me and the book even though it took longer to write than either of us ever imagined. Wow, it has been a very interesting journey so far and there is still more to come. I am looking forward to our next incarnation together, perhaps we will meet in Avebury again.

Contents

Foreword

I'm a pragmatist. I deal in the practical end of metaphysics – that's my business. Yet I tend to make many of my more important decisions based on dowsing with a pendulum. This may seem paradoxical but the two are not mutually exclusive.

To the contrary, if you assume your subconscious mind is your personal access point to the primordial consciousness underpinning existence, and is hence privy to all information that has ever, will ever and does presently exist, it's perfectly feasible to also assume your subconscious will, on asking a yes/no question, move the small muscles of the outstretched, pendulum-holding arm, almost autonomically, and cause the pendulum to circle one way or the other.

It's fascinating to experiment with reality by basing the way you negotiate with it on the direction a pendulum swings – perhaps merely a game for the foolhardy – but so far my own experiments have overall yielded splendid results, not just in terms of discerning the correct choice but also in deciphering what's going on behind the scenes of daily life, in respect of my negotiations and transactions with others.

But dowsing with a pendulum, however effective, is just playing at baby-level – the real dowsing-rod-toting heavyweights manage to reach a deeper level of insight altogether.

So, as a relative lightweight in the dowsing field, it's an honour to be invited to write this Foreword by one of its most eminent exponents.

Ultimately, of course, dowsing is a tool to aid the intuitive flow, and it's this aspect that personally excites me most. For as more and more of us wake up to our hitherto hidden powers and the so-called psychic faculties develop – the capacity to see more of the sound and light spectrum and so become more cognizant of what we were seeing all along, but hadn't registered – tools like dowsing are naturally gaining more and more popularity.

While at the fringes of the metaphysical movement there will always

1

be those who espouse the most glorious mumbo jumbo, at its core lies a relatively vast body of people coming from a scientific or business background, who underpin their life's work with the wisdom of the ancients in a sensible and productive way. It's to these people I most relate and I am always delighted to chance upon someone from this background, who has managed to encapsulate their findings succinctly enough to be of service to the layperson.

Adrian is one of these, a wonderful, sincere man, who has developed the ancient art of dowsing to a high degree and has yet managed to share the method in a generous, clear and helpful way, so that anyone can use it to optimize their living conditions in all respects.

This book will be an invaluable aid in removing negative energies from your living and work environments, and instigating a healthier flow, and will set you on the road to developing a failsafe intuitional aptitude applicable to all aspects of your life.

Barefoot Doctor

Introduction

Do you sometimes shiver when you walk into someone's house?

Do you feel tired all the time?

Are there cold or uncomfortable areas in your home?

Are your children or other members of the family unnaturally irritable?

Is your house not selling?

Are you always ill or have niggling pains?

If you have answered yes to any of the above read on:

After the tenth person said to me, 'You should write a book about what you do.' I decided that I had better do so – and here is the result. I was sitting in my then home, in Godalming, Surrey, wondering how on earth I had got to this stage, and thanking 'the powers that be' for placing me fairly and squarely on my path.

I want this book to be in every home in the world, not for fame and money, but to know that people are helping themselves back to health. Not having to suffer in silence or make yet another visit to the doctor to get even more pills.

I wanted the book to be a practical guide on clearing geopathic stress from your own home, without having to rely on others to do it for you. We are all given special powers, 'healing powers' that we can use for ourselves and for the greater good of others.

Once I began to realize that many of us suffer from geopathic stress, and that mainstream medicine would never understand the effects and symptoms, I started to look for practical and straightforward ways of dealing with this naturally occurring noxious energy.

It would be wrong of me to say that geopathic stress makes you ill. However, it is a major contributory factor to wearing down your auric field. This, in turn, affects the way in which your immune system operates.

The unseen world exists, it is all around us and we interact with it all the time. With experience, it can be understood – and if it can be understood, we can work with it to our mutual advantage. Most energies are either positive or negative, but a few can be detrimental. This is how I deal with the latter.

Most healthy and well-adjusted people cope with the negative bits quite naturally, although the natural stress of life can make you susceptible to these noxious energies. When our immune systems are low, or the detrimental energies are particularly strong or focused, we aren't able to cope as well.

I have therefore put together a checklist to show you the areas and detrimental energies that need to be worked on and this will be found at the beginning of Part 2: Diagnosing Your Home. It will help you to deal with the more straightforward problems up to say -5 on my scale. If you have a line or area in your home above -5 and feel out of your depth or fear that you might get out of your depth, please contact me for help.

After many miles, courses and conversations, I started to develop my own particular style of dowsing for geopathic stress. I then began to 'work' on friends and relatives, before launching forth on unsuspecting members of the public. I was never quite sure how successful 'Dowsing Spirits' would be. However, I needn't have worried, as clients have found me from all over the globe.

The phrase 'I always feel better when I am away from the house' has been mentioned so many times to me during my initial conversations with clients. I am always staggered at how low people seem when they finally find me. They have probably been 'under the doctor' for many months, or even years, trying to find a cure for what ails them. Blood tests have probably been run, antibiotics have been prescribed and maybe a second or third course with no effect. Once in the grip of these 'earth energies' running within and beneath your home, there will be no let up without moving house or finding an experienced geomancer (earth healer).

That the earth produces noxious energies has been documented for many years by those 'in the know'. However, unsuspecting members of the public are left in the dark. Doctors scratch their heads when it comes to finding a cure for the cause, rather than just the symptoms.

The word geopathic can be split into two syllables:

Geo: The Greek prefix geo- signifies earth (e.g. geology is the study of the Earth)

Pathic: 'Pathos' meaning disease or suffering

Stress: an organism's total response to environmental demands or pressures.

Therefore, we have disease or suffering coming from the earth that affects humans and animals within their own environment.

Type the words 'Krebs Houses' into an internet search engine and see what appears on the screen. Way back in the 1920s, the effects of water veins and underground streams were documented, by Von Pohl in Germany, as causative factors in the onset of cancer, leukemia, arthritis and rheumatism. This information has been freely available ever since, but has seemingly been completely ignored by medical practitioners. Think how much money could be saved by preventing these painful and deadly diseases, if everybody's house could be cleared of geopathic stress.

My journey has been a fascinating one – learning about these earth energies. Perhaps 'learning about the mysteries of the earth' would be a better way of putting it.

With all the advances that science has brought, we are still missing the point. Living in houses and offices 24/7 is just not good for us. We, as humans, need to be outdoors, to be in the fresh air as much as we possibly can. This is because geopathic stress gathers and is trapped inside buildings. The way we live our modern lives means that we are falling into the clutches of this ancient natural energy. My mother was always one for throwing open the windows, even in the depths of winter, to 'clear the house' as she put it. I didn't know what she was talking about as a child but I do now.

Our body's rate of recovery is remarkable when left alone without external or internal interference. When we sleep, our body's internal healing system should spend 100% of its time repairing the damage that we have inflicted on it during the course of day-to-day living and working. If we are living above, or in, a geopathically stressed zone, then our immune system will expend part of its valuable resources protecting us from this detrimental energy. It will consequently spend less time repairing the body, as this will happen for the entirety of the period that you are asleep in your beds. Gradually, the percentage of healing versus protection will start to change, and fighting off the effects of geopathic stress will become more important than repairing the body. The immune system is compromised – and dis-ease occurs.

Earth energy lines, water veins, energy spirals, stress/disturbance lines and Toxic lines all form a natural part of the problem. They are joined by technopathic stress, spirit lines and place memories that are caused by humans – especially the emotional outpourings that permeate through our homes and workplaces.

I believe that people should be able to sleep soundly in their own beds – and that is the reason for writing this book. I want to present a practical guide on how to work with and balance geopathic stress and other issues in your home. This will help you, and your family, to live a happy, harmonious, balanced and peaceful life.

I have tried to write this book to enable every reader to understand and use the information it contains. Many people involved in the so-called 'new age' use words that confound, confuse and cloud everything they do in coded or clever sentences. So, to make things clearer, I have thrown out terms like sha streams, hara, dragon lines, chi, yin and yang, and I have replaced them with more basic modern words like energy line, energy vortex or spiral, balance, harmony, heart centre, etc.

I have set out the book in three sections: **Part 1** is a general guide to dowsing, auras, chakras, belief systems, Angelic realms, healing and protection techniques.

Part 2 is a full description of what there is to find in your home, working through a detailed checklist to give you the full picture of what ails you and your family. There you will also find detailed case studies, describing some reasons why my clients sought my help and why their homes needed healing.

The Healing takes place in **Part 3**, where I have given detailed descriptions of all my healing techniques and belief patterns to enable you to work on and clear your own family and home, I feel that this is a unique and important aspect of this book. As the Chinese proverb states, 'Give a man a fish and you feed him for a day. Teach a man to fish and you feed him for a lifetime'. I am passing you the rod.

Please enjoy this book. Use it as a guide to help you live a better life, and also to help heal our beautiful planet.

Throughout this book there are images to help guide you. To see them in full colour please visit my website www.dowsingspirits.co.uk.

Part 1:
Why Dowsing?

Chapter 1.

Dowsing – What is it, and how do you do it?

To get the best from this book it will help if you know how to dowse. Dowsing is something that we can all do instinctively. In fact, we are all built with the natural ability to 'feel' through our bodies. However, many of the skills that we were born with have been 'switched off' in today's scientific age.

Dowsing is a journey beyond our five senses (touch, taste, sight, sound and smell), connecting us with the spiritual aspect of our lives. Using external devices (such as L rods and pendulums) helps us gain answers to questions that we should naturally and psychically know – but that we are unable to tap into without expert help.

Dowsing will help you to cultivate your sensitivity and your psychic ability; it is a practical way of training the brain to think outside the head. Using dowsing rods or a pendulum externalises what you already know, the message has been received psychically and the movement of the instruments is the body's way of giving you the answer.

Picking up a pair of dowsing rods for the first time, asking for a 'yes' response and then watching them move is something that you will never forget. My DVD Intuition – Your Hidden Treasure (which can be purchased from www.dowsingspirits.co.uk) helps to explain the dowsing process.

To get started, I suggest that you get hold of two metal coat hangers and a pair of pliers; this is the cheapest way to make L rods. Cut off the twisted parts and straighten the wire. You now need to bend the wire into an L shape (90° angle) with approximately 3½ to 4 inches on the shorter side and 7 inches on the longer side. Alternatively, heavier brass rods can be purchased from me.

Get two plastic Bic/Biro pens, strip out the innards and take off the tops. Insert a single L rod into each sleeve, which will then allow them to swing easily. You now have a pair of rods – and you can start dowsing.

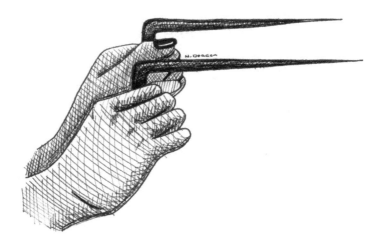

Figure 0. Holding the rods.

Hold them comfortably in front of you. With the rods parallel and tipped down slightly from the horizontal with your arms by your side, start to walk. This forward motion is important as it helps the rods move, and it relaxes your body and mind, allowing the dowsing process to take place. If you do not move forwards you may still get a response, but it will be less pronounced.

On a recent trip to Guernsey, I was asked to hold a workshop entitled 'Perfect Planting', which involved getting twenty-two people to start dowsing in order for them to get the best from the following two hours. Only three of the twenty-two people there failed to get a reaction from their rods at the first attempt. After a few minutes' coaching, all twenty-two people were dowsing. The sight of twenty-two people walking towards me with rods extended is quite frightening, but it is so rewarding watching their faces when the rods move for them.

The technique I used was to stretch a rope (the target) across the lawn, and to get the people to ask for their rods to move as they walked over the target. This technique helps in several ways: it gives the brain something to concentrate on, and it gives the eyes something to fix on. The brain, as usual, will operate on logic – the left part of it, anyway – and is inclined to dismiss anything unseen, like an underground stream or an earth energy line, as not being there. The right part of your brain, the feminine intuitive part, knows that there is something there and it will react accordingly. It will get the rods to move through an unconscious muscle action (yes, it's you moving the rods).

Back to the rope. Try this experiment yourself. Walk towards the rope, asking your rods to cross or move as your foot travels over it. Both parts of your brain will register the fact that the rope is there, and they will send the necessary impulses to the muscles in your arms – getting both the muscles and the rods to move.

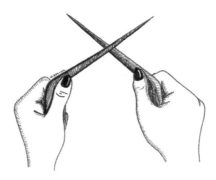

Figure 1. Crossed rods

If this does not happen for you the first time, do keep trying. You are learning a new skill, asking your brain to combine the right and left hemispheres, which it rarely does, and this takes time to master. Dowsing uses the masculine, logical left brain to form the questions and the feminine, intuitive right brain to provide the answers.

If you still haven't got a reaction, don't panic. Sit quietly, take a deep breath (or two) and try the following:

Dowsing Exercise

Place both feet firmly on the ground and relax your body. Imagine both feet sinking into Mother Earth: that you are part of her and everyone else living on the planet, and that a beautiful white light is gradually moving up your legs, through your body and your head and eventually covering you fully.

Empty your mind, as much as you can, to allow new energy to flow into you. Dowsing is about being connected to the universe, so if your head is full of everyday junk, nothing new can enter. Be calm and still for a few minutes: give yourself time. Now, try again. Don't force the situation: just relax and see what happens.

Don't be discouraged if mastering this technique takes time. You don't run a marathon the day after you start walking. The same applies to dowsing, whether you use a pendulum, L rods or the traditional hazel Y rod.

Once the movement of the rods has become natural, the next step is to ascertain your 'yes' and 'no' responses. This is done, as before, by moving forward with the rods parallel and asking them to show you your 'yes' response. Note what they do. In most cases they will cross (see Figure 1), but of course everyone is different. Your 'no' response is usually an outward movement (see Figure 2), but because we are all unique, responses can be different. My 'no' response, for instance, is no movement of the rods – my brain feels that's logical.

Now, what can we do with the rods once we have mastered the 'yes' and 'no' response?

Much of the practice that you carry out will come under the heading 'Trivial Dowsing'. However, I prefer to use the phrase 'Fun Dowsing'.

You will find that the better you get at dowsing the worse you will become with fun dowsing. It is as though the universe has moved you forward. It's a bit like getting up in the morning and having to teach yourself to walk or talk again. Once you have learned your lesson, it is full steam ahead and no looking back.

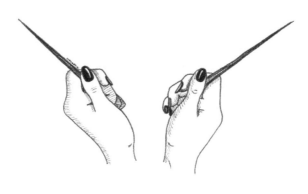

Figure 2: Outward movement

We have seen the rods cross over the rope, now it is time to hone your skills further. Dowse the edge of a table, a shadow falling on the floor, the edge of a carpet, anything that you can see so that the brain can also acknowledge its being there. The balance needs to be struck, during your early dowsing experience, between your eyes 'seeing' and your brain 'knowing' that there is something there to aim at – a tangible target.

Ask a friend to place six pieces of coloured paper into six envelopes, marking them 1 to 6, and then to place them on the floor in a random pattern. Now, start to dowse to see which colours are in which envelopes. Mark down your answers, and then open the envelopes to see how you have done.

A note of caution here – your ego can get in the way, especially as your dowsing skills improve. I was on a weekend course some years ago, being tutored by the late Hamish Miller and his wife Ba. The Saturday went, and I thoroughly enjoyed the whole experience. I felt that I had dowsed well and I gave myself a proverbial pat on the back. Sunday came, and I dowsed everything that Hamish threw at the group – tree auras, our auras, underground water . . . It then came to the coloured paper in the envelopes. I took a few seconds to dowse them, feeling very smug that I would get them all right – and I sat down with a satisfied look on my face. Hamish then started to tell us the colours in each envelope. I had got the first one wrong, and the second, and the third, and the fourth and the fifth and, finally, the sixth one as well. What was the chance of getting all six wrong? I looked over at Hamish, who just winked. He knew, just as I did, that I had learned an important lesson: whatever you do in life, remain humble and don't let your ego overtake you.

Try dowsing when your post will arrive, what time a guest will turn up, if your train is running late, what time will it stop at the station, anything that you can verify easily.

Chapter 2.

A Brief History of Dowsing

The art of holding a forked stick that twitches in our hands to find water has been with us for thousands of years. Ancient civilizations in China, Egypt and Africa all used it to good effect. The Chinese, in fact, seem to have been the first race to have actively looked for, and located, areas of detrimental energy that today we would call geopathic stress. They actively avoided building, or even living, near them.

Eventually, this led to the practice we now call Feng Shui, the bringing into balance of energies through building practices, such as ensuring that your home faces in a certain direction and putting windows in the most auspicious place. I believe that in the early days the 'Shaman' could, by intent, clear these lines, rather than perhaps having to move beds and generally disrupt a person's home to achieve the desired results.

Especially in the UK, it seems that dowsing or divination is viewed with suspicion. It has been associated with witchcraft or Devil worship, particularly by the mainstream church. I do go to church – not often – but when I do, I don't suffer any side-effects when entering the door or singing a hymn.

Way back in the sixteenth century, Martin Luther decided that divination was not good practice, and therefore dowsers were obliged to go underground, carrying on their trade in secret. Wouldn't you, if the punishment was torture and then burning at the stake? I believe that dowsers were an integral part of the community, because finding water was then, as now, of great use to a village or town. Perhaps the local vicar or priest turned a blind eye to the other 'goings on', including dowsing for herbs and medicinal plants with, maybe, a little healing and alchemy thrown in.

Books were published in Britain intermittently over the ages, including *Cosmographica Universalis* by S. Munster (1550) and *A Discovery of Subterraeneall Treasure* (1639), by Gabriel Plattes, describing how to dowse for metallic ores.

It wasn't until Victorian times that dowsing re-entered the public realm, through John Mullins, a very successful water dowser, who drilled wells on several large estates. He came to the attention of a sceptical Sir William Barratt, then a physics professor at the Royal College of Science in Dublin. Once he saw Mullins' work, he was convinced that dowsing actually worked. Barratt was one of the founding members of the British Society of Psychical Research, publishing the results of his research on dowsing in the society's journal. In 1926, he and Theodore Besterman wrote *'The Divining Rod: An Experimental and Psychological Investigation'*, which is a fascinating insight to the world of Divining.

Our Continental cousins, on the other hand, faced less opposition, with the clergy and scientists all regularly dowsing. Indeed, much of the early work on geopathic stress was undertaken either in France or Germany. They remained so enlightened that in certain parts of Austria geopathic stress surveys are carried out as part of the planning process. Can you imagine that in the UK?

Arguably, modern dowsing in the UK stems from finding water. The British Society of Dowsers was founded by Colonel A.H. Bell OBE, DSO, MRI and other retired officers of the British Army – a distinctly grounded set of gentlemen. In his book, *Dowsing: One Man's Way*, J. Scott Elliot, himself a decorated officer, talks about such down-to-earth topics as finding water, lost objects, minerals, precious stones and even people. He tells us that this can be done remotely and urges us to use our 'natural sensitivity'. Interestingly, he also believed that dowsing was the work of the mind, not the brain.

American troops used dowsing rods during the Vietnam War to locate enemy tunnels, but today dowsing is mainly used for more peaceful

18

purposes. Typical uses are finding leaks in water pipes, tracing cables and locating other underground utilities, health, earth energies and archaeology.

The British Society of Dowsers embraces all forms of dowsing and I would encourage you all to become members. It doesn't matter if you are just starting to dowse or have been doing it for years; there is a place for you within the Special Interest Groups and the regular events that they hold throughout the year in various parts of the country. Contact details are at the back of the book.

Chapter 3.

The Question String

How to ask the right question is a valuable lesson to learn – and one that most people find very difficult. It is probably the most important aspect of dowsing, in that if you get it right, it leads to repeatability.

Scientists love repeatability – and this is where dowsing has fallen down over the years. What one dowser finds, another one won't.

The difficulty is that we all have our own unique thought patterns and visualizations. If I asked two people to dowse for an underground stream, for instance, one person would imagine a stream ten feet wide and forty feet deep, but the other person might imagine one that is thirty feet wide and eighty feet down. You would not find the same stream, ever. Parameters have to be set to gain repeatability, especially in the early days of your dowsing. Be specific in what you are looking for and start asking questions – a wide, all-encompassing one to begin with, and then narrowing it to a finite point as quickly as possible.

With practice, the questions will start to flow. One answer will lead to another question, and so on. Before you know it, you will be dowsing for very specific targets or questions – and getting very positive results.

As you progress, start to look at other ways of testing your dowsing. Ask a friend or member of your family to hide something, say a set of car keys inside the house, and then go and find them using dowsing.

Question strings are similar to flow diagrams:

Are the car keys on the ground floor?

Yes/No.

If no - Are the car keys on the first floor?

If yes - Are the car keys in one of the bedrooms?

No.

In the bathroom?

No.

In the airing cupboard?

Yes.

Which shelf is it on? Top?

No.

Middle?

Yes

I hope that from this you can get the idea of how the questions and answers flow. It is the right side of your brain supplying the logical bits – and the feminine side giving you the intuitive answers. It may not come easily at first – however, practice will make perfect.

Once you have carried out these tasks successfully, it is time to move onwards, upwards and outside.

When you are outside, ask the rods to point at a member of your family, or a pet, and see what happens. This is a great way to find someone during a hide and seek game, and again it's easily verifiable. Ask the rods to point North or South. You will find, with practice, that they can become an excellent compass – they will also act as a Sat Nav, guiding you to where you are driving or walking if you are lost (or just misplaced, if you are a male).

Ask the rods to show you where the nearest earth energy line is, and watch the way the rods point. Follow them until they cross, then mark that point with a flag or something similar. Then, find the other edge of the line and mark that, too, when they cross again. It doesn't matter if you don't know what an earth energy line is at this stage, as the rods will show you where it is, anyway – just have faith. You can now trace an energy line in your garden, either by following the edge lines or by walking in a criss-cross manner, marking the relevant edges until a full picture is gained.

Do the same with a soak-away pipe or an electrical cable, moving on to an underground stream or a water vein – marking them with flags, so that you can stand back to see where you have been and what you have found.

Now you need to know how to ask for the depth of the targets, in which direction they run, and whether it's good or bad for you to stand or sit above them.

Counting with dowsing rods or a pendulum is also an important lesson to learn. This will allow you to date a particular artefact, work out how deep an underground stream is, how detrimental an area is for you, or when a particular event might have happened in the past. Many dowsers make this look tortuous. However, most people find it relatively easy once they get the hang of it. Remember, ask the wide question first and then narrow down the answer as quickly as possible.

For example, having already ascertained that there is one, the question is: How deep is a particular stream running beneath your garden?

Question string regarding the depth of an underground stream

Are we having to count in thousands of feet?

No.

Hundreds of feet?

No.

Tens of feet?

Yes.

Is it over 50 feet down?

Yes.

Over 60 feet down?

Yes.

Over 65 feet down?

No.

61...62...63... (waiting for the rod to move)

64 feet (rod movement happens, showing the depth of the stream)

We have, within a few seconds, ascertained that the stream is sixty-four feet down. If you started at one, and then counted up to sixty-four, it would take a few minutes. If the stream is 250 feet down, then you could be there quite some time.

Now that you have found the depth of the stream you will need to ascertain which direction it flows and whether it is detrimental to you or not. Standing above the stream with dowsing rods in the search position, ask to be shown the direction of flow and wait to see what the rods do. If they don't move try walking forwards, slowly, asking the question again, this time the rods will move, showing you the direction of flow.

Now ask if the stream is detrimental to you, if the rods move inwards then it is, if they don't or they move outwards then its affect is not harmful. If the rods have indicated that the stream is harmful use the 0 to -10 scale to find out how bad it is. A tip is to ask whether the detrimental effect is above -5, if the rods indicate 'No' then you can quickly count from -1 to -5 and watch the rods swing when you get to the correct figure.

Chapter 4.

Pendulums and How to Use Them

Using a pendulum is a very convenient way to dowse, as it can be stored in your pocket when not in use – unlike an L rod. Anything tied onto a piece of string, cord or chain can be used as a pendulum, such as a necklace, a crystal – or even a wedding ring.

Ideally, the 'heavy bit' at the end should be symmetrical to the central cord, with the string somewhere around six inches in length. There are so many different pendulums on the market, and it is very much down to personal choice. No one pendulum works any better than another, but do try a few different types before buying, as the balance and feel are important.

Although I have been dowsing for years, using the pendulum was the most frustrating thing for me. Just trying to get the blasted thing to move at all was so exasperating – and several were destroyed when I used them for conker practice! I am not prone to bouts or fits of temper, but trying to use a pendulum used up all the patience that I had, and then some.

I would sit patiently, in the beginning, waiting for the pendulum to start swinging, showing me my 'yes' response. Nothing happened. It was like time-lapse photography: everything was moving around me but the pendulum wasn't, and my patience was starting to wane. I tried everything that the books told me to do, but nothing happened. That was until I met David Lockwood, now a very close friend, who showed me a simple technique that worked. In fact, it worked so quickly that I was in a state of near shock.

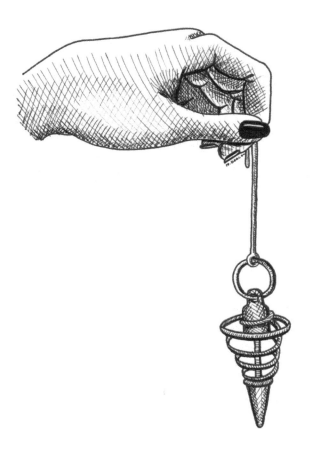

Figure 3. Holding a pendulum

David's technique is as follows:

Hold the pendulum, so that only two to three inches of cord shows (see Figure 3). This will enable the lump on the end to give a quick and smooth response; the longer the cord, the longer the response time will be. Set the pendulum in motion, swinging gently backwards and forwards (this is your neutral position). Then ask it to show you your 'yes' response and note the movement. Keep the swinging motion going, don't stop as this helps the speed of the response.

Follow this by asking for your 'no'. You can use either hand to dowse with, although I tend to only dowse with my right (my master hand). Do check your responses regularly; by asking three verifiable questions (for example, is it raining outside? Am I wearing a blue shirt today? Is it Monday?), as they can change, although this normally only happens after a trauma, operation or emotional upset.

Pendulums are used by many people all over the world who still don't associate them with dowsing. Whether using L rods, a hazel twig, bobber/wand, kinesiology or just using your body responses, it is all dowsing one way or another.

Generally, pendulums are used when dowsing for health as they are much more client friendly. They are less invasive and you are not so likely to poke the person that you are treating/healing as L rods can be quite difficult to use in close proximity to the body.

Pendulums are also easier to carry in your pocket or handbag although the British Society of Dowsers do sell some wonderful extendable rods (rather like the old car aerials in the 70s) that fit into a small pouch and are very convenient should you prefer using L rods.

Pendulums are also easier to conceal when dowsing in a church or indeed a shop. They're useful for deciding on which is the best food for you to buy, which organic foods are truly organic, etc. But be careful as I have been thrown out, literally, from several supermarkets, caught red-handed dowsing over vegetables, wine, frozen foods. I was working out if a) they were good for me to eat and b) whether there was any calorific value in them.

Apparently, the customers didn't like it. Funnily enough, I have had many conversations with shoppers asking me to dowse for them once they knew what I was doing. Food intolerances are on the increase and dowsing is a good way to keep you safe and eating wisely.

My pendulum is never far away from me as you never know when it might come in handy. On a recent motorbike trip to Brittany for instance, it came in very handy when looking for a Chambre d'Hote (Bed and Breakfast) to stay at, running my finger down a list and watching for the pendulum to give me a yes response. I have never been let down yet.

Dowsers generally have a favourite instrument to use but both the rods and pendulum are good for different things and knowledge of both is useful. In Part 2: Diagnosing Your Home, you can use either, as both can show you the direction of an energy line or water vein and both can be utilised to count when working out how detrimental an area is.

As I mentioned earlier, no one pendulum is better than the other, it is purely how they feel to you. I like one that is reasonably heavy, as it gives me a very quick response when using it. Try before you buy, you can dowse to see which pendulum is the best one for you and don't buy with your eyes. Some crystal pendulums looks stunning but a brass one might suit you better, depending on its reaction time to a question.

If you do buy a crystal pendulum you will need to clear and then program it. All crystals vibrate and we need to fine-tune these to our own needs. First of all, apologise to it, (yes, that's right, talk to your crystal). Say how sorry you are for what it went through on its journey to get to you.

Having grown happily underground for so long, only to be dug up, broken up, sometimes dipped in acid or tumbled for hours on end, it won't be happy. Clear away all the detrimental energies that it has picked up, by filling it with light and love; see the healing section of this book to find out about the ultra-fine mesh net method.

Once clear, ask the crystal to work with you, to harmonise its energies with yours and to work for the highest good. The pendulum will then be a loyal and faithful friend for many years to come.

Chapter 5.

MORA and Vega Machines

I always look for verification of my work. I have sought ways of doing so, mainly to convince myself in the early days that remote healing and dowsing actually worked. It is all well and good diving headlong into the work, but it's a little like jumping onto your white charger and rescuing the damsel in distress. First, you need to make sure that a) she needs rescuing in the first place, and b) once rescued, she will be better off.

Obviously, feedback from clients is an important way of confirming that what I am doing is working – and that they are beginning to feel better, or that the house feels warmer, etc. I do strive to keep in regular touch with my clients and to fine-tune the work as we go along.

Because scientists are still finding it difficult to prove how dowsing works, and even where the dowsing response comes from, they are inclined to dismiss dowsers and healers as being 'away with the fairies'. It is therefore wonderful when verification of this type of work is unexpectedly provided by a scientifically based machine.

Bio-Resonance or Bio-Feedback machines have been used for some years now and are getting more and more complex in their design and how they work. Several types are made in Germany, where they are used regularly to test for signs of geopathic stress in people and animals, Crossgates Bioenergetics for instance based in Settle use their machines for testing Cows, Sheep, Horses, Chickens etc. and treat with homeopathic remedies.

MORA (trademark) is just one type of bio-resonance machine in use today and Jo-Anna Coxall, a practitioner from Lancashire explains:

MORA Therapy is an internationally renowned comprehensive assessment and treatment. Engineered in Germany more than 30 years ago, and used to reduce or eliminate just about any disease. Its practice is based on the well-known scientific principle of bio-resonance, whereby a wave form of a particular frequency can be cancelled by inverting the wave form and feeding it back. When applied to the human body, it has been found that biological frequencies can also be measured and inverted. More than 20 years of research carried out in Europe can confirm that a person's own vibrations can be used to prevent illness and to heal the body.

MORA Therapy combines the ancient wisdom of Chinese Acupuncture (TCM) and the effectiveness of homeopathy – enhancing the natural healing process, by regulating and unburdening the body. The MORA system provides a non-invasive means to assess the degree of disorder in the body as a whole, as well as simultaneously assessing the activity of individual organs and various biological systems within the body. Besides healthy vibrations, ill health creates disharmonic vibrations within the body. With the help of a series of tests, it is possible to obtain a great deal of information about the present condition of the body. MORA Therapy is particularly successful in measuring, and subsequently desensitising, individuals to foods, chemicals, environmental toxins and geopathic stress, which put the body under stress. When geopathic stress is alleviated, it has been found that people respond much better to treatment, as they have greatly increased their energetic resources, given that the body is no longer fighting geopathic or electromagnetic stress.

Jo-Anna worked at The Sanctuary of Healing in Langho, Lancashire. During many of her tests, carried out before treatments were started, she noticed that geopathic stress was registering highly with many of her clients. She contacted me and we had a discussion about how my healings work, and what I needed from her clients before I could start working with them. I then got my first of many clients from her and The Sanctuary. Little did I know the power of the MORA.

One particular client had been suffering from ME for some years, and was looking for help, either to relieve the symptoms or to totally cure the problem. The MORA machine showed a high reading of geopathic stress in his house. Jo-Anna therefore decided to refer the client to me, to see if I could reduce the problems that he faced.

I worked on the floor plan and typed up the report, sending a copy to my client and to The Sanctuary of Healing. It showed two water veins crossing beneath his bed, an earth energy line running through the centre of the house, various energy vortices, two disturbance lines and a lot of detrimental emotional areas around the house. He and his wife were also affected by various attachments that were causing relationship problems. The dining room table was also causing a lot of psychological problems. It was one of the worst power objects that I have found over the years. I rated it at -10 – mainly because the scale only goes up to -10.

The combined effects were causing many of his ME symptoms. However, his emotional and business stress weren't helping either. He was a perfectionist, and this pursuit of an unachievable goal was not helping his cause. Figure 4 shows how badly affected he was. Twenty-two of the bars were above the red line, which were abnormal readings. The number of red bars needed to be reduced, to help his immune system and body do what they do naturally – that is, heal from inside out. We needed to get all the readings under the red bar and preferably under the green, too.

I wasn't shown this graph until a few weeks after I had finished my work. In fact, I was completely unaware of these readings, or indeed that the MORA machine was capable of producing such a detailed image.

(To see the following graphs in colour to really appreciate the difference, please go to my website – www.dowsingspirits.co.uk.)

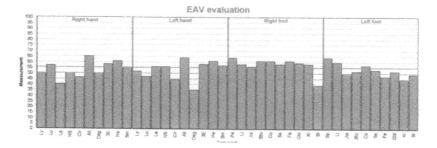

Figure 4. EAV evaluation for ME sufferer. (EAV Evaluation – Electro Acupuncture)

I went through each of the problems that I had found using distant healing (intent/prayer), to bring the house and family back into balance and harmony. I spoke to my client about one week later, and found out that he and his wife were suffering from flu-like symptoms. This was a typical sign that the healing was progressing and that they would very soon be feeling a great deal better. I wasn't prepared for just how much better, as the MORA machine was again used to find out how successful the treatment had been. The results, after four weeks, are shown in Figure 5.

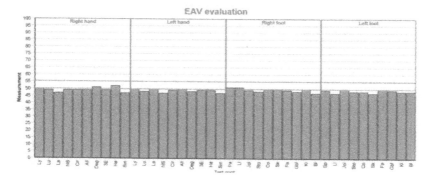

Figure 5. Revised EAV evaluation for ME sufferer

I know what I do works. I know that it can have a profound effect on my clients and their families. However, I didn't anticipate this type of verification. All the bars had dropped below the red line, and many of them had dropped below the green line too. Rarely do we, in the alternative healing profession, see such tangible results in such a vivid and matter-of-fact way.

Chapter 6.

Belief System or the Power of Intent

We need to start with the basics, before we can move on to tracing and healing geopathic stress and other issues within your home. We all need a belief system, even if we don't believe in anything spiritual. We also need to be true to ourselves, and to believe that in each of us we have something good to give to others. We are all of the divine – and we hold within us the God-spark.

Keep an open mind. Scepticism is fine, but to be closed-minded is not logical. You will never learn anything that way. Look around you – miracles occur everywhere – rainbows, clouds, sunshine, water, people...

When people become disenchanted with their materialistic lives, or become ill from stress, they will often turn to the 'spiritual realm' for answers. Sometimes, this starts with a visit to a healer.

People involved in healing others generally call themselves 'healers', but this is the wrong title. They have become channellers.

Let me try to explain.

Albert Einstein, who believed dowsing to be an unexplored branch of science, has been attributed as saying:

Everything is energy and energy is everything.

All that a 'healer' does is manipulate that energy – a form of spiritual rewiring if you like. They use an external force – which some people

33

refer to as God, while others would perhaps prefer 'the highest of the high', 'the management', or 'the universal consciousness' (there are many words and names used), but it is by tapping into this higher energy, and by channelling it through themselves, that they can 'heal'.

You do not have to be religious, and in fact you can be downright sceptical, but you will need to be open-minded and aware of this higher power. Otherwise, you will soon become unwell if you purely use your own energy to help your family, friends or clients.

There are many different religions, and all approach healing in different ways. I feel that if you come from the heart, this signals to the higher power that you wish to send healing to others. Sometimes, that is all that is needed.

I started on my 'healing' path by learning Reiki, moving through levels I, II and III, and eventually becoming a Reiki Master. It was a wonderful stepping-stone, and I am eternally grateful to my teacher Andy Roberts for his wit, wisdom and insight. I was originally seeing him for healing, as I was going through a very stressful time, trying to sell a business with a partner who was reluctant to move in any direction – let alone sell it. Regular doses of Andy's healing kept me sane and strong throughout the transaction. Then, one day, he said the immortal words, 'You can heal too – and you will be doing so quite soon. By the end of the year, you will be helping people and shifting some big stuff.' Little did I know what was waiting for me.

I still feel that the title Reiki Master should be earned over many, many years, and not given to someone who has just completed the three levels. I always picture a Master with a long grey beard and hair, around eighty years old, rather like the man with the funny grey eyes in the TV series Kung Fu. I only have the grey hair – and not much of that either.

However, being taught the basics in the art of 'healing' will certainly help when it comes to Earth Healing (geomancy), and when dealing with geopathic stress.

Most healers look towards spirit and channel their healing energies from above, but I do feel that we are here, on planet Earth, for a reason

34

and therefore we need to combine the healing element of Mother Earth in what we do. I always make sure that the healing energies that I use come to me from above, through my crown chakra as well as from Mother Earth through my feet, meeting at my solar plexus and then I channel this energy to whomever I am working on.

Just recently however, in a guided meditation, my animal guide came through, a Phoenix, and told me that I needed to include healing energy from the Sun in what I do. So now I combine all three energies, in what I call the Holy Trinity of Healing: The Father (Spirit), the Mother (Earth) and the Life Giving Sun. It's very powerful.

The angelic realms are also important. Yes, they do exist – and they can help you in many ways. All that you have to do is ask.

I ask that you suspend your disbelief, as detrimental thought patterning is mostly pre-programmed. Children, for instance, at least before entering mainstream school, are free thinkers. They will often see spirits (imaginary friends), and will have the most wonderful insights into life. Once at school, these experiences are 'educated' out of them. They will, more often than not, leave these gifts behind. Only when they get to their mid-forties will they start to look around for what is missing in their lives – the so-called time of 'finding oneself'.

Whether it is called the power of intent, the power of prayer or just sending beneficial thoughts to someone, it doesn't matter. It is one and the same thing. I don't bring religion into dowsing when tutoring courses, as everyone has their own ideas, depending on their race, religion and creed. However, I do bring a spiritual aspect to all my teachings. It is important and, frankly, it makes the world go round.

A good way of proving that intent works is to sit and concentrate on one particular person for five minutes. Send them good thoughts, and see what happens. More often than not you will receive a telephone call within minutes, or perhaps later that evening if they are busy at work. The person's subconscious would have 'felt' you tune in and would have sent a message to the brain to say, 'Hey, remember so and so? I think we should give them a call.'

Human intent is everything. Just by thinking a good or beneficial

35

thought you can change someone's life, even if they are living on the other side of the planet. Such is the strength of the gift that we are born with. We are connected to everything on this planet, all animate beings and inanimate objects. Yes, even to the coffee cup in your kitchen, your pet and to people that you don't even know.

Whilst writing this chapter I am thinking back to my days as an estate agent in Surrey. I am wondering what the 'me' then would think of 'me' now, talking about healing, angels and God. I think that I would have been mystified, and perhaps a bit envious, but most of all intrigued.

I also work with spirit guides, protectors, friends and relatives that have passed over into the light.

There are many beings in the 'spirit realm' that are here to help us – but also a few that are here to hinder.

Detrimental Energy Patterns are All Around Us

Most people don't realize that by being negative or 'down' they can easily project those thoughts and words outwards – and that these energies can create 'entities', which as I mentioned before, I prefer to call attachments.

Attachments are literally other people's bad thought patterns and words that have formed into a 'ball' of energy, and that have attached themselves to a poor, unsuspecting victim – perhaps someone who was feeling a little under the weather themselves. They will now begin to feel a lot worse.

Just sit and think how many arguments you have had over the years that were never resolved. How many unkind comments you have made to others and how many unkind thoughts you have had. That gives you an idea of the problems that we can face on a day-to-day basis. These detrimental energies form a fog all around us. Thankfully, most of us cannot see it – if you could, you probably wouldn't go out.

Couples that argue, and eventually part, can leave behind a 'detrimental energy form' which occupies the space they lived in –

both in their home and in their garden. The next occupants will probably be affected by this, and may add to that negative energy form by also arguing.

So, unresolved arguments leave detrimental energy, thought forms or attachments. Depending on how they were created, they will have different energy needs and you will need to protect yourself and your family against them (see Chapter 8 on Auras for further details).

Why Psychic Protection?

At its most basic, 'psychic protection' is all about keeping your body and mind healthy. You wouldn't go out in the rain without a coat on, would you? Well, then, don't go out into the world without some form of psychic protection either.

People with a robust constitution and a positive approach to life are much less likely to pick up detrimental energies. If their aura (the energy shield around them) is kept strong and clear, any negativity will just bounce off it. It will therefore also be much harder to be 'psychically attacked'.

A healthy diet with enough rest and relaxation, no smoking or drugs and little or no drinking will also help to keep you well at every level – physically, mentally and spiritually.

What is a Psychic Attack?

We humans are very complex energy beings and when we simply ask a question using a dowsing instrument, or during meditation, our energy state changes.

Effectively, we 'open up' to explore the question, and we receive the response. Our energy centres, called chakras, open up to allow us to work and to receive dowsing responses.

Some signs and symptoms of a possible psychic attack or an attachment include:

- Feeling that someone is looking through your eyes;

- Feeling down or angry with no real cause – especially if this is out of character for you;

- Feeling drained or very tired for no particular reason;

- Having odd or unusual thoughts that just aren't you;

- Feelings of being out of control;

- Losing your temper for no reason;

- Feeling irritable;

- Having a bad headache;

- Feeling that you can't settle or are on edge;

- Bad dreams.

All people who are involved in healing, dowsing, or spiritual activities of any kind should protect themselves. In fact, we should all do so, all the time. It would make our lives so much easier and less fraught. Detrimental energies are all around us – in our homes, shops, schools, hospitals, etc. – and we could be affected at any stage, at any time.

Here are some simple methods of protecting you and your family.

Cloak of Protection

Imagine a blue (or your colour choice) cloak being placed over your shoulders with the hood over your head. The cloak is longer than you and tucks under your feet and ties at your waist. You can further protect yourself by adding a lining of a different colour.

A Bubble of White Light

This is one of the easiest methods to use, and is instant in the way that it works. All that you need to do is to visualize a bubble of white light surrounding you entirely, asking the *Source* to protect you and your family from anything detrimental that might be around you.

Multi-colour Layer Protection

The main method of protection that I now use, was given to me by Andy Roberts. Every morning, before I leave the house and before I start working, I do the following:

(For more detailed information about the chakras and an image of where they are located, see Chapter 8.)

Breathe the colour red in through your base chakra and then out forming a 2" layer around your body.

Then breathe the colour orange in through your sacral chakra and out forming a second layer around you.

Now breathe in yellow through your solar plexus and out to form a third layer around you.

Through your heart chakra breathe in green and on the out breath it forms a fourth layer around you.

Now breathe in the colour light blue through your throat chakra and on the out breath it forms a fifth layer around you.

Through your third-eye chakra breathe in dark blue and then out to form a sixth layer around you.

And through your crown chakra breathe in purple (the divine light) and breathe out to form a seventh layer around you.

Now through your crown breathe in silver light and out to form an eighth layer.

Then gold through your crown and out to form a ninth layer.

Finally breathe in divine white light filling up your body from your toes to the top of your head.

You are now fully protected inside your very own rainbow. This helps protect against psychic attacks and spirit attachments. It might sound easy and simple – but it does work.

If you find that this is difficult to visualize, try drawing yourself inside the bubble on a piece of paper – that should also work for you.

Your Higher Self

This is a term that you may not have heard of, although those in the healing profession will be familiar with it. Again, it is open to interpretation, and I would think that each person will have their own idea of what it means.

I tend to feel that I am a 'chip off the old block'; the old block being my higher self that remains static in, let's call it Heaven, for the want of a better word. The chip is me living as Adrian Incledon-Webber, in this incarnation on Earth. I often refer to my higher self as a mainframe computer, gathering and holding all the information and lessons that I have learned over thousands of lifetimes. Each time I incarnate on the planet, I am given certain information that will be useful for me during my current life, if I can remember or rediscover it. I am therefore like a portable hard drive, gathering external information whilst alive, then delivering it back to my mainframe once I pass over.

Therefore, an essence of Adrian is always in Heaven, and it will help the Adrian on the planet by passing wisdom via dreams and/or meditation. You are never alone, as you are being looked after from 'above'. Life can seem very hard whilst living on the Earth, and sadly we often only learn from the difficult lessons. Then again, if life was always easy, wouldn't we get bored?

Try talking to your higher self – preferably in private, as you can and will get some funny looks if you do so in public. A thought is all that it takes. I often ask for help three times in a row, as I feel it shows intent and your higher self is more likely to take you seriously. If you ever have a problem that you can't solve, ask the question of your higher self before going to sleep; you could be surprised how easily the answer can come in the morning.

Just because you choose to live a spiritual way of life, it doesn't mean that it will automatically be easy. Hard lessons will have to be overcome in order for you to know yourself, so that you can walk your true path.

Chapter 7.

Angelic Realms

This title still brings a smile to my face – me, believing in angels? When I first started out on my new pathway, little did I know that it would bring me not only to work with these heavenly beings, but also to come face-to-face with one of them.

When I set off on my new venture, leaving a very commercial life behind me, I had no idea about what awaited me. The phrase 'babe in the wood' comes to mind.

I started from a sceptical background, trying to discount anything that I had been told or already knew about the subject of Archangels, Angels, Cherubs, et al, so that I could look at the whole subject afresh. I needed to pull apart the dogma surrounding them, in order to work out for myself what was true from what was written purely for a gullible public (and I was a member of that group myself at the time).

I picked up a book in a charity shop called *The Light in Britain* by Grace and Ivan Cooke. Grace, a natural clairvoyant, channelled information from White Eagle, a Native American Chief and Shaman. She set up The White Eagle Lodge, initially in London, but now the lodges can be found all over the world. In her book, she quotes from Dr Edmund Szekelys' book *The Teachings of The Essenes from Enoch to The Dead Sea Scrolls*, giving us his views on 'Angelology'. He tells how the Essene, an ancient Middle-Eastern tribe (second century BC to the first century AD), called in an Angel for each day of the week to commune with, and to enjoin in reverence:

First day (Saturday): they called upon the Earth Mother asking for her energies to flow into them and the earth.

Second day (Sunday): they called upon the Angel of the Earth with thoughts of fertility (for example, causing the grass to grow and the flowers to bloom).

Third day (Monday): they called upon the Angel of Life with thoughts of the life-force or vitality stored in the trees and forests, drawing on those energies to revitalize their bodies.

Fourth day (Tuesday): they called upon the Angel of Joy, thinking of all the joy manifested in nature's flowers, songbirds, bright clouds, sunshine, the beauty of the dawn and sunset. By drawing all these together they felt closer to Mother Earth.

Fifth day (Wednesday): they called upon the Angel of the Sun to appear, thinking about the rising sun and the feeling of warm sunlight entering their solar plexus chakra, where light infused their being.

Sixth day (Thursday): on this day the Angel of the Water would appear, dedicated to seas, lakes, rivers, falling rain and the rising sap in trees; they identified their own blood with pure water flowing through their body, purifying it and the blood stream.

Seventh day (Friday): this day was set apart for the Angel of the Air, filling their lungs with its power; filling their whole being with healing air and renewing them.

This to me is a beautiful concept. Wouldn't it be wonderful if we could all spend a few minutes during our busy lives, thinking about and calling in a beautiful angel each and every day, asking for their blessings and guidance – just like the Essene?

The Benefit to Us?

On average, the Essene lived to be 120 years old, and were resistant to pain, illness and weariness.

Since starting on my path, I have spent a lot of time with mediums, palmists, clairvoyants and seers (or see-ers). From these gifted people, I became aware of unseen 'things' around me. The more that you work with the spirit realm, the more you become aware of them. However, in the early days, the term 'Thick as a brick' would probably have sufficed – even to the point of stepping on a ghost at West Kennet Long Barrow that I didn't know was there. The ghost was not amused, and made his feelings known by giving me an instant headache.

Getting clarification and verification of what I experience or feel is important to me. I knew that for this form of healing to work, I would need more than just 'me' to do it. I started going to Mind, Body and Spirit fairs and, on one occasion, a medium stopped me and said, 'Do you know how many Angels there are with you?' I hadn't got a clue, nor indeed had I ever given any thought to the subject. 'You must be a healer,' she added. Actually I was an estate agent, but I had been stepping off that path for a long time, and I'd had yearnings to venture into the 'alternative' field. I told her that I wasn't, but she replied, 'You will be – and Archangels will play a big part of your life.'

During meditation, I will often see colours. These differ, depending on what is occurring in my life at the time. I dowsed to see why they changed, and what they meant. The answers surprised me – Archangels and Angels. I needed to know which ones were present and why they were there.

I started to research the subject, but got completely bogged down. There were hundreds of different Angels and Archangels; where could I start? I attended a Flower of Life course in Glastonbury, where various Archangels and several Ascended Masters were channelled by Amarna Sinclair. I had my first tangible experience of a visiting 'super power' – and it left me feeling humbled (which was unusual for a former estate agent). The sheer bliss and wonderment left me wanting more.

I decided that as I was a dowser, I should be able to dowse to find the names of the Archangels that were with me during my healing sessions – both when clients were physically present, as well as during my

43

distance healing work. I started off with 'numero uno', Archangel Michael (well, I had to start somewhere), and I received a positive response. I couldn't believe it. Archangel Michael was working with me! No wonder some of the healing sessions had a blue light or haze appear in the room whilst I was working.

I then dowsed my way down the alphabet. A got a response and I dowsed the other letters that spelled out Azriel. Then to G, which turned out to be Gabriel, and finally S for Sammuel. I found out by dowsing that I was working with, or invoking, four Archangels to guide and help me.

I now have a further four with me, notably Feriel, who helps with some of the 'darker stuff' alongside Azriel. The other three come in on different coloured rays – blue, emerald green and aquamarine. As I write, I haven't got names for them. It seems the more work you do with spirit, the more help you receive.

The most profound experience was to happen some years later, whilst working with medium Linda Monjack, during a three-day course that my wife and I were running for a number of close friends. After two intensive days, four of us were ready to do some trance mediumship; literally allowing a spirit to come into your body, either to give you a message or, if you are able, to let them speak through you. Linda prepared us well and, fully protected (psychically), we went into meditation, then trance, and waited.

I felt a presence, and a young girl came in. I have never experienced anything like it before. She just came to say hello, but immediately as she did so, she was replaced by a bad-tempered and dominant character. I was completely unprepared for this second visitor and I felt him straight away. My body seemed to change, to fill out and then to become stooped, as though I was looking down from a judge's bench, passing a sentence on some poor soul. He was exactly that – a judge. He had many attachments, and a very deep and guilty conscience. I found myself carrying out a healing on him, as I would for a client, even though he was a spirit, it felt like a natural thing to do.

Once I had finished, off he went, quite happy, calm and free of the 'dark energies' that had been haunting him before. Then I was filled with what I can only describe as total and utter bliss. It was such a feeling of calm and love that I could only gasp. An Archangel had come in to thank me for working on the judge – a spiritual pat on the back that left me floating for days.

I have no doubt that the angels exist. They are here to help us when we ask them, and to guide us to be able to carry out remarkable healings. Call on them; asking something three times shows that you are serious. Don't ask, 'Can you please help me?' Of course they could – but you are not asking, you are enquiring. 'I want you to help with . . .' is a request, and one that is likely to be listened to.

Chapter 8.

Chakras and Auras

Much has been written on the subject of chakras and auras over the years. Depending on which book you read, there are anything from seven chakras to several hundred, if not thousands.

Chakras

Chakras are the energy centres of our body. They can be seen as rotating vortices, and they connect with the meridian system to supply the body's subtle energy needs. The word chakra comes from the Sanskrit for wheel or turning, and they rotate constantly, supplying 'prana' or external energy to our body via its meridians.

Some books say it is most beneficial if they all rotate in a clockwise direction, whilst others state that a counter-clockwise direction is preferable. Some say that they spin in alternate directions as you move up the body. The colours can also vary, leaving the reader totally confused, and not sure what to believe.

They do exist – that is the first question out of the way. There are at least seven; they rotate; and they are linked to all of your bodily systems, including the central nervous system, the endocrine system and the immune system. If one chakra is out of balance, then your body is affected, probably in a detrimental way.

Energy is therefore constantly flowing into our body through the top of our heads (the crown chakra) and travelling down the spine, feeding each of the other chakra centres – although all chakras also receive this energy directly.

Each chakra is responsible for maintaining the health of specific organs and bodily functions. These centres also correspond with the major nerve centres.

If your chakras are all in balance and spinning correctly, you should be in a healthy state, mentally and physically. If not, then both physiological and psychological problems can result. Chakra balancing can be carried out with healing – although a good diet, a stress-free life, being true to yourself and clean living will certainly help them stay in tune.

Overview of the Chakras and Their Associated Colours

1. **Base (red):** Safety in the physical world; the need to be grounded and of the earth. Being rooted to the ground makes you feel safe and then able to conduct your life the way that you want to.

2. **Sacral (orange):** Power and control in the material world; money, sex and the control of other people. The ego/self centre of the body. The ability to be in control of your life and the situations that you find yourself in, which can lead to becoming self-assured and, in some cases, arrogant. The subconscious needs to be kept under control.

3. **Solar Plexus (yellow):** Personal power; fear of intimidation and rejection; lack of self-esteem and the survival instinct. The body's power house; the energy centre; helping you to work, rest and play. If this chakra is out of balance, then lethargy, feeling undesirable and thinking that everyone is 'out to get you' can become symptomatic.

4. **Heart (green):** All issues concerning love, heart's desire and the love of other forms of life. Unconditional love comes from the heart centre; it helps us with all our relationship matters including friendship. The ability to communicate with work colleagues and family; to be able to 'be' with others. When you catch someone's eye and you feel a spark of excitement, or a

link, then that is the heart chakra at play.

5. **Throat (light blue):** Development of will-power and self-expression. The need to be listened to, to express your true feelings and to communicate with others comes from here. We all like to be listened to, and we should be able to say what we feel to others – whether they are family, friends, work colleagues or loved ones. If we don't exercise that right, this can lead to the throat chakra becoming out of balance or blocked, leading to a sore throat, laryngitis, tonsillitis or worse.

6. **Brow or third eye (indigo):** Use of knowledge, higher reasoning and intuition in your life. Using and developing this chakra leads to you becoming more 'spiritually aware'. The intuition that we were born with starts to function again. You become more aware of it, and start to listen to what it is telling you. How often do you hear people say, 'I should have gone with my instinct and not done what I did'? We are born with an innate knowledge of 'what we are here for, or to do' however we lose that ability during our school years. Working with this chakra brings you into touch with the higher realms, and your spiritual path is beckoning.

7. **Crown (violet/purple):** The acceptance of one's life; having the capacity to fulfil one's purpose and find meaning in life. Violet robes are worn by those in the high church. It is considered the holiest of all the colours; it is the one closest to our Maker. Violet or purple is therefore a very spiritual colour, and it can often be seen during healing sessions, by both the healer and the client, as a violet flame. Working with this colour and chakra helps you to develop your higher consciousness; to bring about changes in your earthly life and to see the bigger picture. It is through this chakra that healing is channelled. Opening the crown allows 'Prana' (vital life, in Sanskrit) to flow into our bodies then, via our brow chakra, throat and heart, to exit from our hands into the client to give them the healing.

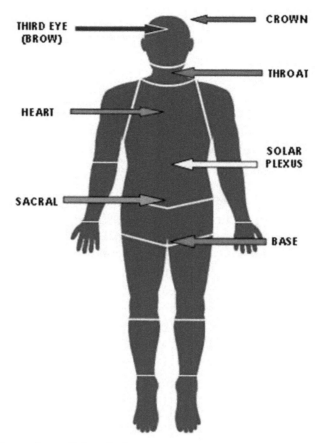

Figure 6. Location of the chakras

As I have already mentioned, colours are also linked to the seven main chakras. It is sometimes interesting to observe, both on yourself and also on others, which colours are prominent in their (or your) dress code each day. It can sometimes show which chakra is out of alignment or balance, and which therefore needs healing.

Red (base) can mean that you are not grounded, or that you are feeling rather unsure of yourself and need to show outwardly that you are in control of your feelings and emotions.

Orange (sacral) is to do with your wants and needs in the physical world. The ego is coming into its own. Power, money and control over

50

others is very significant to you, sex can be seen as part and parcel of this.

Yellow (solar plexus) can mean that your personal power is being questioned and you need to give yourself a boost with the Sun's energies.

Green (heart) can demonstrate that you need true unconditional affection or love in your life – either from a friend, a family member or a partner. It may also mean that you are not happy with your current situation and need to look more closely at your life.

Blue (throat) may mean that you are not expressing yourself correctly or not being allowed to say what you mean.

Indigo (third eye or brow) shows that you want to work in the spiritual realm and are starting to use your intuition in various aspects of your life – perhaps starting some form of healing or looking into an 'alternative lifestyle'.

Purple (crown) perhaps shows that the spiritual aspect of your life is calling and you are not hearing. All to do with the meaning of life and finding your true self.

If you concentrate on the ego (orange), then the spiritual (violet) may well be out of balance. If you are coming totally from the heart (green), then you may not be grounded (red) and you may appear to float through life, giving unconditional love to all and never getting anything done. Life is a balance – and the chakras show that if a person is too ego- (self-) based then the heart cannot function correctly. They will appear hard and uncaring, whereas deep down they are a beautiful, caring person. Chakras help us to communicate with our fellow human beings; they connect us to the outside world; they are our subconscious link to the world.

When we see something that makes us go 'aaaaahhhh', our chakras open up, like the petals of a flower in the sun. In fact, the shape of our chakras is likened to that of a lotus flower in Hindu and Buddhist texts. Walking around with your chakras fully open can be both exhausting and dangerous – they allow all sorts of 'spiritual junk' to become linked or attached. It is rather like leaving the landing light on and the window open at night– moths will be attracted into the house. Having a continuously open chakra is exactly the same, except that detrimental attachments will be attracted, rather than moths.

Once this has happened, problems such as bad headaches, sharp pain in the stomach, feeling down/depressed can be activated. Therefore, it is always best to protect yourself psychically before you leave the house.

Auras

As with chakras, I had heard a lot about the 'Human Energy Field' surrounding our bodies, but I didn't really know what to believe, what it did or how it got there.

Reading books on the subject certainly helped this time, as many of them describe the aura in similar ways. The rest was done with dowsing, meditation and, well, experience.

I gave a talk to a U3A (University of the Third Age) group on dowsing recently. When I asked for a volunteer to demonstrate the workings of the aura and its various layers, the lady who had booked me for the event said, 'Work on my husband, he's a scientist and doesn't believe in anything like this.' Talk about a lamb to the slaughter. So I sat him down, asked him to remain calm and not to think about anything. I then approached him with my dowsing rods, looking for the outer edge of his emotional energy field. The rods crossed about two and a half feet away from the gentleman, showing that he had a reasonably healthy emotional field. I then asked him to look at a group of happy pictures on the screen (a PowerPoint presentation) and measured his emotional field again. This time it had grown to about twenty feet, showing that the happier and more positive you are, the bigger and stronger the auric fields and therefore the healthier and more protected you will be.

Then came a picture of slugs (he was a gardener, I found out later on, so the picture was very apt). Immediately, I felt his field diminish. I measured it with my rods to find that it had shrunk to about twelve inches from his body. He did look puzzled as, in his own words, 'I didn't feel a thing whilst it was happening.' He then turned to talk to someone – and I moved towards him and stood a few inches from his back. He immediately turned around and looked quite shocked, 'I felt you standing there. I actually felt threatened, even though I didn't know that you had moved towards me and stood close behind me.' He was convinced.

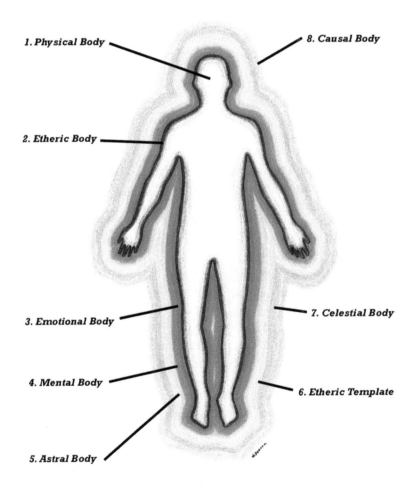

Figure 7. The auric fields

Our aura not only surrounds us, it interpenetrates our physical body and contains many different levels. It contracts and expands with our moods and thoughts. The bigger and brighter the fields are, the healthier we will be. Inversely, the weaker and dimmer, the more chance we have of negative energies becoming attached and affecting us in detrimental ways.

The main auric fields are:

Etheric body: rather like a second skin, it is the lowest in frequency and it regulates the human body, keeping it in shape.

Emotional body: this regulates the emotional side of us and processes our inner feelings.

Mental body: this processes all of our thoughts and beliefs and gives them structure.

Astral body: This connects the physical to the spiritual aspect of our lives and also to the higher dimensions of our physical, emotional and mental levels. It combines with the...

Etheric template: to form our soul. This to me is our essence; it contains all that we are and all that we will be. Our complete life experiences, character, thoughts, personalities etc. This is what moves from our body on our passing.

Celestial body: This helps us with our healing abilities, connecting to the universal energies surrounding us and helping us to channel the prana (divine energy) through our bodies.

Causal body: This level contains our life plan, our soul path or our purpose. It acts as an outer sheath for all of our etheric fields.

There are people that can naturally see auras clearly. Some carry out Auric Readings, giving an insight into 'why you are the way you are'. Our auras are contracting and expanding constantly. They not only react to our thoughts, but to other people's thoughts as well – and they also interact with other people's energy fields and thought patterns. As a result of this, they can easily become muddied. If a black blob of energy becomes attached to, or nestles within, one of the layers, it can cause you to act out of character, become bad tempered, have irrational thoughts, suffer headaches or depression, or feel just downright yucky.

These blobs of energy are sometimes referred to as entities. However, Hollywood entities are the not the same as these chaps – so I prefer the word 'attachments'. They are created by our thought patterns, actions and hurtful comments – remember, 'everything is energy, and energy is everything'. Any action that you make will produce a reaction, a bad comment or outburst will produce a detrimental pattern, while a kind or thoughtful comment or action will produce beneficial energy. Once these 'black blobs' have been formed they can move away and attach themselves to another person. This can be within one of their auric fields – or, worse still, in one of their chakras. We must all be aware that we give life to these attachments, and that they can directly affect other innocent parties who have played no part in their creation.

Future illnesses will first manifest themselves in one of your auric fields. The trick is to catch them early and to clear them before they get too close to your physical body. Our auric field is like a filter that keeps the bad stuff out for as long as it possibly can. However, if we are mistreating our bodies with smoking, alcohol, drugs (both recreational and medical), late nights and stress from work or families, this weakens our aura and can allow the illness or attachment to move closer to our physical body. The first sign, as explained, is when you act out of sorts. However, as the energy moves closer to your physical body there will be changes, starting with mild symptoms, which can worsen until you become physically ill. We have a duty-of-care not only to ourselves, but also to our friends and families, to prevent this from happening. Therefore, protection is as important as regularly clearing your aura.

Here are some of the colours linked to your energy fields. It is by no means an exhaustive list. It is only intended to be a guide to help you understand the workings of your body and mind, as you progress through this book. This list comes from a Dowsing for Health course, run by myself and fellow healer and dowser, David Lockwood:

Red: Represents materialism, materialistic ambition, a focus on sensual pleasures and a quick temper.

Orange: Represents thoughtfulness and creativity.

Yellow: Represents intellectual development, for either material or spiritual ends.

Green: Represents balance, peace, and often indicates ability as a healer.

Blue: Represents serenity, contentment and spiritual development.

Purple/Violet: Represents higher spiritual development.

Indigo: Represents a seeker, often of spiritual truth.

Grey: Represents narrow-mindedness and an inability to bend. It can also mean illness or depression.

Black: Represents some kind of blockage, or something being hidden. It can also indicate an attachment/entity.

Pink: Represents unconditional love; love requiring nothing in return. It is also the colour of friendship and conviviality. In the aura it signifies balance.

Brown: Represents 'down to earth-ness' and common sense.

Gold: Represents understanding and luck. Remember that nothing comes from nothing. It is the most powerful healing colour. In the aura, it represents service to others, for example, through healing.

White: Represents a high level of attainment, a higher-level soul incarnated to help others.

Silver: Shows that you have a strong healing ability and have started to use it for the good of others.

The human aura is something that I had desperately wanted to see for many years, but somehow was never able to – until once it just happened, unexpectedly.

I was on a Buddhist retreat in Chalice Well, Glastonbury, and it was about the third day of a five-day stay with a delightful Buddhist monk called Khenpo Chimed Tsering Rinpoche. I noticed a bright light on a wall behind him, surrounding his head and shoulders. It moved whenever Khenpo moved, and it looked like a silver liquid (as fluid as mercury). It was very intense.

I was fascinated, so much so that Khenpo noticed me staring at him. He stopped what he was teaching and asked me why my gaze was so focused. I told him and he smiled – that enigmatic sort of smile that says, 'why are you so surprised?'

I knew then that I had seen his aura. In fact, I had been seeing auras all my life, but I was unaware of what they were. It sounds daft but it's true. It wasn't until I was in a relaxed state of mind and not trying too hard to see the aura that it appeared.

The trick is not to try too hard to see the aura – and then when you do see it, practice, practice, practice.

Hold both your hands up in front of you with a light-coloured wall behind them and then 'unfocus' your eyes. Don't look directly at your hands, but beyond or through them, just like you do when viewing one of those 3D magic-eye images that were so popular in the periodicals several years ago. You should be able to see a faint outline around your fingers and, as they start to move closer together, you may see the energy move from one finger to another. This will get brighter and stronger the more practiced and skilled you get.

Don't mistrust what you are seeing – it is there and you just have to be open to it.

Now, do the same with a friend or member of your family, by asking them to sit in front of a pale wall. This time, you are looking for the aura, the human energy fields that surround them. Try moving around, observing them from different angles; this should help. Remember to keep your eyes looking beyond or through the person and let your image of them become unfocused.

Chapter 9.

What is a Ley Line?

The term ley (an Anglo-Saxon word meaning a cleared strip of ground or meadow) is confusing to most people and that includes many dowsers. Sir Norman Lockyer used 'British Megalithic Alignments' to describe the lines running through ancient sites but it was Alfred Watkins in his book *The Old Straight Track*, published in 1925 that brought the word ley into the public eye. He was a self-taught amateur archaeologist, antiquarian and a pioneer of photography, who noticed straight lines (alignments) in the landscape running through notches in hills, churches, archaeological sites, etc. He used the word ley to describe these alignments. Sadly, many of the sites that he noted have been lost to us, due to the development of houses and commercial premises over the years.

My interpretation of a ley is a line of human intent, laid down by man as a guide or map on the ground. I believe that our ancestors could see or at least feel the energies coming from the ground, and could easily follow this intent line from their village to a sacred site, holy well or any other destination. With the country being far more wooded then than it is now, it would be easy to get lost in a forest and stumble around for hours, if not days, before finding your way out. Following a guide, or a line of intent, would be so much easier. The village Shaman or holy man could easily set up this spiritual pathway, making the journey quicker and safer for his people.

An earth energy line is something different. I believe these are lines that were set up on this planet as it was being created – and they allow us, as humans, to survive here. Other planets, such as Mars, had them, but they started to disappear millennia ago.

Birds follow these energy lines, thereby easily returning to their nesting grounds each year. There are also colours associated with these lines; just imagine them as rainbow serpents circling the planet – what a kaleidoscope of colours. It's a beautiful picture that gladdens my heart.

I was asked by Richard Nissen to dowse how the albatross navigates the globe, and how it can then return to its place of birth so easily. I wasn't sure where to start, but when sitting quietly (meditating) the questions started to formulate. I then dowsed the answers:

1. They have excellent eyesight and can recognize landmarks;

2. They use their sense of smell to guide them;

3. They feel/sense earth energy lines;

4. They can see the colours associated with the energy lines and follow those to their birthplace.

Black Lines

Healers and dowsers often talk of black lines. So, what exactly is a black line? So often, if you ask that question you get a blank stare back.

'Well, black lines are black lines!'

'So what, exactly, are black lines?'

'They are lines and they are black, and they are harmful to people.'

'But how are they harmful, how are they formed and are they actually detrimental to the family in the house?'

Let me explain with an adage:

Several years ago I was asked by a lady in Buckinghamshire to carry out a house healing. This was more out of curiosity than her having

60

any health problems but, on talking with her before I carried out the work, there was a great deal of unhappiness in the house. There was 'stuck' energy, and she was finding that her life was a little like 'walking through treacle'.

I received a very detailed floor plan from her in the post. However, I had to work through a waiting list of several other clients before I could start the healing work on her house.

There was a great deal of stuck emotional energy there, mainly due to the lady's divorce. The couple were amicable by the end, but during the early days – and before the financial aspects were resolved – tempers flared. The situation became quite tense and heated, and don't forget that energy is expelled during an argument, and it has to go somewhere. The lady had also inherited some problems from the last owner of the house, which wasn't helping her at all. There were the normal water veins, energy lines and vortices – as well as a couple of spirits that had taken up residence in the house. I did a complete healing on the house and its occupants. This was followed up regularly, and healing was given to any new layers that appeared. The feedback after two months was very good, and she was happy with the feeling of the house – 'very peaceful,' as she put it.

Several months went by and I bumped into another dowser who mentioned that he had met the same lady at a recent talk he had given – and was invited to the house for a cup of tea. Whilst there, he said that he had picked up on a 'black line' running through the house and he had healed it. The questions started, 'So what exactly is a black line?' and so on.

He hadn't got a clue. He just knew that it was a black line and it was detrimental.

'To whom?' I asked.

This got him thinking, 'Well it was a black line and it needed healing.'

I repeated my question, 'Detrimental to whom – to you or to the lady?'

'Well, to me.'

'So, did you check to see if it was detrimental to the lady that owned the house?'

'No, just that it was a black line and it needed healing,' he replied.

'Okay, so can you dowse now and ask if it was harmful to the owner?' I asked.

He did so, and found out that it was only harmful to him, but not to the lady concerned.

'Oh!' Was all he said.

I explained to him that the line running beneath the house was actually beneficial to the owner and that I had cleared away anything that might have been detrimental to her; the line was very energizing for a female, but not so for a male, who would find it very draining.

Be careful what questions you ask – the gentleman concerned was not guilty of anything but naivety. He thought that he was helping, and he did so out of the kindness of his heart, but he ended up changing the energies in a non-beneficial way.

Finally there are the energy channels that wrap themselves around a ley, for example, The Michael and Mary lines of Hamish Miller and Paul Broadhurst fame (as featured in the book, *The Sun and The Serpent*) that intertwine with the Michael Ley running from Cornwall to Norfolk. They are described as having male and female attributes, or a positive and negative current. This provides a balance to the main ley and to the sites that it crosses.

These wonderful feeder lines dance a merry jig around the countryside, connecting and interacting with many sacred sites, including Glastonbury Tor, Chalice Well and Avebury. The node (crossing) points are very special, and it is worth seeking them out, purely to feel the heightened energies there – but make sure that you are protected first.

Part 2:

Diagnosing Your Home

Introduction

As with most things in life, the better prepared you are, the better you can proceed. This is the case with healing your home and family too. Dowsing is a wonderful medium, and if practised regularly it will hold you in good stead for the future.

This book has been written as a guide to healing your home of detrimental energies, both man-made and from the earth. I would suggest that you read it from cover to cover and only then start the process of working on your home and family.

I have found that carrying out the healing work in one go is better than doing a bit at a time, but you can, however, diagnose it over a few sessions. Once the information is complete do all the healing at once. The energies will take time to settle and you can always carry out further healings later on.

I find that drawing a plan of your home is beneficial as you can always refer back to it in the future and to colour code the lines as you dowse making them easier to identify as you do the healing.

I work through my checklist when working on clients' houses. I never deviate from this, and I make sure that each item is covered fully, before moving on to the next. I check with the question, 'Have I found all the problems associated with this item, before I move to the next one?' If the answer is 'yes' then I move on, if 'no' then I need to start up a new question string.

Once the healing work has been done, do look for changes in behavior or a breaking of patterns, this will be the verification that what you have done is working. Sleep patterns can be disturbed; family members (including pets) can be a little moody whilst the energies in the house are changing and old challenges might be revisited. A shift in energies will bring a shift in behavior but it will all settle after a few days.

Keep notes of the changes together with the map of your home, it will be interesting for you to look through this later.

Retest in a few months (or weeks if you prefer), to see if all the detrimental areas in your home are now beneficial. If not, then carry out another healing on this problem area and dowse again in a few weeks. Layers do exist and sometimes it will take several healings to change the detrimental energies there.

It is also important to make sure that you, as you will be doing the healing, are in the right frame of mind to carry this work out. It is important to ensure that you are ready to do the healing work, to find out if you are, you can dowse 'Is it a good time for me to do this work?' Also 'Do I need to do any healing on myself first?' Check down the list to find out which areas you need to work on, dowsing which number etc.

In this part of the book, I will itemize my checklist, then tell you what to look for and how to plot all the information you need to find. In Part 3, I shall detail the healing process for each of the problems. First, though, there are a few more general questions which have to be resolved.

Please don't forget that this work is new to you and you will get tired, especially in the beginning. We use the logical left-hand side and the intuitive right-hand side of our brains many times during the course of the day but only fleetingly at the same time. With dowsing and healing you are combining both halves all the time and the brain is just not used to it, therefore, do take your time, keep hydrated and go outside to get some fresh air if you start to lag, then come back and continue.

BEFORE CARRYING OUT ANY DOWSING PLEASE MAKE SURE THAT YOU ARE FULLY PROTECTED USING THE METHOD DESCRIBED ON PAGE 39.

How Badly Are You or the Family Affected by Geopathic Stress?

I like to show my clients just how badly they and their families are affected by geopathic stress, and its effects on the environment in which they live. I feel that a percentage scale is the best one to use in this instance (0% being the best, and 100% the worst). From this figure you can often tell who goes out to work (they often have a lower figure) and which of the family members are most sensitive.

The figure is derived by mentally bearing in mind all the checklist items, and then dowsing for the percentage of how badly each person in the family is, or has been, affected by living in the house. The ultimate figure can be an accumulation of the years that they have lived there, or the time that they have spent in the one location. You can also use this simple formula if you are looking to buy a house or have perhaps just bought one. The questions to ask include:

- Is this house badly affected by geopathic stress?

- If the answer is yes, on a scale of 0 to 100 how detrimental is it for me/the family? Use the counting method to ascertain the figure as a percentage.

- Can this be healed, so that we/they can live safely in the house?

- Is there anything on the checklist that needs to be specifically looked at? If 'yes', then run your finger slowly down the list above until the rod or pendulum moves to the 'yes' position. However, don't stop there – finish the list, as there could easily be something else. Note down the results, and consult the relevant section in the book on how to bring healing to the problem.

Due to the nature of geopathic stress, and the problems that you and the family may face, I would suggest that in the first instance a total clearing/healing is carried out. Then you can carry out individual healing, as necessary, later on. I was once asked, by the editor of a spiritual magazine, to carry out a healing on her home – but not to do it all in one go. She asked me to heal the problems that I had found four items at a time, as she wanted to see and feel the effects of the changes

67

as they happened. Although I had never done it this way before, I agreed, because I felt that her sensitivity would give me feedback as to the effects of the healing on her, the family and the house.

I carried out healing on the first four items on my checklist, namely lost souls, detrimental attachments, human-manifested forms and lower animal life forms. The changes were apparent, and the house immediately felt lighter, warmer and friendlier. The atmosphere stayed like that for a week or so, but then gradually declined. The next week I worked on the next four items, and so on until I reached the end of the report. After each healing, the effects were felt and the atmosphere in the house improved, but again this was only for a week or so. I dowsed to find out whether working on a house and family like this was the right way to carry out this work and I was told 'no'. It seems as though it is all or nothing – there is no halfway house.

I now do a complete healing on each member of the family and the house, all in one sitting. It allows the family and house to get into balance within a few days, because by doing it little-by-little no one knows quite where they are in the process, and it allows the healing to slip a little each time.

Don't forget that we are only looking for detrimental energies here, not beneficial ones, as once the 'bad ones' have been dealt with the 'good ones' are naturally enhanced. The only positive question asked is the final one, 'Are there any beneficial areas to sit, heal or mediate?' Whatever healing work you then do on the house, these areas will remain very special, as they are further enhanced with the curing of the geopathic stress zones.

For all other geopathically stressed areas and zones I tend to use a 0–10 scale, to show how detrimental the lines and areas are in the house. It is a great deal quicker than having to count to 100 all the time.

What We Are Looking For and How We Find It

I suggest that, to begin with, you generally dowse around your home getting to know it, checking each room, each corner, asking to be shown areas of geopathic stress, water veins, detrimental areas of stress . . . Draw a floor plan of the house, so that you can note down each location or run of a particular water vein, energy line, etc., so that when you come to do a healing, you know which areas you are working on.

Gradually, with practice, you will be able to pinpoint accurately the problem areas and your plan should start to look something like this:

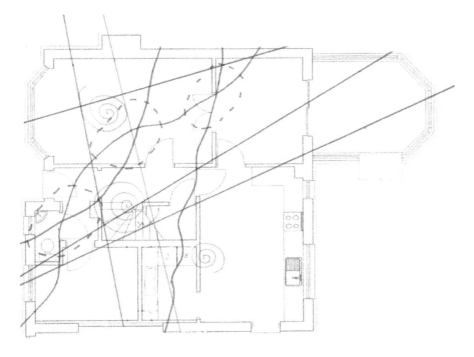

Figure 8. Floor plan of a house with geopathic stress lines

How to Draw Geopathic Stress Lines on a Plan

If I am working for a client, I am rarely sent a plan as well drawn as the one in Figure 8. Mostly, they are sketched. I generally scan them on to a computer, and then clear as much writing off as I can, to leave just the outline of the rooms. I then print off a copy, lay it flat on my desk with a heavy crystal holding the plan down, and start to dowse the questions from the checklist.

As I dowse I make notes – brief ones to begin with, as I like to return to work in greater depth later on. This is just a snap-shot or a review of the problems.

With Spirits, for instance, the question string is:

Are there any Spirits/Ghosts in this house that are detrimental to the family?

Yes.

How many are there to be found today?

Start counting and note the answer. (Say there were two)

I would then write:

1. **Spirits x 2**

   a) **Spirit 1**

   b) **Spirit 2**

The deeper information – how detrimental they are, their sex, when they died, etc. – will be dowsed for later on.

When we come to the first item that we need to plot on the plan, in this case 'water veins', I would ask a similar question string:

Are there any detrimental water veins running beneath this house?

Yes

How many are there?

Start counting and note the answer, in this case three

I like to number and colour-code my lines, to avoid confusion and also to make life easier for both my clients and myself. Once the number of lines has been dowsed I would then write:

9. Water Veins x 3 (coloured blue and numbered on plan)

a)

b)

c)

It is now time to plot the lines on the plan, and this I would do as follows:

I use the dowsing rods to show me the direction in which the water vein is flowing, and I note the angle mentally.

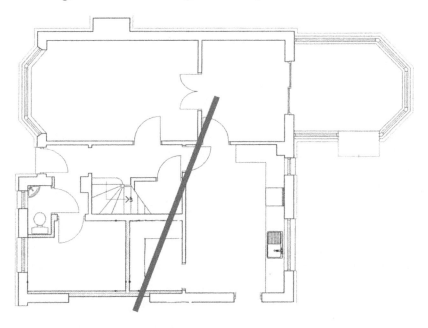

Figure 9. Dowsing the direction of a water vein

I then run my finger from left to right along the top of the plan, and make a mark when the rod moves (point 9 on the plan). Then I do the same along the bottom of the plan, marking the point when the dowsing rod moves again (point 1).

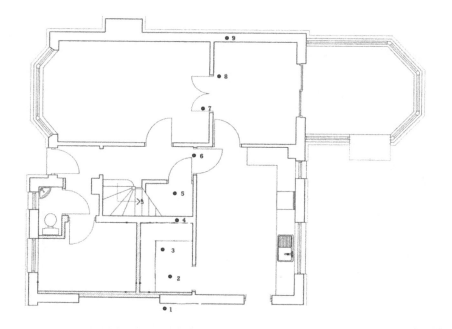

Figure 10. Following the direction of a water vein

From here, move your finger up the plan by an inch, then run your finger from left to right, marking the next point (2) when the rod moves, and so on until you reach the top, marking as many or as few points as you wish, this way, you are tracking the true course of the water vein. After that, it is simply a dot-to-dot exercise – join them all together and view the results.

You can see me doing this exercise on my DVD *Intuition*.

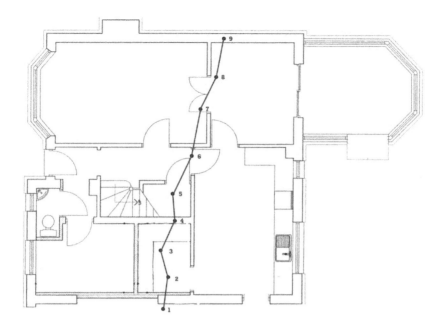

Figure 11. Joining the dots

Then do the same for the next two water veins, plotting them on the plan. Water veins are the only items where I show the actual deviation of their flow. This will give you a better idea of why a particular member of the family is suffering from the effects commonly associated with water veins. Earth energy lines, for example, tend to run much straighter.

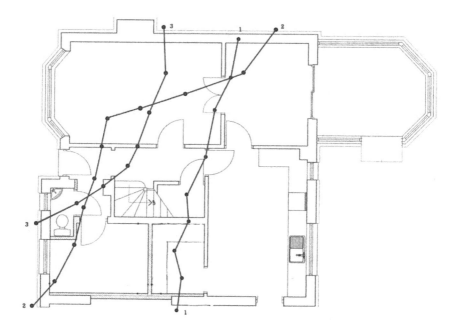

Figure 12. All water veins

We have now plotted the three water veins on the plan – note where they cross as these areas are particularly detrimental to humans (normally -10 in detrimental effects) and most animals. I do tend to highlight these areas for my clients as they will often explain sleepless or restless nights, feeling drained of energy, and so on. I use a dashed line to show how far from the crossing points the effects of the energies are felt. The other two crossing points would need to be shown as well.

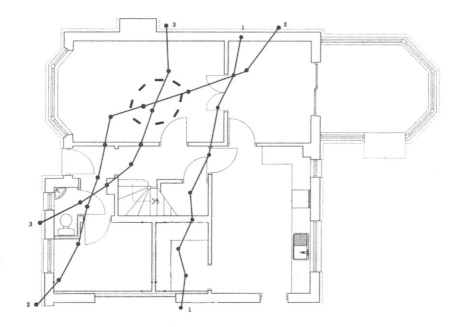

Figure 13. Crossing points of water veins

Having shown you how to plot these lines we can now move on to the checklist and compiling the report. If you are not happy about map dowsing then walk around your home plotting the areas on the ground or taking the plan with you and sketching the lines as you move from room to room.

I tend to work purely on the ground floor as the lines will be generally echoed on the floors above; I have been asked how an apartment on the twelfth floor can experience the same problems as a flat on the ground? Well, to me the whole building acts rather like a huge chimney or funnel: the exterior walls seem to enclose the energies and push them upwards so that the effects can be felt as much on the top floor as on those below.

The colour codes that I use are as follows:

Blue lines for water veins

Green lines for Earth Energy Lines

75

Red lines for Stress/Disturbance lines

Pink lines for Toxic Lines

Light brown lines for Ley or Holy Lines

Orange lines for Energy Spirals or Vortices

A light brown * for a Sink Hole

A green * for a Power Artefact

If I then need to plot anything else on the plan I will choose some other shade to mark the item or area.

We will work through the process, drawing up floor plans and noting down all the information that we need before carrying out a healing. The following is the checklist of the questions that I dowse for each house; the terms are fully explained in the following chapters.

DON'T FORGET THAT WE ARE ONLY LOOKING FOR DETRIMENTAL AREAS IN YOUR HOME, USE THE SCALE OF 0 TO -10 TO RATE THE PROBLEMS THAT YOU HAVE FOUND.

The Checklist

1. Ghosts, Spirits, Trapped souls, Tricky spirits, etc.

2. Detrimental or Inappropriate Attachments

3. Human-Manifested Energy Forms

4. Lower Animal Life Forms

5. Black Magic

6. Psychic Cords

7. Fourth-dimensional Portals

8. Water Veins/Underground Streams

9. Earth Energy Lines

10. Toxic Lines

11. Reversal Points

12. Fractured Souls

13. Stress/Disturbance Lines (Man-Made)

14. Ley Lines/Holy Lines

15. Energy Spirals

16. Sink Holes

17. Karmic Problems

18. Human Conflict or Emotional Energy Areas

19. Power Artefacts

20. Technopathic Stress

21. Guardian of the Site/Spirit of Place

22. Place Memory

23. Elementals

24. Tree Spirits

25. Animal Spirits

26. Spirit Lines

27. Chakra Balancing or Blockages

28. Anything Else Running Through the Site

29. Fabric of the Building

30. Curses or Spells

31. Anaesthetic Traces, Vaccinations and Heavy Metals

32. Anything Else to be Considered Regarding Your Health

33. Human Interference Lines

34. Psychic Attack

35. Parasites

36. Energizing/Healing Rays

37. Beneficial Areas to Sit, Heal or Meditate

If you begin to feel out of your depth or nervous at any stage please contact me via my website, it will always have my current telephone number noted.

1. Ghosts, Spirits, Trapped Souls, Tricky Spirits, etc.

This is one of the most intriguing and enjoyable aspects of being a geomancer. Soul rescue, the ability to release a lost spirit to the light (Heaven or Haven) is such a wonderful and worthwhile thing to do – setting someone free, who is stuck in between this world and the next.

In times past, if someone had told me that I would be working directly with lost souls and ghosts, I would have laughed at them. I was so scared of the dark that I would not walk down my family's garden path by myself. The thought of a ghost in the house would have terrified me and given me nightmares for weeks. But here I am, carrying on conversations with 'the dead', helping them to continue their interrupted journey into the light.

I have never been comfortable with the Heaven and Hell scenario. It seems illogical that just because someone does something bad in this life, he or she would be damned to spend the rest of eternity burning in Hell. I feel that we are on this planet to eventually reach enlightenment, and the way we do that is by making mistakes and learning from them. If we don't, then back we come to learn the same lesson again, and so on. How, then, can we move forward safely, to evolve into a perfect human, if the prospect of Hell awaits us if we err? Religion has a lot to answer for; never content to allow us the freedom of choice, or to allow us to make naive mistakes without the full force of the Lord bearing down on us.

I am sure that when we eventually pass over and reach Heaven/Nirvana (your choice of word), we will look back and scratch our heads, wondering how or why we allowed ourselves to be deceived in this way. Perhaps the person who coined the phrase 'Hell on Earth' was right; maybe we are living the hard one here, and then all is forgotten once we ascend. Time will tell.

Spirits are energy, just as we are, only subtly different. They have lost their outer shell (physical body), and exist only as energy patterns. However, they can still affect us – it really depends on how sensitive we are to their presence.

All souls should move on from the earth plane. However, when they pass over, some get lost in the fog, whilst others die so suddenly that they don't even realize they are dead – especially those killed during a war or murdered. They can become trapped here on the earth plane.

It is possible that some lose their faith just before they die. For example, they may have lived a happy and Christian lifestyle during this incarnation, doing only good for others, and then developed a terminal illness (cancer, for instance). It is then possible that their overriding thought could be that God does not exist, because if he did, why would they develop this illness when all they have done is good in this life? That hesitation could mean missing their calling when they die, ignoring the light that would guide them to 'Heaven'. They could become earth- bound, living on instinct where time will have no meaning to them, regardless of whether they passed on recently or more than a thousand years ago. They will wander endlessly, living what to them is a normal life, interacting with other spirits who are also stuck here. A film starring Nicole Kidman called *The Others* is an excellent example of this.

I have found all spirits that have not gone to the light will naturally give off detrimental energies, because they should not remain here in the form that they take. They need to be released for the good of all, including themselves.

Contrary to popular belief, a spirit does not have to have lived and died in your home, or indeed have any connection to it at all. They are often attracted by your energies, and can follow you home from the shops, hitching a lift in your car, to become an unwanted house guest. Be aware of your children's comments about an old lady sitting on their bed reading them a story, or perhaps they might mention a child who tugs at their quilt asking them to come and play.

Our children, before reaching school age, have very open and uncluttered minds. Many are able to see trapped souls or ghosts and even communicate with them. They haven't been told that there are no such things as ghosts, or that if science can't prove something, then it doesn't exist. That so-called 'imaginary friend' might just exist, and has come to the child to ask for help to move on. It is us grown-ups who are blinkered, stressed and ungrounded.

Because childrens' life energies are so vibrant, spirits can be attracted to their 'buzz', and can often become attached to them. Rather like surrogate grandparents, they care for them, look after them and can become fiercely protective of them too. Any parent that scolds the child who has a spirit close to them, needs to be careful, as they could be asking for trouble.

Often because children have such open minds, they are a spirit's first port of call, as far as communication is concerned. If the spirit recognizes that it is dead, it may want to do something about it – quickly. It doesn't want to hang around; it wants to move into the light, but sadly it cannot find it. It had its chance, but missed its turn to go. It will seek out anyone that it can talk to or communicate with – mediums, sensitives or children, hoping that someone, anyone, can help in its quest to move on, to continue its spiritual journey to ascend.

These lost souls don't, in most cases, mean to be a nuisance, frighten or harm anyone. However, they can get frustrated, particularly if ignored. In extreme cases they can move or throw objects, or create unusual smells. Creaky floorboards, when no one else is in the house, can be a sure sign.

Once discovered, these lost souls can normally be quite easily moved on. This is not an exorcism; they are not being banished or sent off to bother someone else, but they are merely being given another chance to go to the light, to move off the earth plane. In fact, most are very keen to go, once given the chance. I always ask for a vision of what awaits them to be shown, as this often speeds up the process. Talk to them; they will listen to you and go on their travels.

You will sometimes find a 'tricky spirit', someone who won't move on due to the fear of what awaits them, perhaps retribution for what they have done whilst alive. Or maybe they have a liking for the atmosphere of the house and the family, or, possibly, they just enjoy causing upset and mayhem. Some spirits can attach themselves to people and start to control them. If this happens, you will need to find out why they are here, what they want and why they are afraid to go to the light. Dowsing is a good tool for this. Sit down, write out the question string and then get the rods into action.

Fear of retribution is a major reason for spirits not going to the light; it can keep them linked to the earth plane for many years – sometimes hundreds of years. They may fear what awaits them once they ascend, the possibility that it might be hell rather than heaven.

The following scenario is typical: Many years ago, local vicars, priests or monks would have had many young children placed in their care, perhaps by single mothers who couldn't or were not allowed to look after their newborn child (possibly out of wedlock). Sadly, not all of these clergymen were kindly people. Children were abused mentally and physically, and when it eventually came to the clergyman's passing, he would have been fearful that retribution would be 'smote upon him' and so made the decision to stay on the earth plane. Then, as each child in turn passed over, he would have taken control of their spirit/soul, keeping them here, not allowing them to pass into the light for fear that they would 'spill the beans'. You will have to find a way of releasing the controlling spirit first, before the other trapped souls are able to go.

It is doubtful that you will come across this scenario when moving a spirit on from your home. However, you might want to progress to releasing other souls to the light or join a spirit release circle. Be aware, though, that spirits operate on instinct, and they might be carrying a lot of guilt.

Many houses will have their own 'spirit' or 'guardian'. These are different to the spirits that we have been talking about above. They are generally the protectors of the house that work for the good of the family.

Forget all the Hollywood hype, the word 'poltergeist', for instance, just means 'noisy spirit'.

When dowsing, and before I do a spirit rescue, I like to work out how detrimental the spirit is, what sex they were, and when and why they passed. This helps put a human face to the ghost, and allows me to work out the best way to help them to ascend. It also shows them respect, which they rightly deserve, they were human beings after all.

If you know the basics of their life before you start to communicate with them, either mentally or verbally, you will be able to empathize with them and be in the right frame of mind.

If you have any doubts about moving on a lost soul, dowse the question:

Is it appropriate for me to move this spirit into the light?

No. **(Try to find out why. Inexperience?)**

Is it appropriate for someone else to move the spirit on?

If when you dowsed your first question, 'Is it appropriate for me to move this spirit into the light?' and you got a 'Yes' then you can do so when we get to the Healing section (Part 3)

If we are going to be changing the energies within the family's home, I feel that the spirits in residence should be helped first. They will be very sensitive to any changes that take place, and we don't want them getting upset, as they can cause problems for both the family and yourself. It is appropriate to clear the house of spirits, before you proceed to the next step.

As I mentioned earlier, I look to receive verification of my work wherever I can. This often comes in many different and unexpected ways. For example, I went to visit a medium several years ago. We had never met, and she certainly didn't know who I was, or what I did for a living. I was dressed in a light-coloured shirt and denim jeans, wearing no outward signs of being spiritual. I knocked on the door; she answered it and, before I could take a step into the hall, she said, 'I have been asked to say thank you.' I was a little taken aback and asked by whom? She replied, 'By the hundreds of souls that you have helped ascend to the light'. I was stunned. Even though I have the utmost faith in the work that I do, it is always humbling to have an unsolicited comment like that, especially from those who have departed.

Case Study 1: Judy in Wiltshire

One of my earliest cases of soul rescue came from Judy, who was having trouble sleeping in one room of her house. She slept in the larger of the two bedrooms. But when guests came to stay, she moved into the spare bedroom – and that is where the troubles began.

For the first few months, she did not use the bedroom. She was aware of 'something not being quite right' in the property, but put it down to 'a settling-in period'. She was very sensitive to atmospheres, and was quite spiritual in her beliefs. However, she didn't realize that she had a ghost in residence.

Nothing really happened until a friend came to stay. Judy moved into the smaller of her two bedrooms, switched off the light and was settling down for the night. Then, in her own words, 'I felt a massive kick in my solar plexus. It took my breath away. I wasn't sure what had happened. I switched the light on, expecting to see someone and there was nothing there. I became frightened and I tried to get out of the room, but the door had stuck. I shouted for help, and my friend, who had heard me call, came along and opened it easily from the outside. I slept downstairs that night – and not very well, either.'

'My friend and I went into the bedroom in the morning. It felt so cold. It hadn't been that way the previous night, and we both felt that someone was there. We shut the door, put the kettle on and wondered what we should do.'

I had worked on the house of a mutual friend a few weeks earlier, and they suggested that Judy get in contact with me for some advice. I tuned in and then dowsed to see what the problem was. Sure enough, I found a discarnate soul in the cottage – a female who had passed in the early twentieth century, dying during childbirth. But her baby, a daughter, had survived. Such is a mother's love for her child that she had decided to stay on the earth plane to look after her daughter, even though she was dead and, physically, could do nothing. The daughter grew up and left home, eventually passing into the light herself, totally unaware of her mother's sacrifice, and leaving her mother virtually marooned. Her mother could not follow her into the light, or reach out to her. Can you imagine the heartache that she went through?

She made her presence known to whoever she could. The previous owners were not as sensitive as Judy and, although they didn't like the

84

room, they had decided that it was cold because it was north facing. It wasn't until Judy moved in, and then occupied the room, that the mother could make someone aware of her plight – and not in a subtle way either. That approach hadn't worked on the others, so it was a 'hammer to crack a nut' stance that she adopted to get Judy's attention.

As soon as I tuned in, I got her full attention, and I started the healing process straight away. She didn't need any persuasion, and as soon as she saw the light, she was off. I didn't need to sell her the prospect of meeting family and friends, or that all her pain would fall away as she entered the light. No, she was gone, without any backward glance.

The spare room is now warm and homely. Judy has spent many comfortable nights sleeping in it. She feels that it is the best room in the house, and certainly the happiest.

Case Study 2: Mike and Linda in Hampshire

This was an intriguing case. It involved a parent who did not wish to give up his home, even after death. People can get very attached to possessions whilst living, and this can often continue after they have passed away, which is what happened here.

The gentleman lived in the large house for many years, but unfortunately, due to ill health, it fell into disrepair and needed extensive renovations once his son had inherited it. This wasn't just a DIY venture. It needed re-roofing, damp courses installed, rewiring, re-plumbing, and so on – even before the kitchen and bathrooms were renewed. A major refurbishment was needed, requiring builders, electricians and plumbers to be in the house for many months.

The external work started, and all went smoothly until they started inside the house. They had started to rip out the old kitchen and bathrooms when tools began to go missing. Then, one of the builders had an accident, then another, and so it went on. A workman was uncovering a long-lost inglenook fireplace when he noticed an elderly gentlemen standing watching him work. He said 'hello' to him, but did not get a reply. When he looked up, the man had disappeared. He was concerned that a lot of heavy work was going on in the house, and was conscious that the man had not been wearing a hard hat (health and safety standards) or jacket. He walked out of the room to see if a colleague had seen in which direction the man had gone. But no-one had gone past him. The first worker put it down to his own imagination, and promptly forgot about the incident.

As the work inside the house progressed, the old man began to appear more often, and the workmen started to become spooked. Several of them decided not to come back to the house, as electric tools would suddenly cut out and not start again. Items would get thrown across the room, and work started to decline. The completion date was in danger of being put back. Several people described the energies inside the house as 'like walking through treacle, we always feel so tired there'. Morale was at an all-time low when the foreman decided, after several weeks, to bring the matter to the attention of the owners, who were living off-site until the house was completed. Mike and Linda were spiritual people, and they listened to the foreman's story with interest. Mike asked the foreman to describe the old man – his clothes, age, stature, etc. It was unmistakably his father, who had passed away a year or so previously.

Mike had never enjoyed a good relationship with his father, who had always been a domineering character and had disapproved of Mike's career, his choice of wife and the way in which they brought up their children. Mike had been surprised to have been left the house. 'I always thought that the old boy would have given it to charity rather than pass it on to me,' he told me. When alive, his father would never accept any help from anyone. This was the reason that the house fell into disrepair. He was a hermit, keeping himself to himself, and whilst the family did visit him, such was his disapproval of the children that the visits were kept to a minimum. Mike and Linda lived about four hours' drive away, so it meant staying over should they visit. He didn't want anything done to the house, and defended his lifestyle vehemently, saying that he didn't need a modern kitchen or bathroom – those that he had were sufficient for his needs. The only change he allowed was the installation of a downstairs shower, once he found the stairs difficult to scale and was confined to living on the ground floor.

Mike had received a telephone call from a neighbour, saying that his father had passed away. It seemed that he had fallen in the downstairs

86

shower room, couldn't get up and eventually died. On Monday, the milkman noticed that the milk he had delivered on Friday hadn't been picked up. He immediately called the police, who broke in and found the old man's body.

The house had been in Mike's family for several generations. Consequently, they decided that it would be good to continue this tradition, selling their home and moving into a rented house close by, so that they could monitor and manage the works that needed to be done, to make it fit for a modern family. It lay empty for almost a year, whilst plans were drawn up and quotations for the proposed works obtained.

Both Mike and Linda had felt a presence there, but put it down to an 'old house and its character'. Little did they know that Dad was still there, and that he would make his disapproval of what was about to happen to the house well and truly known.

The final straw was when their bespoke kitchen and bathrooms were delivered and didn't fit. Linda said, 'It was almost as though they were made for another house. The measurements were completely wrong, nothing fitted at all.' The company were distraught as they had never had anything like this happen before. All their measurements checked out, and they couldn't understand what had gone wrong.

Dad had obviously got other plans for the house. He didn't want any changes taking place; it was fine for him as it was – and how dare anyone make unnecessary changes. He was determined to keep the house the way he liked it. Linda was also worried about Mike, as he seemed to be changing, taking on some of his father's less desirable characteristics. He became very dogmatic, didn't want to see anyone and spent more and more time just sitting in the house.

Linda searched the internet, looking for help. She came across my website, telephoned me, and made an appointment for me to visit them. I generally don't meet many of my clients, as I work mostly with distance healing. But I was living near Avebury at the time, and they were just over the Hampshire border. Immediately when I walked into the house, I felt uncomfortable. The air was heavy and uninviting; a strange smell was also apparent. I am one of those people that doesn't see spirits, but I can feel them. I know when something isn't right. I often had these feelings during my estate agency days, and often those houses didn't sell. Linda showed me around the house and the shower room where the poor man fell and died. It was colder inside than out – even I shivered.

I then met Mike who, no pun intended, looked haunted. He certainly didn't look well, and the whole saga was beginning to take its toll. The delays with the work were making him unwell. I then sat quietly by myself and dowsed. Certainly, Mike's father was still here and having a detrimental influence – not only on Mike, but on the workmen too. The earth energy work was not going to be straightforward either, as I felt that Dad was going to dig his heels in. I had psychically protected myself before I reached the house, and mentally doubled it as I sat 'tuning in'. Most spirits, when given a second chance to go to the light, will move on very quickly. Some will need a gentle prod, whilst others require a good 'selling job'. I decided that Mike's father fell into the latter group so, with my best negotiator's hat on, I started to talk, trying to persuade him to leave us and go to the light. He seemed quite happy with what I had said, and went off without a murmur. Looking back, and with the benefit of hindsight, he went too easily. It was a ploy to get rid of me as quickly as he could, so he could be left in peace in his house.

He was so attached to the house that he didn't want to leave it – and he didn't see why he should. So, a few days later I got a call from Linda to say that Mike wasn't well, and hadn't got out of bed. The house felt very heavy again, and the workers didn't want to go in. Could I come again and see what the problem was? I agreed. I dowsed the house to see what the problem was. Sure enough, I found out that Dad had tricked me. He hadn't gone, and was still there, controlling not only the house but Mike as well.

After consulting with Linda, we decided on a course of action, which would involve us both, as well as Mike and Allyson, my wife. Some spirits cannot be moved by just one person, two or more are needed – one to hold the energy (Allyson) and the other (me) to cut the cords that were holding the spirit in place.

I asked Mike to go upstairs and read out loud from a short text that I had prepared for him, basically telling his Father that he wasn't welcome here anymore and asking him to leave the house and let the family live in peace. Once done, he went downstairs and made himself a cup of tea.

Allyson, Linda and I stood in the shower room and linked hands. I asked that we be fully protected whilst we worked, and that the Angels would be with us. Once we had raised the energies high enough, I asked Allyson to hold them whilst I talked to Mike's father – inviting him to enter the light and, at the same time, cutting all the ties connecting him to the house and to Mike. It wasn't long before I felt his energies begin to fade, and then suddenly he was gone. Instantly, there was a smell of lavender in the air and a lightening of the atmosphere – success. I mentioned the smell of lavender to Mike, and it turned out that his mother always wore it. She must have been pleased to be reunited with her husband.

After that day, the house and Mike returned to normal; the work progressed at a rapid rate; the kitchen and bathrooms were installed with ease, and the family now has a beautiful home to live in.

Case Study 3: Jools and Nathan in Gloucestershire

I was called in to generally clear Jools and Nathan's bungalow of detrimental energies; to do a full geopathic stress report, and to carry out a healing.

This was an interesting case, as I found the oldest spirit that I've encountered so far. As I dowsed the direction of three water veins that I had found beneath their bungalow, it became apparent that something unusual was about to be uncovered. They all crossed at one central point, almost as though they had been arranged that way. Often, this phenomenon is found at holy or sacred sites, water being used for its energizing properties.

Further dowsing revealed that a stone circle had originally been on this site, long since demolished. The energies were still there though, very much apparent and affecting the couple and their cat in a detrimental way.

Further questioning showed that several people had been sacrificed there and that one lost soul was still in residence. He died in 154 BC, sacrificed by the local Druids to appease their god. He was a pagan and had been raised purely to be sacrificed, a virgin, dying at the age of 19.

I found two other more modern spirits (a lady, 54 years old, who had died in 1834 and another female from 1994, who died of lung cancer at 68 years old). I released them very quickly in a short ceremony. I had to work on the effects of the now non-existent stone circle, healing the energies and literally 'switching them off'.

We have since found, in their attic, a spirit who doesn't want to leave. This is connected with guilt, and with his attachment to several artefacts that he left in the house when he passed over. Work is still progressing on this, and I am sure he will be in a better place before too long.

Case Study 4: A house in Norwich

This is a tale of caution of what not to do. Ego can easily get the better of you in the early days; actually it can get hold of you at any stage of your life. Your wish to 'help the planet and everyone living on it' can land you in deep water, or at least with a size nine boot up your bottom.

I had gone to see a friend in Norwich, which isn't the easiest place to get to. After a long drive, I walked through the front door and was immediately greeted with a large glass of chilled white wine. It was consumed, and the glass refilled.

As I sat in the living room I became aware of someone else there, not a living soul but a departed one – actually two departed souls. I mentioned this to my friend, who immediately said, 'What can you do about them, as I don't want them in my house?' I should have said that I would tackle them the next day.

However, with an alcoholic glow around me, and feeling all-powerful, I said, 'I can move them into the light – shall I do it now?' Obviously, the answer was 'Yes'. I sat there quietly and tuned in. They were both males, had been there for many years and were happy to be helped on.

So I did my sales pitch – the first ghost went very quickly. The second seemed to linger, but then he went and the house cleared. I didn't give his hesitation much thought, as sometimes spirits can be a little fearful about moving into the light, and need a gentle nudge. Afterwards, our conversation focused on 'things that go bump in the night', why they are there and why they stay on the earth plane.

After about an hour I started to feel very unwell. A splitting headache came from nowhere, and it developed into what a migraine must feel like – all the symptoms were there, from flashing lights to nausea. I rarely suffer from any form of headache, so this was very unusual. It also felt, somehow, unnatural. I pulled out my pendulum, rather than reach for the paracetamol, and asked the all-important question:

Is this a natural headache?

No.

Has something attached itself to me?

Yes.

Was it to do with the removal of the two spirits?

Yes.

Did the last of the spirits leave a little something behind as he went?

Yes.

Was I being disrespectful?

Yes.

Lessons were learned that day – big ones. Treat spirits with respect; don't mix alcohol with work; don't get carried away and finally, as my father used to say, don't be a smart-arse. Although both spirits went, the second one didn't like being moved on in a disrespectful manner. He felt that I should have been stone-cold sober and carried out the process quietly and in a dignified manner – not as he put it 'by showing off'.

He left a little reminder with me, an aching head that I had to work out how to clear and to put matters right. Once I had apologised, the headache went and normal service was resumed.

Dowsing Diagnosis Questions for Ghosts, Spirits etc.

1. You need to find out how many spirits are in the home.

2. Ask how detrimental each one is to you and/or the family.

3. Find out when they passed away.

4. Find out how old they were when they passed away.

5. Find out how they passed away.

6. Are any of them tricky souls?

7. Where are they?

8. Are they all happy to go to the light today?

9. Is there another layer of spirits to move on?

10. Check your car and outbuildings for spirits.

11. Is there anything else that I need to know?

2. Detrimental or Inappropriate Attachments

These attachments are created by us, most of the time unknowingly. It's just that the way we live in today's modern society can cause hundreds, if not thousands, of these little fellows to come into existence. A bad thought, a bitchy comment, gossip, etc. can set up these 'black blobs of detrimental energy'. I really don't like giving them any more form than that; some people will see them as shapes or figures. I don't like to give them that degree of credit, as giving them form gives them more energy.

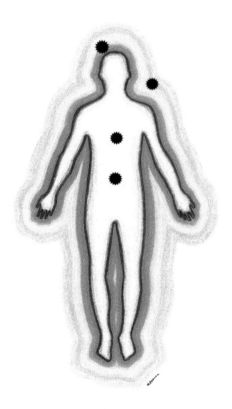

Figure 14. Attachments to the aura and body

You need to be aware of the way you conduct your life. Any angry outbursts – in reality a release of detrimental energy – will cause an attachment to form. This will then be attracted to another source of negative energy caused by you, and contained in your home/office or by someone else, and then gain in strength. The stronger these black blobs are, the easier they find it to attach themselves to you or another human being, either within the auric field or, worse still, to one of the chakras. They are like the sticky buds that you find when walking in the countryside. It doesn't matter how much you try to avoid them, there is always one sticking to you somewhere.

They sustain themselves and they can get stronger, exerting more influence over us, as they draw more and more energy from us. Unfortunately, their sustenance comes from our auric field, chakra system or body, and as this draining of your life force continues, the weaker you will become. It will leave you feeling drained of energy, both physically and mentally. As this process continues, mental and emotional problems can become the norm, leading to depression and illness.

They can attach themselves to you at any stage in your life. A traumatic event, illness or stress at home/work are normally the reasons for the attachment, and the means by which they achieve it. Some can also be with you from birth.

Because many attachments come into existence due to suffering, illness, weakness and anxiety, hospitals are particularly bad places to visit. They are also not the best places to be in if you are ill. Let me explain that comment: If we are unwell, then our auric fields will be compressed, therefore making it easier for these attachments to become lodged within them. This does not help the healing process, as they drain us of our vital energies, just when we need them the most. Hospitals see a massive range of emotions, from the utter joy of the birth of a baby, to the depths of despair from cancer sufferers.

No wonder, then, that these black blobs of energy tend to 'hang around', waiting for an opportunity to attach themselves to a human being. They are like pieces of a jigsaw puzzle – they wait for a match, and then bingo, you have an unwanted guest attached to you, influencing you, sometimes talking to you and certainly playing with your emotions.

If you are going to hospital for a check-up, operation, or just visiting, please make sure that you are fully protected psychically. You wouldn't leave your wallet or handbag lying around for the opportunist thief to steal would you? So make sure, then, that you are not leaving yourself completely open for a psychic thief to steal your energy.

Another way for you to pick up an attachment, is during a healing session, dowsing, or by being very sensitive and open. I have already mentioned that your chakras 'open' to receive channelled healing or information from the universe. By being open, we are attracting all sorts of attention from less than desirable energies, so be aware and on your guard. By protecting yourself psychically each morning it will help keep you clear – it only takes a short time.

All attachments need to be moved on as soon as they are detected. The longer they are with you, the worse you are going to feel and the longer it takes for the effects to wear off.

'The eyes are the pathway to the soul' – how true that is, and a sure sign that a family member or friend has an attachment is the colour of their eyes. Much can be told about the state of your wellbeing by your eyes. For example, iridologists look at patterns, colours and other characteristics of the iris to determine a patient's systemic health. The same can be said regarding attachments. The iris darkens, sometimes appearing black, and you may feel that someone else is looking through their eyes.

Removal is a simple and straightforward process (forget *The Exorcist*), and one that can produce miraculous results in the person that has been affected.

Case Study 1: Susan and John, Norfolk

I was approached in 2009 by John, as his wife Susan was suffering from mild depression. Actually, she had been suffering for a long time, but it was getting deeper and more frequent. Susan had been on anti-depressants for years, and had tried to stop. She found that as soon as she did stop, the dark bouts returned, so she started taking the tablets again.

I had been recommended to John by one of my clients, who'd had her house healed of geopathic stress by me some six months before. She had noticed that her husband, also prone to 'dark days', had responded to my work in an unexpected way. He seemed to be much happier, and his eyes had returned to the bright blue she remembered.

I instinctively felt what Susan's problem was. But I still prefer to go through the whole healing process, rather than concentrate on one item, a 'catch all' for the want of a better phrase. I worked on Susan and John individually, as well as their home. I picked up three attachments on Susan – combined they produced a -8 in detrimental effect (and don't forget that -10 is the worst.). One had been with her for almost twenty-five years, since the birth of her son. John told me that she had had terrible post-natal depression after returning from hospital. She had, in fact, picked up the attachment whilst giving birth. Obviously, her mind and body were concentrating on something else at the time, and this little beastie nipped in.

Soon after I carried out the healing, I received a telephone call from John. He could hardly contain himself: 'I don't know what you have done, but you have given me my wife back after twenty-five years. She has returned to the girl that I married, so happy and loving, thank you.'

Feedback like that is every healer's dream. I was stunned and humbled at the same time. I spoke to John about a year later, as I was curious to see how he and Susan were. Susan picked up the telephone and told me that they had been away on holiday, something that they hadn't done in years due to her not wanting to leave the house, and that they were blissfully happy.

Case Study 2: Julie, Paul and Family, Hampshire

I received a rather sheepish telephone call from Julie. 'I am not sure how to start this conversation, and it might sound odd, but one of my children is acting totally out of character. It just isn't him anymore, and I am not sure what to do.' Many of the calls that I receive start off like that, and I rarely think that anything is odd or strange anymore.

I asked Julie to send me a floor plan. It helps me tune in to the family and house, and it also indicates to me how serious the people are to find a cure to the problems, by how quickly it arrives. This was emailed in about twenty minutes, so I knew that Julie was keen to find a solution to her son – Harry's – dilemma.

I dowsed the problem as an attachment that had joined with Harry about two months previously. I later found out that he had been taken to hospital with suspected appendicitis at that time. He is a sensitive boy and the attachment played havoc with his emotions. He literally became a different person, with a voice in his head telling him to be naughty. The attachment was only a -4, but because of his sensitivity it could influence him easily.

I worked on Harry several times, clearing away all the dross that was contained in his aura – and then the attachment that had fixed itself on his third eye (brow) chakra. He instantly became a different boy. Julie saw it happen, 'It was as though a cloud was lifted from him, I felt the darkness go and his eyes cleared, my son was back with us again.'

Not every healing or clearing of attachments brings about this type of comment. It can be a gradual change and sometimes several weeks go by before the other person notices a change. I never know what time I am going to work on a particular client, and they don't know either. When carrying out a healing on an individual, he or she has often said that they felt the change, as the attachment is removed. It can coincide with the exact time that I am working on them, or possibly a few hours later – they always experience something though.

Dowsing Diagnosis Questions for Detrimental Attachments

1. How many attachments does each member of the family have?

2. How detrimental are they to each member on a scale from 0 to -10?

3. When did they attach?

4. Why did they attach?

   (E.g. during depression, stress, relationship etc.)

5. Can they easily be removed?

6. If I cannot remove them, can someone else?

7. Is there anything else that I need to know?

3. Human Manifested Energy Forms

Again, these forms are created by us. As you read earlier, a bad thought, an unresolved argument, unkind words or actions are enough to set up an attachment or entity – a black blob of energy that can cause us all sorts of mental and physical problems, but these Human Manifested Energy Forms are much stronger, perhaps 'super attachments' describes them better.

The more detrimental energies they pick up, due to the constant repetition of negative actions or thoughts from others, the stronger they become, until they have a life force of their own and can exist without being attached to a person. They can be found in the most unlikely of places.

Once these attachments are formed, they can roam around looking for the perfect fit for their shape, like a jigsaw puzzle.

You must psychically protect yourself at all times – whether shopping, out for a meal, visiting friends or whatever. Everybody has a different energy pattern to you, and they are all detrimental up to a point.

Most of us have been given the ability to live closely with others without suffering too many ill effects. But there is always going to be one person that 'dumps heavily on you' – perhaps a friend unloading all his or her troubles and worries, and you taking it all on board, attachments and all.

Just because you find one in your home doesn't mean to say that it was formed there. I have found these energy forms in a home that was less than twelve months old, yet they were created some eighty years ago.

They can arrive at any time, attracted by a particular energy in the house. Boys and girls, going through puberty, are especially susceptible to attracting these forms. They like to experience the range of emotions that an excess of testosterone or oestrogen will promote.

Depression, illness and stress can also be responsible for setting up or attracting these detrimental forms into the home, office or workplace.

Despair will feed a simple attachment, allowing it to deepen and grow. The more desperate you become, the stronger they get, and so on until they become a free form that starts to create emotional and physical problems.

They can be either 'thought forms' or 'life forms'. In some ways they are very similar to each other, but they are subtly different. Each is dealt with in a similar way, but you will need to double check when dowsing to find out why they are here, and what formed them, i.e. greed, depression, illness, etc. It will be easier to move them on, if you have as much information to hand as possible.

Often, the dark shadow that you see out of the corner of your eye is a human-manifested thought form or life form moving. It can also be a spirit. It's best to be conscious of what is around you, at all times. Spatial awareness is so important, especially when dowsing and carrying out healing. You need to know what is around you, and what effect you are having on not only the house and family but on pets too.

Case Study 1: Donald and Gillian, Lancashire

I was asked to dowse this house by a contact in Lancashire who had been working with Donald and Gillian for several months with a mixture of therapies, including MORA and general healing. The main problem was that they felt wonderful, almost elated, when away from home – not just whilst on holiday, but a short journey to the shops would do it, or even when sitting in the next-door neighbour's garden. This had been going on for years, but it seemed to get worse as they got older. Their energy levels had dropped, and they started not to leave the house, which made matters worse still.

I was dowsing remotely. Even linking in energetically made me feel quite ill at ease. My contact had visited the house several months before and reported that it felt very heavy, almost brooding – and that she couldn't wait to get out.

I picked up that a powerful energy form had moved into the house some twelve years earlier. It had been formed elsewhere sixty-four years previously, and had been brought into the house by a relative who had stayed with them when suffering from cancer. I gave them a

102

date, which they confirmed. He stayed with them until he died – it was not a happy time and he was in constant pain. This life form fed off his suffering and, once he had passed, it then moved to affect Donald and Gillian.

They said that they lacked energy all the time, everything was an effort, people stopped visiting them, but wouldn't say why. They put up with this for many years until we finally started working together on the house. Their home was affected by underground water and energy lines, but the worst problem was the life form – at -8 in detrimental effect.

I dowsed to when the life form was created, and found out that it was caused by the mental abuse of a woman by her husband. It stayed there for a number of years feeding off the detrimental energies, but it moved on to another home and then to the ill gentleman's house, who finally brought it to my clients.

During the healing session, I spent time communicating with the life form, moving it into the light, where it was dealt with appropriately. My clients immediately felt the atmosphere in the house change. They said, 'It was as though the sun came out from behind a cloud, the room and our home was suddenly filled with light, a beautiful smell suddenly appeared just like roses.'

They went to talk to my contact, who couldn't believe that they were the same people. They literally skipped in the door, full of the joys of spring! She went to visit them several weeks afterwards, and confirmed that the house was very comfortable – so much so that she stayed for a cup of tea and cake. That is the trouble with remote dowsing; you don't get to share in the spoils!

Case Study 2: Amanda in the Surrey/Hampshire Borders

I received a telephone call from Amanda's mother, Paula – a lady that I had known during my estate agency years – asking for some advice about the troubles that her daughter was facing. Amanda was a thoughtful and studious, yet outgoing girl, and had achieved good grades in her mock GCSE exams. The real ones were approaching and she was not revising, was very withdrawn and spent most of her time in her room, playing on her sister's X-Box.

Paula wanted her house healed. They had only bought it about six months beforehand, but she mainly wondered if I could do anything for her daughter – specifically to find out what was wrong with her, to find out why she was behaving the way she was, as it had started shortly after they moved there.

The house was relatively clear of earth energy problems, but there were a number of spirits to be moved on, and quite a lot of human dross to be cleared. The last owners obviously weren't happy people, and left some very bad energies behind when they moved. I also found an ancient track way that had a residue of old detrimental energy that needed working on. Though none of those were directly related to Amanda's problem, they did all add to her being generally 'out of sorts'. The main reason for her behaviour was a human-manifested thought form, not created by the last owners, but certainly brought in by them – and it stayed when they left.

This life form was created by extreme jealousy and envy. It started life as a fairly innocent 'black blob' of energy. Gradually, over the following twenty-three years, it became stronger and stronger (-7 for Amanda), so that eventually it became a self-sustaining form, moving from house to house at will. It arrived and stayed at the house that Paula and her husband eventually bought, and it then started to play havoc with Amanda's emotions.

They love the emotional rollercoaster ride, rather like attachments, but these are more powerful. They talk to you and they press all your buttons, they can make you appear hyperactive one minute, and then down in the depths the next. They can become very protective too, as this one had, keeping you isolated from the rest of your family and friends. You can feel as though you have a guiding arm around your shoulder, and you get moved, emotionally, to where it wants you, without you even noticing. You can become more and more detached from normal life.

I dowsed the problem as part of my normal checklist, and I found that the thought form had linked itself totally to Amanda – and it was exerting a great deal of influence over her. I worked individually on

Amanda and the thought form, making sure that it was taken to the light. Some go voluntarily, whilst others need a firm helping hand. This one went quite quickly, but did leave a residue behind which needed clearing a few days afterwards. Always check to make sure that they have totally gone, and that nothing has been left behind to start the process again.

Amanda soon reverted to her old self. The smile appeared, much to her mother's relief, the revision started in earnest and the exam results were excellent. All in all, a favourable result. The lesson is to be aware of changes in family members and friends – if they do something out of character, or become withdrawn, dowse to see what the problem is.

Dowsing Diagnosis Questions for Human Manifested Forms

1. Are there any Human Manifested Forms in the house?

2. How many are there?

3. How detrimental are they?

4. Are they thought forms or life forms?

5. How long have they been in existence?

6. How long have they been in the house?

7. Why are they in your home?

8. Are they easily moved on?

9. Is there anything else that I need to know before I move them on?

4. Lower Animal Life Forms

I first came across lower animal life forms when talking with Barry Witton, a dowser/healer friend living in East Sussex. Barry had studied with Jack Temple before he passed away, and he was the recipient of Jack's library. He telephoned me one day to ask for some help with a client, a young lady that he was working on, who had attachments that Jack called 'Lower Animal Life Forms'. They needed removing, and he wasn't sure how to do it.

This was not a term that I had come across before, so I asked Barry to dowse his client after about an hour, to see if the lower animal life forms had been removed. Before he hung up the phone he mentioned that, 'Their seeds and tentacles also need to be removed. If they are not removed, then they can grow back.' I dowsed to see if I could remove them and got a 'yes' response. I must admit I wasn't sure as to how, but sat there and put my thinking cap on. I like the practical nature of life, and I thought about the animal world first – how do they capture animals in the wild? With a net?

So, I dowsed the question: 'Is a net of light and love good enough to remove the lower animal life forms, their seeds and tentacles?' I got a slight twitch of the rod meaning that I was on the right path. 'Is a FINE mesh net of light and love good enough to remove the lower animal life forms, their seeds and tentacles?' Another slight twitch showed me that I was still moving forward, but hadn't yet reached the answer. 'Is an ULTRA-FINE mesh net of light and love good enough to remove the lower animal life forms, their seeds and tentacles?' This time the rod gave a full swing, showing me that I had reached the conclusion that the ultra-fine mesh net being pulled through the young lady's auric field and body would work. Somehow it seemed too easy, but I carried out the removal process and waited for the telephone call from Barry.

'So, how did you do it?' he enquired.

'Have they all gone?' I said.

'Yes they have, how did you do it?'

I explained the questioning technique that I had carried out, and how I then went about removing the lower animal life forms, their seeds and their tentacles from his client. 'Is that all you did?' He was staggered that it could be so easy and so logical.

These lower animal life forms have lived on this planet before; they are similar to elemental beings but are far more ancient. They come from a time when humans first arrived here on Earth. At that time, humans did not have the range of emotions that we do today and these lower life forms now find this rather unique aspect of humans fascinating. They do have a form but are rarely seen.

I feel that they are here to learn how we use our emotions and how we, as human beings, actually function. They seem to love the roller coaster ride of what we call life. The more emotional the person, the more they like it. They can influence, in a modest way, how we react to given situations and problems.

I have found that most people have one or more of them attached – and generally the detrimental reading is around -2 to -3. It is also apparent that the more important the employment of the host, the more lower animal life forms the person will have attached. One client had twenty-five. When I asked his wife what he did, she said 'Something high up in the MOD.'

Interestingly, I have never found them attached to anyone with autism, Asperger's or any form of mental illness, such as Alzheimer's or dementia.

Though they are mostly found within your auric fields, they can sometimes become attached to your chakras; you will need to check where they are when you are dowsing. They need to be carefully removed making sure, above all, that they leave nothing behind – this includes their seeds and tentacles.

Dowsing Diagnosis Questions for Lower Animal Life Forms

1. How many does each member of the family have attached?

2. How detrimental are they?

3. When did they attach?

4. Why are they here? (To learn about human behavior etc.)

5. Are they easily removed?

6. Is there anything else that I need to know (before I do)?

5. Black Magic

Black magic is a serious business, and one that needs to be treated both carefully and tactfully. Should you feel out of your depth at any stage or feel that you may getting out of your depth, please contact me via the telephone number on my website www.dowsingspirits.co.uk.

Black magic is practised by many people around the world and it can lead to serious problems. Not only in the house where it has been practised, but also to the person that has opened up to a whole new 'dark' world. However, many people just dabble, and they really don't know what they are getting themselves into.

Often a Ouija board can be the first step into a very dark realm because there are as many spirits out there working for the bad as working for the good. As you ask "Is there anybody there?" you open a portal or doorway to the spirit world, if you are lucky you will make contact with a friendly soul, if not then watch out.

A Ouija board invites any lost soul that happens to be passing your front door into your home. Would you go out and drag a complete stranger off the street and have them in for tea? Very doubtful. So why view the spirit world any differently?

Similar spiritual energies are tapped into, whether you are using a Ouija board or dowsing. This is why psychic protection is so important, so before you start dowsing put on your shiny suit of spiritual armour and once finished make sure that you close yourself down. You will need to close any doors that had been opened during your dowsing or Ouija board session and ask that all energies you have used are returned to whence they came.

The word 'occultist' means a seeker of knowledge. However, it has been linked to black magic over the years, and sadly the two are seen as synonymous. My wife walked into our local library recently, to find 'Occult' as the title above mind, body and spirit books, including Angel Cards and Reiki Tuning. Clearly, not the best way to lead people into a more spiritual way of life.

It is always good to find out why any practices were carried out in your home, and by whom, before you start working on the cure. I also like to put a date on when the event occurred, to find out how many people were involved and whether bad intent was the reason for them meeting. The dark energy areas may have been left by amateurs, using a Ouija board to call on dark forces to help them with money, career, etc. – or perhaps by people trying to cast spells without knowing what they were opening up, or the dark energies that they were leaving behind.

If they haven't cleared up the residue, then you need to be very careful. The house will possibly have a brooding atmosphere, which will only deepen in time. I don't come across these problems very often. However, when I do, clients often say the same things, i.e. people who visit their affected home don't stay long, their friends dwindle and after a while no one comes to see them at all.

Case Study 1: A rented cottage in Milford, Nr Godalming, Surrey

This was one of my early house healing cases and I was quite shocked when I found out that black magic had been practised in a village that I once lived in. I was also a little hesitant as it was the first time that I had a positive response from my rods on the question of black magic. I always remember Andy Roberts' words when it comes to dealing with something new: "They (the Powers that be) will only give you something that they know that you can deal with, the more experience you gain the bigger and more complex the problems they will throw at you." So with those words echoing in my ear I set forth knowing that I should be able to deal with what I had found.

First I asked how detrimental this problem was and counted to -5 before the rods moved, my confidence was a little dented at that point but I continued with my questioning:

How many people were involved?

Five.

Did they know what they were doing?

Yes.

How long did they practice in the cottage for? Do I count in weeks?

No.

Months?

Yes **(I started counting and the rods moved at twelve)**

Twelve months.

How long ago did this start? (Use the same process as above)

Eighteen months ago.

How regularly did they meet?

Once a month.

There was a fitted carpet in the room so I dowsed the following question:

Has anything been carved or painted onto the floorboards, leaving a permanent mark?

No.

So we are only dealing with residue or a mental detrimental energy pattern left behind?

Yes.

Can this area be healed by me?

Yes.

Can it be done remotely?

Yes.

I admit to breathing a sigh of relief at that point, I was standing in the cottage at the time and it felt very dark, the owners had left me to it as they didn't like the atmosphere there. The cottage had been empty for just over five months since the last tenants moved out; they were the people responsible for leaving the detrimental energies behind. It appeared that after eighteen months of living there, the couple had split up, the girlfriend had moved out which coincided with my finding, the rituals then stopped.

The owners of the cottage met the outgoing tenant when they collected the keys; they said that he looked haunted, white faced with big bags under his black eyes. They assumed he must have been on drugs.

They'd had a good number of viewings, it was a pretty cottage, but no one wanted to rent it. In fact they said that several people who had seen it were quite hostile as they came out of the house. They thought that it might be the decor in the house and decided to get a quote to repaint some of the rooms. The decorator was a friend of mine and quite psychic, he took one step inside and then backtracked fast saying: "You don't need it painting, you need it healed, it's got bad juju!"

I got the telephone call and went to see the owners; as soon as I walked into the front room I felt the darkness close around me, no wonder that the cottage was still empty. I mentally increased my psychic protection and started dowsing for the answers. I continued from the string above:

Was this the first time that they had practiced the black arts?

Yes.

Was it one person that suggested it and the others followed?

Yes.

Was it very much for self-gain?

Yes.

Great, that made it easier to deal with. Frankly if it had been any deeper then I would have 'phoned a friend' to help me.

Is it ok for me to carry out a clearing on this house?

Yes.

So I went home, prepared myself and my room then did the work. I told the owners what I had found and that I had cleared the cottage of all the detrimental energies that I found there. I asked for them to give me feedback in a week and in fact I received a telephone call five days later to say that they had found a tenant who was moving in two days later. She loved the cottage and said that it felt peaceful and welcoming as soon as she walked through the door.

Job done. Happy owners and a very happy tenant. I heard that she was still there two years later and in fact wanted to buy the house.

Remote healing, from the sanctity of your own home, is so much safer than being on site. Make sure that your room is cleared of all detrimental energy, that you are psychically protected and have checked that it is the right time to tackle the problem.

Dowsing Diagnosis Questions for Black Magic

1. Has black magic been practised in this house?

2. Where did it take place?

3. Is there a detrimental area that needs healing?

4. How detrimental is it to the family?

5. How many people were involved?

6. Was the detrimental energy left there on purpose?

7. Was it someone playing with a Ouija board?

8. Was it more serious than that?

9. Can I clear it with healing?

10. Is there anything else that I need to know?

6. Psychic Cords

These psychic cords can be set up for many reasons including illness, concern, love, jealousy, relationship matters, divorce and death. They link one person to another – normally via the chakras, although they can attach anywhere to your body, front, back, sides, head and feet. You will need to dowse where they are attached, who attached them and how long they have been there. These cords can be draining, both emotionally and physically.

How can you tell if you have a cord, or cords, attached? Feeling drained of energy is one symptom; thinking about someone all the time is another; strange thoughts, feelings and emotions are also classic cord problems.

Sensitives often describe these cords as a thin gold filament leading from one person to another – transferring emotions, images, psychic and physical energy.

Any strong repetitious emotion can establish a link, and love is the first and probably most common reason for one person to link to another. As you fall in love, your heart chakra opens, and a cord can easily be generated, subconsciously, between you and your partner. This can be healthy between a loving couple. However, it can sometimes lead to inter-dependence, a diffusing of individuality and eventually a lack of self-worth. I do recommend that individuals remain as individuals, after all, that is how we have all been brought up – and that is the person that you fell in love with, after all.

Illness is another fundamental way that cords are set up. A daughter's or son's concern for a sick parent, for instance, will see the subconscious transfer of their healthy energy to the ailing parent. It cannot be avoided, as that is what we do naturally. Unless the cord is cut, this energy drain will go on indefinitely, even beyond the grave.

Friends and colleagues are also a great source of cords. The friend who always needs support and is full of woe can become a so-called 'Psychic Vampire'. They subconsciously feed from your vital energy.

Sometimes a work colleague, who is perhaps jealous of you, can also psychically drain your life force from you.

The list below is by no means exhaustive, but will give you an idea of the type of people who are most likely to set up a cord:

- Chronically ill or sick parents, family members or friends;

- Alcoholics;

- Emotionally damaged relations, family, friends or work colleagues;

- Aggressive people;

- Drug addicts;

- Needy or dependent people, or those lacking in self-worth;

- Loved ones.

Case Study 1: Pam and Her Ex-Boyfriend

I received an email from Pam asking for my help. She described herself as an outgoing person, normally very confident (she had her own business) and happy. However, in recent weeks, she had started to feel very 'down'; she didn't want to go out; she lacked energy and kept having strange thoughts or 'daymares', as she called them. She also mentioned, at the very end of the letter, that she had 'just come out of a long-term relationship with a "cold and controlling" man'.

I asked her to telephone me, which she did. The relationship had started well, and she said that all her friends had welcomed Steve into the fold. They shared a common interest, and consequently spent a great deal of their leisure time together. As the months went by, she noticed that they were seeing less of her friends; the telephone calls between them reduced and she found herself alone – apart from her boyfriend. She felt as though life was passing her by. They had stopped going out as a couple. She didn't go out by herself, as Steve didn't like it, and their common interests had dried up.

This had gone on for about two years before she decided that enough was enough, and called a halt to their relationship. Steve didn't understand why – and apparently, to this day, still doesn't. He became very vocal at first, and then resorted to emotional blackmail, before she finally closed the door on the relationship – although she still received intrusive telephone calls and emails from him.

Shortly afterwards, the strange thought patterns started. She couldn't get Steve out of her head, and she felt as though all her energy was draining away. The 'daymares' became more frequent, and with them came mild symptoms of depression. 'I couldn't believe that I, of all people, was going to the doctor for anti-depressants,' she commented on the telephone. 'I took them for about two weeks, but didn't feel any better, so I flushed them down the toilet. Then a friend recommended that I contact you, so here I am. Can you help me, please?'

The recent break-up of her relationship and her current symptoms led me to believe that Steve had attached a psychic cord – and it was this that was detrimentally affecting her. I dowsed and found that she didn't just have one attached – she had three. One to her heart chakra, one to her brow chakra and the final cord to her solar plexus chakra, but attached at her back. I wasn't surprised that she was feeling under the weather. Steve really was 'doing a number' on her. However, it was all subconscious and I don't think that Steve was aware of what he had done.

I cut the cords and put Pam into a mirrored pyramid for a few days, to give her extra protection against these cords re-attaching. The strange thoughts stopped almost instantly, she started to feel lighter and she said, 'It was a though I could breathe again; I felt free and happy.' I did warn her that Steve would probably telephone her in the next day or so. Once cords get cut, the responsible party will suddenly feel a great loss, or that something is suddenly missing in their life, and they will get the urge to make contact. He did just that – the very next day. He subconsciously tried to attach even more cords, but Pam's protection stopped this happening. She never heard anything from him again.

Case Study 2: Maggie and Her Father in Kent

I gave a talk to a dowsing group on geopathic stress and was approached by Maggie at the end of it, asking if I could help her with a problem. We agreed that she would contact me the next day, when I had more time to talk.

Maggie's symptoms were similar to Pam's, in that she was suffering from a general lack of energy, had lost weight and felt quite depressed. However, she also added that her father was in her mind constantly, at night and during the day – his image just wouldn't go away. I asked if she was worried about him for any reason, and she replied, 'He's been dead for five years.'

I checked to see if he had gone to the light, and discovered that he had. I then dowsed further, never imaging that my questions would lead to a psychic cords. I would have imagined that, as you pass over, any psychic cord would automatically be severed. But here was proof that that was not the case at all. I asked Maggie how he had passed, and she replied that he had suffered from cancer – and that it had been a long, drawn-out death. During that time, she had carried out much of the nursing, and had obviously set up a cord by transferring some of her energy to her father, in the hope that it would help him to fight the disease.

Because of the timescale involved, Maggie had been exhausted by the time her Father died – not only physically and mentally drained, but also psychically through the cord. Because the cord had not been severed on his passing, the tiredness had continued for a further five years – it was no wonder she wasn't well.

I asked if the cord could now be cut – and the pendulum indicated 'yes'. Would it be beneficial for both parties if it was? I got another yes response. Was the cord also affecting Maggie's father in a detrimental way? Yes, it was. So, by cutting the ties between them, we were affecting both this world and the next in a beneficial way.

Once done, Maggie started to feel better and she went on holiday with her mother, feeling refreshed when she returned. She started to gain weight and to sleep properly again. She went to see a medium, who said that her Father was now at peace – and he wished her well.

Dowsing Diagnosis Questions for Psychic Cords

1. Do you have a psychic cord attached?

2. How many?

3. Who attached the cord, you or the other party?

4. Who is the cord attached to? (i.e. parent, child or friend)

5. When were the cords attached?

6. Where are they attached? (i.e. to the physical body, aura or chakras, don't forget to ask whether at the front, back or both)

7. Can they be severed? (if yes, then do so, if no, ask when you can do this days, weeks or months)

8. Is there a good time in which to do this?

9. Will this be beneficial to you?

10. Will this be beneficial to the other party?

7. Fourth-dimensional Portals

This is a spirit doorway to a different dimension, which can be opened by a careless thought, depression, illness, playing with a Ouija board – or perhaps on purpose – allowing demons or spirits to enter our world and to cause us all sorts of problems, both mentally and physically.

Once these beings are in your home, office or workplace, they can spread melancholy throughout the entire building, making people feel very uncomfortable, edgy, unhappy, depressed, listless, tired or even unnaturally elevated. These spirits can spread a detrimental feeling over everything and, once found, need to be returned to their own dimension as quickly as possible.

I have said that anyone playing with a Ouija board (who doesn't know what they are doing) can – and will – open many different portals. Some may be good but mostly they are bad. Unless these doorways are closed, then the problems can – and probably will – get worse, rather like a deepening depression shown on a weather map.

Doing anything psychically unprotected is like leaving your front door open all night, with the lights on in a busy part of town. You are more than likely to get unwelcome visitors or guests.

Before you close the doorway, you will need to make sure that all the beings that have come through are returned to their own dimension. Once this is done, you then close the door – and make sure that it is locked for all time.

Case Study 1: Jonathan From Near Farnham, Surrey. (Aged 25)

Jonathan's mother called me one day asking for my help. She had been a friend for several years, knowing me as an estate agent initially, and was therefore rather dubious about what I did. It must have taken a supreme effort for her to approach me; however, this was all to do with a mother's love for her son.

Jonathan was a sensitive lad, and picked up 'vibes', both good and bad, in his home and also in other people's houses. Over several months, his mother had noticed a change in him. He had become rather like a hermit, and had virtually confined himself to his bedroom. He was even eating all his meals there. He had been an open, friendly young man, although he always had been, as he put it himself later on, a little 'geeky'. He worked with computers, writing software and games for various IT companies, and this meant that he spent much of his time alone in his room. However, it was the dark moods and melancholy feelings that were unusual. His code-writing dried up, and he was just sitting in his room, often staring into space.

Because they lived near me, I went to visit the family. I sat talking to Jonathan and his mother, trying to find out why the dark feelings had started. I felt that it might be an unwanted spirit in the house, and I tuned in. Nothing was apparent, so I needed to look elsewhere for the root cause.

After further investigation, the story began to unfold. It often needs an 'outsider' to come along to ask questions, before the family can see the cause of the problem – and it doesn't matter how obvious it is.

Because Jonathan was getting busier, he needed more space for his computer equipment, and his father had offered to swap rooms. This swap took place over a few days, and Jonathan began to expand and to settle into his new office. After about a week he began to feel low, and flu-like symptoms developed. He just thought that he had 'burnt himself out' during the office move, and felt that a few days' rest was all that was needed. Sadly, rest was not the answer, and he spent most of his time either asleep or sitting in his chair, feeling 'dazed and confused'. He didn't want to see anyone, or talk to his parents, who were becoming very concerned and wanted him to see a doctor. He flatly refused, saying that 'all they do is give you pills'.

Luckily, his mother called me to see if I could do something for her son, rather than push the mainstream medical route and an endless supply of tablets.

I carried out my normal dowsing of the house for geopathic stress, and found many different problems there. However, when it came to the question, 'Are there any portals here?' I found the answer was more of

124

a scream in my head rather than just a movement of the pendulum. There certainly was one and it was directly affecting Jonathan; it fact it was in the very room he was now occupying. His father hadn't done him a favour, after all.

When asking how long the portal had been there, I got just over five years. When asking the family what happened five years ago, the answer was, 'Oh, that's when John (the father) was made redundant; it was a difficult time for the family, and he spent many hours in his office telephoning other companies, trying to find another job.' John then spoke about that period in his life, saying that he often became quite depressed, sinking into some very dark places.

There are many different ways of opening up a portal, and depression is a classic one. Sitting in a room on a chair for hours, with dark thoughts or worries going through your head, the energy has to go somewhere. This energy can easily open a portal, allowing detrimental beings through. These beings can 'mess with your head', especially if you are feeling down, or are unprotected psychically.

Because Jonathan was so sensitive, he was targeted by these dimensional beings, and he felt the full force of their energies. His emotional rollercoaster ride helped feed their requirements for energy, to sustain them here on Earth. Once I had found the problem, it was straightforward to solve, I sent the beings back to their own dimension and then shut the door.

Jonathan made a full and speedy recovery. His artistic flow returned, his sleep patterns became normal (for him), and he became part of the family again. John became self-employed and has never been happier – and Mum has become a healer.

Dowsing Diagnosis Questions for Dimensional Portals

1. Does the house have a dimensional portal?

2. Where is it?

3. Is the dimensional portal open?

4. Is it detrimental to you and the family?

5. How was it opened, i.e. depression, stress, on purpose?

6. When was it opened?

7. Can it be sealed?

8. Does the house need to be cleared of any beings that have come through the portal first?

9. Once sealed do the energies then need clearing?

8. Water Veins/Underground Streams

I prefer the term water veins, as underground streams can mean, in people's minds, anything from a large river to a small trickle of water. Water veins are rivulets of water running beneath your home, somewhere between ten feet and forty feet under the ground, carrying human emotions and/or earth radiation. They can be extremely detrimental to you and your family.

Water creates an energy field of great intensity, and this can have a profound effect on you. Stand by any river, swollen from the rain, and feel the energy as it rushes past. A water vein gives off the same energy, as it runs beneath your home. Unfortunately, as the energy rises, it gets trapped in your fully-insulated house and can't escape – unlike an overground stream or river, where the energies can easily dissipate into the air.

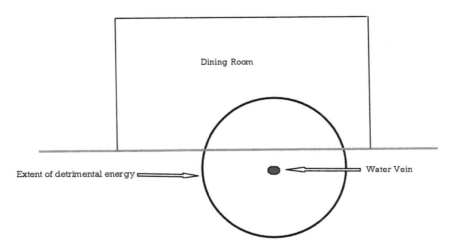

Figure 15. How detrimental energies affect people and houses

A famous piece of research into dowsing and healing circles was carried out in 1929 by Baron Gustav Freiherr von Pohl of Germany. He approached the Mayor of Vilsbiburg, a small town on a tributary of the Danube in Bavaria, near Munich, to carry out research into clusters of deaths due to cancer. The majority of the houses had been owned by the same families for generations, so he could look at the hereditary factor as well as the effects of underground water.

While carrying out his research, he was escorted by a policeman, to ensure that he would achieve an 'acceptable scientific result' for the dowsing work and the cancer research. First, he dowsed where the significant streams ran underground (over grade 9) and mapped them. He later cross-referenced them with the deaths from cancer of the people in the town. His dowsing showed that all the cancer deaths occurred above strong underground currents and their crossing points.

He repeated the experiment in Grafenau, with much the same results as before. All the people that died from cancer had, in Von Pohl's own words, 'slept in radiated beds'. His resulting book *Earth Currents – Causative Factor of Cancer and Other Diseases (Erdstrahlen als Krankheitserreger)* is a must for all earth energy dowsers, medical students, doctors and researchers alike.

Try typing in 'Krebs Houses' on the internet – much of his research is available there to read. He felt that water veins were, and are, probably the main factor of many of today's illnesses – including various forms of cancer, leukaemia, rheumatism and arthritis.

The same ideas were looked at after the Second World War by Dr Joseph Wurst, a German scientist, and Jakob Stangle, an engineer and dowser. Between them, they carried out a similar experiment to Von Pohl, but this time citing gamma rays as a potential cause of illness. There were other such experiments carried out in France too.

Kathe Bachler's book *Earth Radiation*, published in 1975, continued looking into cancer caused by earth energies and water veins. In looking at over 11,000 cases of illness, she was able to show a strong correlation between them and the noxious energies from the Earth. She also looked at learning difficulties in children and matched these to where they sat in class, again often over detrimental areas.

Sadly, these experiments and research could not be repeated these days due to the Data Protection Act. Can you imagine knocking on the door of your local hospital and asking for all the information that they have on local cancer deaths over the last twenty-five years?

For me, it is one of the most important aspects of a geomancer's work – looking at the water running beneath the house; moving the water vein both physically and energetically and allowing the affected person's immune system to do what it does naturally – heal the body.

Yes, you read that correctly – most geomancers are able, by intent, to move water veins physically and energetically from running beneath a house. Once this has been done it will, in most cases, allow people to sleep in a more beneficial way. This is necessary for the whole healing process.

Don't forget that when dowsing your home, we are looking for all things detrimental. There may be other veins and streams running beneath the house or office, however, *if they are not detrimental, leave them alone.* The healing work, once done, should enhance the beneficial aspect of these other veins and streams.

When I dowse, I like to know where the underground water runs and plot this on a floor plan of the house. I will also dowse how far the detrimental energies extend from the water, noting this on my report. Showing the meanderings of the water can often help to explain health problems in people, especially if they are sleeping above a detrimental area. Crossing points of water are particularly bad, and will normally show up as a -10 (the worst) during my investigation and dowsing.

Water has been proved to carry and store human emotions. Masaru Emoto conducted many experiments, and his findings can be found on the internet easily. As he froze water samples, he played various forms of music, from meditational to heavy metal, in the room. The results were staggering. The more 'sacred' the music, the more beautiful the ice crystals. The heavy metal music (which I do enjoy myself) didn't fare well – the crystals were malformed. There were also experiments using human intent as the water was frozen. Thoughts of love and peace produced some wonderful shapes – however, the obverse was that crystals subjected to hate and disharmony were almost formless.

Avarice, greed, hate, jealousy, etc., all produce energy, as do thoughts and actions of love, peace, harmony and healing. The former, though, produces detrimental energy that can then influence others, especially if the bad thoughts happen over a water vein that carries them beneath other people's houses. If, for instance, your next-door neighbours were always arguing and fighting – and the water vein ran in the direction of your home – you would be directly affected by those harmful emotions. The more sensitive you are, the more detrimental the effect could be.

So, when dowsing the water, check on the emotional level – and deal with it accordingly.

Case Study 1: Me

I was renting a spacious apartment in Godalming. When I first started dowsing for geopathic stress, the universe decided that I needed a direct lesson as to the effects of underground water on me – how detrimental they are to the healing process and how easy it can be to clear them.

I have found that when looking for a geopathically stressed area, it is best to start with where you sit most of the day – where you work, if you are working from home, or where you sit in the evening when you get home. It is very likely to be the worst location in the house. This is how it turned out to be for me. I started dowsing the apartment, and I found that the most detrimental water vein ran directly beneath where I sat whilst working on the computer. No wonder that I had started to get headaches, felt a little nauseous and sometimes quite faint.

I decided that I needed a safe haven to work within, as it was no good trying to heal others when I was living in a 'sick building' myself. I set to work and found a number of energy problems that needed to be healed, as well as two very detrimental water veins. Before working on them, I wanted to do a 'blind test', to see if I could not only clear them, but also move them away from the building. I had heard that water veins could be moved, and I was interested to see if I could do this.

I called my son Charles from his bedroom and asked him to dowse the room to see if he could pick up on any water running underneath. After protesting, as all teenagers do, he picked up the rods and asked to be shown where the water was. The rods moved, and he went in the

130

direction that they were pointing. They crossed exactly above the edge line of the vein that I had found, and did so again on the opposite side. He asked how detrimental the vein was, got a -7, muttered something and went off to work. I set to work on the water vein running beneath my feet, asking it to be healed of all things detrimental to Charles and myself, and that it be moved, both energetically and physically, away from the apartment, in a direction that was appropriate.

Four hours later, I dowsed and found that it had moved about six feet from its original position. Now, was I imagining this? Was my need for results influencing the rods, or was it actually moving? The only way to know for sure was to wait for Charles to come home. I hadn't told him what I was doing, so he would be working completely blind. As he was doing a long shift at 'The Cricketers' pub around the corner, I had to wait up until nearly midnight. I pounced on him as soon as he had shut the front door, poor lad, and gave him the dowsing rods.

'Can you dowse that water vein again for me?' He gave me a pitiful look, as much to say, 'Get a life.', but he took the rods and walked purposefully to where they crossed last time. Nothing happened. He could not find the water. I asked him to walk towards the window and dowse. As he neared the window, the rods crossed. The water vein had continued moving, and it was now only about two feet from the outside wall. It had moved eight feet from its initial location. Charles didn't understand, and went back to dowse the original position – nothing – turned and walked again towards to the window, where the rods crossed.

I explained what I had done with the water vein. To me, it was a momentous occasion, an epiphany moment. He just looked at me and shook his head. 'Goodnight, Pa,' was all he said.

Case Study 2: Jools and Nathan in Gloucestershire

As I mentioned earlier, their bungalow was, and still is, a challenge. As I dowsed for detrimental water veins, I found three – they all crossed at one central point, something that you rarely see in someone's home, but quite often in stone circles and sacred spaces.

Their home was built within the original site of a henge and central stone circle – both now demolished. However, the energies and the water crossings were still there, and they were having a very detrimental effect on the couple.

According to Jools, you could cut the atmosphere with a knife. Items were being moved; Larry the cat was being terrorized by who knows what and generally life could have been better. Jools is what we call a sensitive. She can pick up on energies, both good and bad, in a house. She knows when changes have happened, so she could give me good feedback, which in this instance was critical.

We dealt with the spirits there, separately from the one in the attic, as it is good to rescue the souls before you start changing the energies in what is tantamount to being their home. A ley ran through the house and bisected the central crossing points of the water, as did an earth energy line. All told, it is a very energetic place to live, but not the right form of energy for a family to be close to all the time.

I worked on the lines and harmonized them, then came the water. As the water veins had been encouraged to cross there by man, many centuries ago, to energize the henge and the stone circle, it needed carefully dismantling. It wasn't a matter of just asking the streams to move, I first had to work on dissipating the energies of the original henge, and then the stone circle. Once this had been done, sorting out the streams became relatively simple.

Jools reported that the atmosphere in their home lightened very quickly. She and Nathan felt so much better, clear-headed and able to move forward with their work on the bungalow. Often, living above water veins can feel like you are being dragged down, and once their influence has been broken you feel free, thoughts become more positive and that in turn will lead to positive changes.

We did have an episode of a missing bunch of keys, shortly afterwards. They were the only set of keys to their van, which they were looking to sell. If they couldn't find them, then the sale would be in jeopardy. 'Can you dowse where they might be for me please? We have been through everything in the place and cannot find them,' requested Jools. I did so, and told her that she needed to walk from the hall into their living room – and that the keys would be found in the first item on the left as you go through the door. 'It's a bureau,' she said. 'That's where we thought that they were but we have gone through it with a fine-toothed comb and they aren't there.' 'The keys are definitely in the very first thing on the left as you walk into the room.' I repeated. They said they would look again in the bureau, and call me with the news. I received a telephone call two days later, saying that they had found them – not in the bureau but in a jacket hanging on the back of the door leading to the living room. It was the very first thing on the left as you enter the room. Perhaps my dowsing was a little too literal.

I would suggest that after heavy periods of rain you dowse to make sure that no further water veins have opened.

When drawing in these lines I use a blue fine-tipped pen.

Dowsing Diagnosis Questions for Water Veins

1. Are there any water veins affecting your home?

2. How many?

3. Where are they?

4. How detrimental are they (0 to -10)?

5. How far from the centre of the water vein can the detrimental energy be felt?

6. How deep are they beneath the ground?

7. How much of the detrimental energy is human emotion?

8. Can I heal the whole water vein?

9. Can I divert them all from underneath my house?

10. Can I divert them away from other houses that they affect (always ask if appropriate)?

9. Earth Energy Lines

These are the big power lines of the Earth, necessary for life to exist on the planet. Each one stretches around the globe, taking energy to where it is needed. There are various strata and bands within these lines, however I do not normally show these when drawing up the floor plan of a house, as they can over-complicate the diagram.

When dowsing a sacred site, you will find these lines are prevalent. They are different to ley lines, which to me are created by human intent and by their male and female feeder energy channels, as with the Michael and Mary lines.

It is interesting to dowse the other planets in our solar system, to see whether any of them have had similar energy lines in the past. You might be amazed at what you find – especially on Mars.

When working with more earthly lines, I would normally draw them in as straight lines on a house floor plan. They can, however, meander a little, but for all intents and purposes it is easier to show them this way. The choice is yours.

Again, as with the water veins, these lines can also carry a certain amount of human emotion within them. It would be worthwhile dowsing to find out exactly what detrimental patterns are held and, if possible, where they come from. That way, you could carry out a healing at the source, which will be much more effective. You could use a map of the world to help you track down the culprit and, don't forget, a date can be very useful.

I also note down how detrimental they are (e.g. -6), how far the detrimental effect is felt (the line runs within a conduit/tunnel just like a water vein) and, if appropriate, do a healing on the whole line surrounding the globe. I often imagine the line running through an area of conflict and, as the healing happens, a peaceful thought goes through the minds of the people there.

Don't forget that when healing is carried out appropriately, it doesn't matter what you want or ask for, if the 'highest of the high' doesn't want change or healing given, then it won't happen. However, never forget the power of negotiation – always ask for a second time, or even a third.

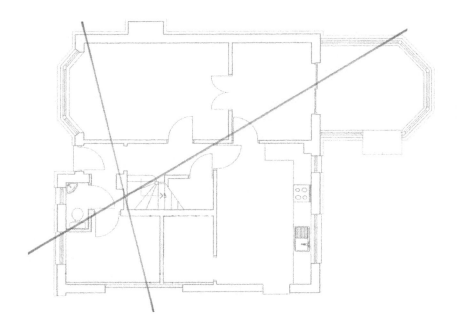

Figure 16. Earth energy lines on a floor plan

Case Study 1: Godalming High Street

Now, this case is very close to my heart, as this particular earth energy line runs straight through my old office – and almost exactly where I used to sit in the days before I had started to look at the complex energy patterns around us – when I really knew no better.

After I had sold the business, I was able to start studying geopathic stress and all its facets. To be honest, I found it very difficult to lead what I felt was a spiritual life, and also be involved in the day-to-day running of a very commercial business. The two, for me, never went hand in glove. It was rather like trying to push together the opposite poles of two magnets – not joining, but actively repelling. There is, of course, a balance to be stuck, but I never found it. So, in order to fully embrace the spiritual side of life, I knew I had to leave the material behind.

The line that runs through Godalming High Street is a particularly powerful one, and it is able to drain, as well as to energize, the buildings and the people it touches. I really became aware of it in two separate places. At the time, I didn't realize that it was the same line, until I dowsed it remotely on a map – and then walked it.

I quite enjoy the occasional foray into the shops. You never know what you might find. Clothes, food, gifts for others, earth energy lines, shoes, ley lines, music CDs, energy spirals – the list is endless. I always have a pendulum in my pocket, just in case I am asked a difficult question by my wife, such as, 'Should I buy the green dress or the red one?' I dowse the answer; I know it's a little like passing the buck, however I feel that the heavenly ones do give us a little leniency.

It was on a trip like this that I sat at the back of a boutique, whilst various dresses were being tried on. Other women were there, looking at the rails of clothes, and I became aware that one section of the shop was being avoided. The articles hanging on a rail, and on the rail opposite to it, were untouched by everyone. I kept watching as new customers came in and started to browse. Every time they walked up to the 'suspect' rails, they gave them a cursory glance and walked straight past. I was fascinated. Out came the pendulum and I started asking questions:

Is there a detrimental line running through the shop?

Yes.

Is it an earth energy line?

Yes.

Is it affecting this particular section of the shop?

Yes.

Are people subconsciously picking up on this?

Yes.

So, we had an earth energy line that was running straight through one wall and out the other, affecting two clothes rails, and also the settee that I was sat on. I was beginning to feel light-headed and faint. I moved to the front of the shop, as I wanted to get away from the energies, and also to speak to the lady running the boutique.

'Do you ever sell any clothes from the two rails at the back of the shop?' I asked.

She looked at me rather strangely – you do get used to this when dowsing – thought about it, and said, 'No we don't'. She continued, 'I think that it is something to do with the lighting. It doesn't show off the clothes properly there. We have to keep moving them to other rails, otherwise they wouldn't sell.'

'It's got nothing to do with the lights, and all to do with an earth energy line,' I replied. 'Come and have a look at this.' I grabbed a pair of coat hangers and walked towards the rear of the shop, telling the assistant what was about to happen when I reached the energy line. The coat hangers crossed as my right foot went over the outer edge of the line, and they crossed again at the other side.

'There it is – that energy line is putting your customers off buying these clothes. It runs directly through both rails,' I said, but she didn't look impressed.

So, I tried a different tack. 'Here, you have a go and see what you can find,' handing her the coat hangers. She declined, and gave me that strange look again. I described what an earth energy line is, what it does and how it affects people. I thought that might help, but it didn't. So, I told her what I did for a living, and gave her one of my business cards. I added that I would like the opportunity to do some healing work on the line, to see if we it would make a difference to her sales from those rails. She said that she would talk to the owner and get back to me. Sadly, I never received the call.

It was a great shame, as verification is so important to dowsers and healers. It would have been interesting to see if, by harmonizing the

138

energies in the shop, it would have made any difference to their sales.

Several days later, I walked into one of Godalming's supermarkets to buy supplies for the week. As I pushed the trolley towards the top of an aisle, I noticed that the items stacked on a shelf in one particular section looked untidy. The opposite side of the aisle looked the same. Intrigued, I turned the corner and looked down the next aisle, and saw it was exactly the same – and the next, and the next. Out came the pendulum again, and I started asking questions, 'Are we looking at an earth energy line here?'

The pendulum started describing an anti-clockwise movement meaning 'yes'.

As I was dowsing, I was aware that a man was approaching me wearing a supermarket uniform. I looked up and recognized him; he had been to my local dowsing group a couple of times. He was intrigued at my dowsing in the shop, and asked me why. I pointed at the shelves and asked, 'Do they always look this dishevelled?' 'Oh yes,' he replied, 'We are always tidying them, but they never stay that way. Turn your back and, hey presto, they are all messed up again. Why do you ask?'

I told him of the earth energy line running through that section of the supermarket, and we traced it from one end to the other. It entered by the cold meats section, and exited through the wine and beer shelves.

'Funny that,' he continued. 'We also have a problem with the meat in that area, it goes off very quickly. We have to keep a very close eye on it; the sell-by date seems to have no relevance there.'

I asked what the manger was like, and if he was open to 'our kind of stuff'. My friend looked rather dubious and said he wasn't. He had discussed dowsing with him, but was met with disbelief. However, business is business, and I felt that there was no harm in trying. He was just finishing talking to a colleague when I found him.

I told him what I had found and offered to show him, but was met with a blank face. He did admit to believing in ghosts, but dowsing was going too far, as was the premise that earth energy lines would play any part in messing up the shelves. He added that he didn't want anything done, as Head Office wouldn't approve. I saw his point.

It wasn't until seven years later, when I started to write this section of the book, that it occurred to me to see if it was the same line in both places. I looked at Godalming on Google earth, and lined up the boutique and the supermarket. I discovered that it was the same earth energy line in both shops. Not only that, it ran through my old office, and also through my desk.

Case Study 2: Kate in Farnham, Surrey

Kate and her husband had only recently moved to Farnham and because it was only a few miles away from me I went to visit her. She had not been feeling well since they moved and Kate felt that the house and area had something to do with it.

Kate is a sensitive and is very gifted, she communicates with animals, and I have asked for her help on several occasions since our first meeting. Animals are a wonderful source of information, especially when you have worked on the house and need to find out how their owners are reacting.

The part of Farnham that Kate lives in has always had an 'unusual feel' to it. The town suffered during the Great Plague and there were many mass graves dug for the victims, several of whom had not gone to the light. Kate always felt nervous walking along the main road; she felt that someone or something was following her when she left the house.

When I entered Kate's house the atmosphere felt heavy, as it does on a hot humid day, but this was human emotion and earth energy that was causing it, not the weather. I walked into the living room and started to dowse, and found a large and detrimental earth energy line running almost diagonally across the room – not somewhere that I would have liked to have been sitting for any length of time. Kate told me to follow her upstairs as she wanted to show me something. There on her bed, immediately above the energy line, was a huge cat fast asleep, 'Foss always sleeps there,' said Kate. 'That is my husband's side of the bed and he doesn't sleep well.'

Now, cats are heat-seeking animals and will actively look for the warmest place to sleep, but I have found over the years that their favourite locations are often above or within areas that are detrimental to their human owners. It has been documented that cats are able to transmute detrimental energies; perhaps they are the self-proclaimed guardians of the house.

I carried out some healing at the house but the more in-depth stuff was saved until I got home. I asked Kate to keep an eye on Foss and see if there were any changes in his habits. It didn't take long before I received a call from Kate. 'He's no longer happy sleeping on the bed, in fact he is looking a little lost and can't settle anywhere.'

Foss was aware that the energies had changed in the house, especially in the bedroom. He no longer had to 'stand guard' and use his energies to protect his owners. I did some further work and he did start to settle, spending more time outside underneath a wonderful apple tree that had been cleared of a detrimental elemental. Kate's husband started to sleep better and the house started to feel like a home with all the past emotional energy cleared.

I also carried out healing work to the road, local cemetery and a plague pit, but that is another story.

When drawing in these lines I use a green fine-tipped pen.

Dowsing Diagnosis Questions for Earth Energy Lines

1. Are there any detrimental earth energy lines running through your home?

2. How many?

3. Where are they?

4. How detrimental are they?

5. How far to either side and above can the detrimental energies be felt?

6. Am I allowed to heal the whole line?

7. Will it stay healed or is there another layer to deal with? (If yes, then go to next question)

8. When will I have to deal with it? (Then find out when and put that date in your diary)

10. Toxic Lines

These are not often found, but they do exist. I find that human corruption of the land or pollution from past or present industry is more than likely to blame. On the properties that I have worked on over the years, the lines only seem to clip the houses and only rarely have I seen a line run straight through one.

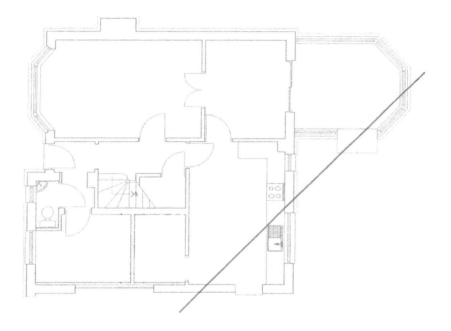

Figure 17. A Toxic line

I used to call this an Earth Cancer line but changed it to Toxic Line after tutoring a Heal Your Home II course in Ashurst, Kent. The students there felt that the term was confusing as the line is more of an illness of the land caused by man-made pollution or toxins. Although, having said that, this form of line came to my attention when I was working on two separate houses in Surrey, only about three miles apart. One person in each house had developed an unusual form of cancer. It was only when working on the second client that I realized the same line must cross both houses.

Out came the Ordnance Survey map, and I traced the direction of the line. Sure enough it went through both, only just clipping each house. Both men had contracted, and were being treated for, cancer. The line seemed to be the link, although that is supposition on my part, and it might be a complete coincidence. However, is there such as thing as coincidence?

Humans had created the line, and this time is was the burial of noxious substances – something to do with the Second World War. I dowsed further to find that munitions had been buried just after the war and had caused this detrimental line to form. The energies seemed somehow to create a cancerous line that was harmful to men.

I have heard that some geomancers will dowse for what they call 'black lines'. However, most of them don't seem to ask what they are or how they are formed. This is important when it comes to clearing and healing them; to know the cause makes it easier to work on the lines.

When detailing these lines I draw them in pink.

Dowsing Diagnosis Questions for Toxic Lines

1. Is there a Toxic Line affecting your house?

2. How many?

3. Where are they?

4. How detrimental is the line?

5. Is it detrimental to both men and women?

6. When was it caused, what date?

7. Why was it caused?

8. Can it be healed?

9. Do you need to heal it at source first, then your home?

10. Can you heal it for other people too?

11. Do other layers exist?

11. Reversal Points

I hadn't come across a reversal point until reading an article by Billy Gawn, published in *Dowsing Today* – the magazine produced by The British Society of Dowsers – although I was aware that there was an anomaly in some people's houses that needed some explanation.

Billy explained that areas in a house, office, workplace or garden can be found that are completely neutral, and have no effect on people whatsoever, until they are covered by an object, which can be as mundane as a table, chair or flowerpot. This will then allow detrimental energies to flow into other parts of the house or office, causing health problems for the family or the workforce. Billy uses kinesiology to demonstrate how this works, and the effects that these detrimental energies have on the body – especially the muscular system, which collapses quickly once a reversal point is covered and you happen to be standing in the wrong place. It only takes a matter of seconds for the harmful energies to take effect, and it's quite dramatic.

To find one, just ask the question. See which way the rods point, and follow them until they cross – you have yourself a reversal point. I don't find them often, but they can exist anywhere in the building, and also the garden. Once found, they are simple to deal with, but when the detrimental energies are rising, due to one being covered, it can be very uncomfortable for the family.

You can obviously dowse this remotely for someone else, by just asking the question, 'Is there a reversal point in this house or garden?', and noticing what the rods or pendulum do. If you get a 'yes' response, find out what room it is in and the exact place. Then, either carry out a healing, or warn the family to leave the area uncovered at all times.

Case Study 1: The Johnson Family in Wimbledon Village

This was an intriguing case, and one that I worked on before I fully understood, or had actually heard of, a reversal point. I knew that something wasn't right in my client's home, but couldn't put my finger on exactly what it was. Now, I always carry out a spiritual update on all my past clients' houses, rather like a computer upgrade, when I find a new problem that comes under the title of geopathic stress.

Their home was badly affected by spirits and inherited human emotions – it had been the scene of several divorces, had once been a small school and was used by the armed services just after the war had ended. All in all, it was a bit of a mess, and the family were suffering, having moved in about two years before they contacted me.

The telephone call started, as many of them do, like this, 'Now this might sound odd and you will probably think that I am crazy but . . .' I must admit that very little sounds strange these days – the telephone ringing will always bring a new, and sometimes unexpected, problem to deal with. Luckily, I enjoy a challenge.

Jenny Johnson explained that when they had bought the house, it was in a bit of a mess and they had to do a lot of work to it. This took about six months to complete because of various problems, including several of the builders and workmen downing their tools and never coming back. This was due to unexplained noises, apparitions and items disappearing or being moved, when there was no one else in the house.

'If I had known about the problems we were going to be facing we never would have bought the place,' she said on the telephone. 'It is so cold, unnaturally cold, and it never seems to warm up, even during the summer months. We cannot live in the house as a family; we seem to be falling apart; there is melancholy in every corner and something needs to be done. Can you help?' No pressure there then.

I asked for a floor plan to be sent through. However, I already knew that the house could be sorted and that I could once again bring happiness into the family's life. Sometimes, the message just comes through loud and clear.

It turned out to be a detached Victorian three-storey house with six bedrooms. What an estate agent would call a 'substantial house', in a very sought-after location. However, when the floor plan arrived through the post, it seemed to have a strange energy about it – even the envelope looked as though it had gone through the wars to get to me. I had to deal with clearing and healing the plan, before I could tackle the house.

Much of the house was as expected, full of stuck emotional energy – and eight spirits that had made themselves very much at home there. They didn't like all the banging and clattering that had gone on during the renovation of the house, and had made their dissatisfaction known during the work. After I had tuned in and made them aware that they could easily move into the light, and that they could be reunited with past family and friends, they went very quickly. This immediately lifted much of the gloom in the house, and the children started to sleep at night. However, that was not the full story, and a lot more work had to be done, including earth energy problems, water veins, emotional energy areas and human-manifested life forms.

The house took on a much better feel; the arguments stopped and the family started having meals together. 'Harmonious' was the word used several weeks later, when following up on the healing work. A few days after that, however, I received an email saying that the house was feeling strange again. The cold was creeping back in and the children didn't want to go to bed at night as they felt that someone or something was there. Layers exist, especially in a house as troubled as this one. Once the main layer has been healed, then a lesser one can rise to the surface and start the problems all over again. This is why feedback from my clients is so important – you can't always sort out all the problems in one go. Time is needed for the family and house to adjust to the new energies, and then you have to wait and see if any further niggles arrive. They did in this case. But they seemed to occur during the day, the night time was quiet.

I carried out a further healing on the house and family, clearing the next layer away. All indications were that it was the last of the detrimental energies, the house should now be clear . . . but it wasn't. I did a further clearing, and all would be normal for a few days – then, wham, it would start again.

I dowsed and asked:

Is there something here that I haven't found before?

Yes.

149

Does it allow detrimental energies to flow in the house?

Yes.

Is it located in one particular area?

Yes.

I dowsed the house plan again and found it located in their kitchen/breakfast room. I dowsed the extent of problem, and it appeared as a small area, about three feet in diameter. I telephoned Jenny and asked what was there. 'Nothing, just an empty space,' she replied. I was no further forward.

Ten minutes later she called me back and said, 'We tend to keep the house tidy, and in the evening we put the children's toys into a box which then goes into a cupboard. During the day, however, the box normally sits exactly where you said that the problem area is, does that help?' It certainly did. I dowsed and found out that when the box was put away at night the detrimental energies stopped, but when it was brought out of the cupboard, and placed on what I now refer to as a 'reversal point' in the morning, it caused the detrimental energies to rise, and start the cycle all over again.

Once I had an explanation, I needed to find for a cure. Healing is, in most cases, intuitive – however, you sometimes need to look at the physical world to find a solution. Being practical helps you deal with problems in the real world, for instance, plugging a hole in a water pipe. You can bring much of that experience into the spiritual world, when carrying out a healing and trying to find a solution to a physical problem.

I picked up my pendulum and started to ask questions:

Can this reversal point be sealed?

Yes.

Is it a simple process? (I kept my fingers crossed at this point)

Yes.

So, I thought, what in practical terms could you use to cover or seal a hole that causes energies to rise in a room? A manhole cover sprang to mind. The next question therefore was:

Is a spiritual manhole cover suitable?

Yes.

So that is what I now use and this will be fully explained in the Healing section of the book.

When showing these on my plan I use a black *.

Dowsing Diagnosis Questions for Reversal Points

1. Are there any reversal points affecting your home?

2. How many?

3. Are they inside or outside the house?

4. Where are they exactly?

5. How detrimental are they?

6. Can I seal them?

7. Do I need to clear the house of their detrimental effect first?

8. Will they remain sealed for all time?

12. Fractured Souls

The big question is, 'Do we have a soul, and if so, where is it?'

It is a question that I have pondered many times over the years. My answer is, yes, we do. However, it is not within us, like our heart or brain, but surrounds us like a shroud, contained within the human energy field. Our very essence is contained within it, reacting to our thoughts, wishes and actions, expanding and contracting with our emotions.

Scientists have now discovered an impulse that stimulates the brain before it sends a message via the central nervous system to our muscles, so that we can move. Does that impulse originate from our soul?

I believe that the soul is found within the auric field that surrounds our body; it is formed between our 4th band (Astral) and the 5th band (Etheric Template) and the fracture is more like a splitting of the energies.

Most of us are born with our soul intact, having survived our last incarnation complete and whole. However, as we grow and mature many things can upset us, and until we know how to fully protect ourselves, both physically and spiritually, your very soul can be at risk – and it is easily affected by people and situations around you.

A parent scolding a child, for instance, bullying at school, stress from work or family life, parents divorcing or trauma from losing a loved one can easily fracture your soul. Adoption is something else that can fracture parts of the soul. The very fact that the child is being taken from, or is given away by, its birth mother can, and probably will, cause major problems for it later on in life. If a fracture is found, it needs repairing.

There are many different ways of restoring a soul. Shamans, for instance, will journey into the underworld and retrieve the missing parts from whoever has taken possession of it. I like to keep things as simple as possible, and I enlist Archangel Michael to help restore the fractured piece.

I dowse to find out why the soul has been fractured in the first place, and the date when it happened, what percentage of the whole is missing, and who or what is responsible.

When dowsing the question for someone else, please be careful as you can, and probably will, be touching on some very deep-seated feelings and problems that have, perhaps, been buried for years. In some cases, the person might not even know that something is wrong – as in this case study.

Case Study 1: Tom from the Midlands

I was originally approached by Tom, as he felt that he had a couple of attachments and a possible ghost in his apartment. After finding my details on the web, he contacted me to discuss his problems – little did he know what was going to transpire.

As I was talking with him on the telephone, a great sadness came over me. I do not usually feel anything when talking over the telephone, as the psychic protection that I put around me stops this from happening. However, this time I was being given a strong message that I had to be wary, and that something unusual was going on.

Tom was in IT, and held a high position within a London-based company. Recently, he had been noticing that when he used a computer it would switch itself off, or the program would suddenly become corrupted. It was happening more and more frequently, and he was becoming very irritated – as was his company. He felt that it must be the electro-magnetic charge coming from his body, and had looked at various methods of reducing this with bracelets, de-gaussing, rubber-soled shoes and grounding exercises, but nothing had really worked, and he was getting increasingly frustrated.

He was right about the spirit. However, it was not confined to his apartment, but followed Tom around constantly, almost like a jealous lover. It was the spirit of a female, and she didn't like him spending time with anyone else, or anything else, including computers. I tuned into her, and I found out that she had passed away in the early 1900s, having committed suicide after her fiancé dumped her rather unceremoniously. She had latched onto Tom, as he reminded her of the man that she had lost all those years ago. I tuned into the young lady, and I mentioned that her fiancé was waiting for her in the light. She went without a thought, and is now blissfully happy in the right place. This left a few other problems that needed to be cleared up, including Tom's attachments and, what turned out to be, a fractured soul.

The attachments had been with him for a number of years, but this is quite commonplace and they were cleared easily. The computer problems cleared up, but during my dowsing I had picked up an upset that he suffered when he was six years old – an upset so big that it had fractured fifteen percent of his soul.

I asked him about his sixth year, and had anything unusual happened around that time? He was rather taken aback at this unexpected question. It turned out that his parents had separated just after his sixth birthday, and a rather acrimonious divorce had taken place. He ended up living with his father, although his choice would have been to live with his mother. Seemingly, his early years had been very happy and for Tom, the break-up was completely out of the blue. He remembers being desperately unhappy and unable to comprehend what it all meant. This had shocked the lad so much that his very soul was affected, and during this torrid time it fractured.

Since that day, he'd had difficulties with getting close to anyone. When he was sent off to boarding school by his father, he felt as though he had been abandoned, and this feeling stayed with him until his fractured soul was discovered – and something done about it. He had not seen his mother or father for years, as he felt nothing for them.

I normally bring healing to fractured souls separately to the main house healing session; I find that it deserves respect and special treatment. How this is done is detailed in Part 3.

After I reunited the fractured section of his soul he said that he began to feel like a different person (although this is not always the case). Shortly afterwards, he started to date a young lady that he had met through his IT work.

I had an email from him about a year later, saying that he was now engaged and was shortly to be married. His personal life had turned around. He had been in contact with his parents, and he had established a relationship with them. Although the relationship was still a little strained, it was getting better day by day. Both his parents came to me individually for healing, which helped the re-unification process further.

He is still in IT; the computers are quite happy, as are his parents, who now have a grandson to dote upon.

Dowsing Diagnosis Questions for Fractured Souls

1. Do you or any of your family members have a fractured soul?

2. Who?

3. How bad is the fracture in percentage terms?

4. When did this happen?

5. Why did this fracture happen?

6. Can you heal it?

7. Which Archangel do you use to carry out the soul retrieval?

8. Do you need to put protection (white light) around the soul?

9. How long for?

13. Stress/Disturbance Lines (Man-Made)

These lines are man-made, resulting mainly from emotional upset and suffering. They can be caused by battles, murder, suicide, muggings, foundations being excavated on a building, bad farming practices, mental and/or physical abuse, suffering after a car accident or trauma. The list can seem endless, and they differ from Toxic lines, which are mostly caused by noxious materials being buried, or by long- term pollution.

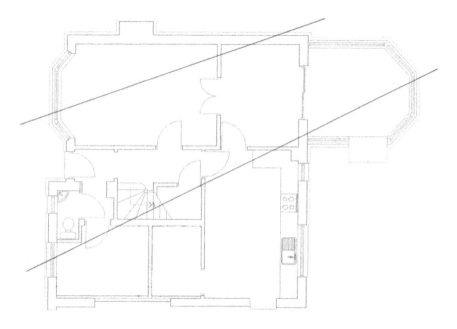

Figure 18. Stress/disturbance lines

You can have caused them yourself inadvertently, and you do need to check out why that might have been. However, it is more likely that someone else has created them, and that they are completely unaware of what they have done, just as human emotion can be present in water veins. It can also run through fault lines, cracks, certain minerals and other weaknesses in the earth.

The lines can be upwards of twenty miles or more in length and, although they can fade as the years pass, if what caused them to form was particularly detrimental, for example a murder or a suicide, they might not – they will be there to stay.

When I dowse for myself or others, I like to find out how detrimental the energy actually is on a 0 to -10 scale. I will also dowse the length of the line – when and why it was caused. Trying to find out how a stress line was set up is not easy, as there are so many differing possibilities. First, I look at how detrimental it is. A level of -7 and upwards is serious, and human suffering is more than likely the cause. A murder ranks at around -8 to -10, and a suicide will be similar. A car crash, where the victim or victims suffered pain or anxiety, will be from -6 upwards; a mugging or robbery from -5. Land disturbance is normally lower on the scale, but this does depend again on the cause. Quarrying, for instance, will be around -3 or -4, however, when explosives have been used, the figure will shoot up. I would start by asking, 'Is the line caused by human suffering or land disturbance?', then move on to find out how serious it is and finally work out the cause.

The more questions you ask, the more experienced you will become. Often, I will find that the answer just comes into my mind, however obscure the reason for the forming of the line.

Case Study 1: Freya in Manchester

I was approached by Freya, in my early days of starting up Dowsing Spirits. She had an apartment in Manchester that she had lived in for a while, but then rented it out. She'd had major problems with all her tenants, and the current one was the worst. He stopped paying the rent two months into a six-month contract; he refused to allow the agent access to check on a leak that had been reported by the owner of the flat beneath, and so it went on. She was at her wits end, and asked if I could help.

When she had first met the tenant, he seemed to be a decent chap. He was well dressed, with a good job, and she felt that he was ideal. She did say though that all the other tenants had appeared that way too. She felt that something in the flat wasn't right, but didn't know whether it was a spirit affecting the men, or the inherited energies of the place.

I dowsed to see if there was a problem with the flat and the answer was 'yes'. I could help, but I wasn't sure at that time what the problem might be. There were two spirits in the apartment, but they registered as quite low on the detrimental scale. I moved them into the light, as I worked through my checklist. When it came to stress lines, I have never seen the rods move in such a positive way. They started spinning and almost took off, something that I normally don't allow. I figured that I was on to something big. I dowsed that ten stress lines crossed the apartment, with the highest at -10 in detrimental effect.

I went through all my normal questions – mental cruelty got a response, physical cruelty also got a response, so did murder and suicide. I was at a loss generally, so I tried dating the most detrimental line and counted back to the seventeenth century, narrowing it down to 1652. Then the word 'slavery' came into my mind. My higher self was helping me, and the rods moved – I had picked up a slavery line. Even after 356 years, the detrimental energies measured -10 – the worst that they can possibly be – no wonder the tenants had had problems. I guessed they might have been having nightmares and feeling abject terror and helplessness. Sadly, I could never speak to them to find out.

I worked on bringing healing to all the stress lines affecting the apartment. The other lines were a mixture of murder, mugging and land disturbance. I worked on them all, sending healing, not only down the lines, but also to their source. I hoped that by doing this, others would be spared the agonies that the tenants had experienced.

I reported my findings to Freya, who was stunned. She had never liked living at the apartment herself, and informed me that the whole building was constantly having problems with break-ins, general disruptions and graffiti, and arguments could always be heard. I received feedback from Freya some weeks after to say that the tenant had resurfaced. He was paying his rent, and he had got the leak fixed himself. He continued living in the flat for a further twelve months, was always on time with his rent and caused no more problems. The next tenant has been the same.

Case Study 2: Restaurant in North London

I was asked by the owner's wife, Devi, to dowse a popular fusion restaurant in North London. They had been open for business for five years, and been very successful from day one. However, takings were now down, they were having problems with staff and generally the place seemed very subdued. Not what you, as a customer, would want to feel when going out to eat.

I decided, in this particular case, to visit the restaurant. I was living in Godalming in Surrey at that time, so it was an easy trip by train and tube. The journey time gave me the opportunity to tune in to the restaurant, and I did some general human emotional clearing before I got there.

Please remember that when visiting a site, it is so important to psychically protect yourself. Walking into a known detrimental area without protection is rather like walking out of the house when it's raining – completely naked.

I met Devi at the restaurant. Although the lights were on, it felt that there was nobody at home. The atmosphere inside was very off-putting; it felt like a south coast town on a wet dreary day . . . uninviting and miserable. I had picked up various energy lines running through the restaurant, as well as three spirits, various human-manifested forms, elementals, power artefacts, and human conflict areas. However, the underlying trend was misery, distrust and suspicion – not the ideal mix for people going there to enjoy themselves.

Just outside their front door, I picked up a particularly bad area that had been formed by human emotion. However, the feelings that created it had gone so deep that it had now become a place memory (as described fully in section 22 of the checklist). I felt that a murder had been committed here and, talking with Devi, she confirmed that only a few months ago a fatal stabbing had occurred. The victim had collapsed in their doorway and died – it was put down as a revenge attack.

I won't go into full details here as to why human emotion turns into a place memory, but the suffering of the victim and the hate behind the murder had left an emotional imprint that the human subconscious can pick up. As people approached the doorway to enter the restaurant, they visibly recoiled and walked on, even though they already had a reservation.

That was not their main problem, though. There's more. Nine stress lines ran through the restaurant – two very strong and seven lesser ones, crossing in the kitchen.

When I showed this to Devi, she immediately said that her normally placid head chef, who had been with them from the start, had suddenly developed a vile temper. This had worsened in the past few months, and he had threatened several of his staff with a knife. Needless to say, they had walked out and not come back. Staffing was, therefore, becoming a huge issue, and they could not find anyone to work there. Devi said that they would normally have a queue of people wanting employment, but this had completely dried up. She had even started to work as a part time waitress herself, and this was having an impact on her children.

The two strongest lines were caused by acts of violence, both within half a mile of the restaurant. The first was a drugs-related murder, about five months previously, and the second was the murder of a prostitute some eight weeks earlier.

The other six lines were formed by two muggings, a gang-related beating, two lots of mental abuse and the final one by land disturbance from the foundations of a large extension, being built down the road.

The combined violence, suffering and hatred of these acts came together in the kitchen. No wonder the chef was having problems. The most detrimental line ran through the dining area of the restaurant; the second ran through the bar and waiting area – was it any surprise that people didn't like it there?

Due to the severity of the lines, they had to be healed several times. Going directly to the source of the problem helps. Clearing the place where a murder has happened is good practice. Once done, the lines should disappear, but do check again in about a week's time to make sure.

When I last heard from Devi, the restaurant was back on its feet and very busy. The chef was back to his normal self and several of the old staff had returned. Business was very brisk, in fact better than it ever had been.

When I draw stress lines on my house plan I use a red pen.

Dowsing Diagnosis Questions for Stress Lines

1. Is your home affected by stress lines?

2. How many?

3. Where are they?

4. How detrimental is each one?

5. How were they created?

6. When were they created?

7. Were you or your family responsible for setting any of them up?

8. How long are they?

9. Are you allowed to heal them all?

10. Do you need to heal the source of the line first?

14. Ley Lines/Holy Lines

Ah, good old ley lines – a term widely misused, even amongst dowsers. Ley lines are seemingly blamed for all our ills. The tabloids, when news is quiet, will often come up with a sensational headline on the effects of living on a ley line; UFOs use them to navigate by; animals walk along them – and people? Well, people just suffer.

Ley, an Anglo Saxon word, means 'a cleared strip of ground'. Watkins himself only used this term himself for a few years, before discarding it in favour of 'old straight tracks' – the title of his book, published in 1925. These tracks ran from hilltop to hilltop, passing through churches, way points, marker and standing stones and a myriad of other points of interest.

It wasn't until the 1960s, and the start of the 'new age' movement, that ley lines returned to public attention. John Michell's seminal book *The View Over Atlantis* introduced us to the Michael Ley that runs from Cornwall to the Norfolk coast, through some of the most famous megalithic monuments in the South of England.

Should you be interested in finding out more about ley lines, see the appendix at the rear of the book for further reading.

There are two schools of thought; one states that ley lines are purely dowsable energy lines, the other that they are purposely placed and created by man for ceremonial purposes – such as the Nazca lines in Peru. Why can't they be both?

To me, they are lines created by human intent, often set up by the village Shaman or holy man, showing the way to a sacred site, such as a spring or a stone circle. Rather like sheep paths, they do have a dowsable energy, mainly from the people that have used them over the years, leaving their emotional imprint indelibly etched on the earth.

Once this spiritual pathway had been created, the people would then be able to follow this 'emotional energy ley' easily to a specific site from a village or local community. They would have been able to feel or sense the specific energies within the line; they might also have been able to see them in colour, picking out the various strata within the leys.

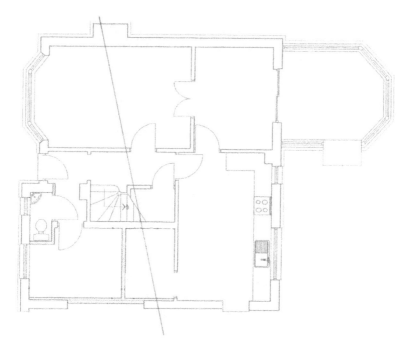

Figure 19. Ley line running through a house

I therefore find that leys do have a dowsable energy – and that this can sometimes be detrimental. However, I rarely find them above a -2 or a -3, at the highest, unless someone has 'dirtied the line' on purpose.

As a matter of interest, I generally dowse the length of the ley and how many sacred sites it links on its journey across the countryside – simple burial mounds, churches or standing stones, such as those at Avebury or Stonehenge.

Case Study 1: Mrs F in Oxfordshire

This was an unusual case, due to the high detrimental reading found on the ley line that crossed Mrs F's house. In fact, there were two running almost parallel through the property.

The less affected of the two leys came out at -2, but the other one was a whopping -7. This line ran almost diagonally through the main bedroom, bisecting their bed.

Mrs F had had trouble sleeping in the bed for several years, eventually moving into the dressing room and sleeping on a camp bed. It wasn't comfortable, but her sleep patterns improved, and she could at least cope with her day-to-day life. She did, however, want to return to the marital bed, and started to look for ways to sort out what she felt were bad energies in the room. How she found me was through a series of coincidences that I won't go into now, but she did ask if I could guarantee that the problem would be sorted. I couldn't, but did say that I hadn't had a failure yet.

The house itself was a large family home made from Cotswold stone. Although the family had done a lot of modernizing work to it, it still felt un-lived in and uninviting. She had two girls, who were never really happy being in the house by themselves. Understandably, she wanted this feeling to go, and for them to be settled. There were four unwanted house guests, spirits that needed moving into the light, as well as a number of human-manifested life forms that were responsible for the girls feeling uncomfortable. I found quite a lot else there too, but it is not relevant to this particular section. Once they had been cleared, the house started feeling lighter and warmer. The girls settled into their home, and all was well – apart from the main bedroom.

This needed to be worked on separately, as the energies in the ley were being manipulated. As it turned out, it was by a man who was envious of the family, and made his feeling show. He obviously knew about earth energies. He'd traced where the ley ran, and sent his message of jealousy, dislike and disruption through it, directly into the house and bedroom.

After having traced where the ley ran, the gentleman concerned set out to corrupt the line. This can be done by intent, or by placing and/or burying an object on the ley. On this occasion, it was through the power of thought. He had sat on the ley, some way from the house, and filled his mind with jealousy and envy. These base thought patterns travelled down the line, causing detrimental energies to be transmitted to my client and her family – although Mrs F was the one targeted and worst affected.

Once I had found an answer to her insomnia, I could work on the solution. I needed to not only carry out a healing, but to block the disruptive thought patterns coming through. I do get a call every now and then to say that she has had a few sleepless nights, but nothing like before. I just increase the protection, and send love and light to the gentleman concerned.

Case Study 2: The Davies Family, London N7

I received a telephone call from Jess Davies, who had recently moved into a house in N7. They had been living in a small town in Hertfordshire, but due to her husband's promotion they had moved the family to London. The house was sizeable, on four floors, and dated from the late-Victorian/early-Edwardian period. It needed a little updating, but was generally in good condition, and the family could move straight in.

They had only been in the house for a few hours when the children, a daughter of five and her older brother of seven, started getting upset and tearful for no apparent reason. Jess asked them what was wrong, but neither of them could say why they felt that way. The moving day had been hectic, and she put their mood swings down to tiredness and feeling unsettled. She fed them, and their spirits picked up a little. However, neither of them wanted to go to bed, and they sat up as long as they could, eventually falling asleep on the settee. Jess and Phil carried them upstairs and put them to bed. Within a few minutes of getting downstairs, both children were awake and crying, 'Sobbing their hearts out,' as Jess put it. 'We couldn't leave them upstairs,' and they, as a family, slept in the living room all night.

The situation got no better and, after a month, Jess was at her wits end – so she started to surf the net for help. She felt that it was spirits that were affecting her children, and she typed in 'Ghost removal', found my website, and I received the telephone call: 'This might sound crazy but . . .' Jess told me the story of the move, and how her children were reacting to their new home. Whilst listening to her talk, I tuned into the house and picked up two spirits there – but neither was particularly detrimental to the family. Actually, they were quite benign; something else was causing the children's unhappiness.

Once the floor plan arrived, I could start my in-depth work. It is generally easier for me to sit in my study and concentrate on a client's home than to make an on-site visit. I have no distractions, and I can spend 100% of my time finding out where and what the problems are – and how to heal them. As I worked through my checklist, I became aware that the last owners were not happy people. In fact, they had divorced, leaving a lot of emotional energy behind, which the children had initially picked up on. Interestingly, I had picked up on a ley running through the house, almost diagonally – when I came to dowse how detrimental the energies were that ran through it, they came out at -10 (my first ever -10). This really was a worst-case scenario.

As I started the questioning process, a picture was beginning to emerge of an underlying trend of hate, despair, evil, sadness, anguish and malevolence, which pervaded the house. I asked how long this had been going on for, and got a date around the mid-1800s.

Is the ley being corrupted on purpose?

No.

Is one person responsible?

No.

So is it a number of people?

Yes.

Is it a large number?

Yes.

Are they in one building?

Yes.

Now, this is where the internet comes in very handy. I logged on to

Google Earth and entered the postcode of the house. The first thing I saw was a football stadium. I asked if that was where the problem was emanating from. My pendulum didn't move, so that was a 'no' (my son would have been happy, as he supports Arsenal). I expanded my search, and my attention was drawn to a large building to the west of the stadium. I scrolled in, and the words 'Holloway Prison' came into focus. Now, all I had to do was map-dowse the ley to see if it ran from the prison to my client's house. It did, and I had my answer. I dowsed just to make sure, and I got a 'yes' response.

I had found the root of the problems affecting Jess and her family – now to do something about it. The energies were very deeply rooted in the ley and a lot of healing was needed. This went on for a few weeks, to get it exactly right. I also worked on the prison, putting it into a bubble of white light, and negating the effect of the detrimental energies on the surrounding area – I did a lot of soul rescue there, too.

Within a short time, the children calmed down and started to settle into their new home. Getting them to bed was no longer a chore, and they started to sleep soundly at night. I am sure that the energies from the prison have affected many people locally in the N7 area; certainly the previous owners of the house are testament to that.

Dowsing Diagnosis Questions for Ley Lines

1. Is there a ley running through your home?

2. How many?

3. Where are they?

4. Are they detrimental to you or the family?

5. How long are they?

6. How many sacred or notable sites do they cross or join?

7. Do you need to send healing to each site?

8. Can you heal the complete ley?

9. Is there a layer system in place? (If so when can I heal the next layer?).

15. Energy Spirals

Energy spirals or vortices are wonderful things, I believe that they, along with earth energy lines, are responsible for life on this beautiful planet. If they disappeared, so would we.

To me, they appear similar to the chakra system of our body, working the same way for Mother Earth. They draw out energies and radiation that the planet doesn't require any more, and suck into the planet what it needs to stay alive, and to support human life. They can be found anywhere that earth energy lines, water veins and disturbance lines cross. They interact with animals and humans, in both a beneficial and a detrimental way – depending on your gender.

Sleeping within, or close to, an energy spiral can be very detrimental to your health. Energies within one of these vortices can easily heighten your emotions; they can promote irrational mood swings as well as give you headaches and migraines. The spiral can be the centre of both positivity and negativity.

Every vortex varies in direction and intensity. When dowsing, I like to find out as much as I can about the individual ones that I have found. By asking questions, I get the answers from my rod or pendulum – finding out the direction of their spin (either clockwise or anti-clockwise), whether they are spinning upwards or downwards, whether masculine or feminine in energy, and how far from the centre the detrimental effect can be felt. As far as their height goes, you can measure them in miles. Certainly they extend high above the earth – try dowsing them from an aircraft; you will still find them.

I always pick up that anti-clockwise spirals in nature are more detrimental than clockwise spirals. Now, this is completely opposite to our bodies, where most molecules are formed anti-clockwise. Perhaps, because they spin the same way, they act against each other – and it is better for the spirals to be diametrically opposed.

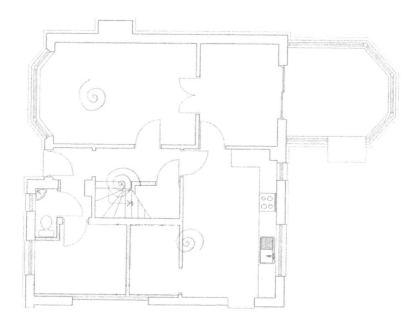

Figure 20. Energy Spirals

The energy spirals should not generally be moved or interfered with, as the energies from them are needed to help bring balance. However, they do need to be harmonized, enabling us to co-exist with them, and ensuring that life continues on this planet.

When dowsing, I normally only pick up on the detrimental aspects of energy spirals. The beneficial ones that surround us and our homes can be left in peace – it is the troublesome ones that we are after, to work on, heal and harmonize, for the good of ourselves and our families.

Case Study 1: An 'Introduction to Dowsing' Course Held at Caterham in Surrey

We are all beginners when it comes to dowsing; none of us truly knows everything there is to know about this ancient art, and we are always learning. This is especially true when tutoring a weekend course. Group dynamics are fascinating, and they have a habit of pushing the boundaries of the tutor's mind. It never ceases to amaze me how often a seemingly innocent question can lead to something so complex.

During this particular weekend, my first as a tutor, we had a number of very knowledgeable people within the group – several of whom were health practitioners, one Shaman, two homeopaths, a sensitive, two Dowsing Spirits clients and Matthew Thompson, who runs Caterham Osteopaths. Matthew's thirst for knowledge is rather like mine, and dowsing brings out the child-in-a-sweet-shop mentality – so much to choose from, but what do you start with? Questions, questions, questions – he and the group were full of them, and answering them, with my co-tutor David Lockwood, helped settle my nerves.

On the second day we ventured into a nearby park and started dowsing for earth energy lines, water, leys, human emotion areas and the rest. I decided to map out an energy spiral with flags. I asked the rods to show me where the nearest one was, and followed the direction in which they pointed me to go. After a few yards, the rods crossed and I found myself in the centre of a vortex. I then tracked and marked the flowing curves with a series of flags, mapping a clockwise spiral on the ground. An audience had gathered to see what I was doing. I explained what I had found and stood proudly in the centre, showing the spiral in all its glory. Suddenly I started to feel very giddy and nauseous – the detrimental effects of being within a spiral. I stepped away from it whilst Amber, one of the group, walked into the centre to feel the effects herself, but nothing happened. She was fine, no ill effect whatsoever. Another lady walked in and felt fine – and another and another, no problems at all. Why?

I dowsed the following questions:

Can some energy spirals be masculine and others feminine?

Yes.

Is this a feminine spiral?

Yes.

Are the affects detrimental to me?

Yes.

Ok, can you show me where a masculine spiral is, please?

The rods obliged, and pointed the way. I walked about thirty feet and the rods crossed. I mapped out the spiral and stood in the centre. My feet began to get very hot, but apart from that I started to feel full of energy. The ladies of the group, meanwhile, had all moved into the centre of the feminine spiral and were in high spirits. Most of the men then gathered in the masculine spiral and started to soak up the beneficial energies there. Onlookers must have wondered what was going on as the banter between the two groups became quite vocal, along the lines of, 'My spiral is better than your spiral'.

Check the spirals in your home, ask first if they are detrimental to you or the family, as many aren't, then check to see if they have a masculine or feminine energy attached. One might be the cause of your sleepless nights; a child's temper tantrums or just general fatigue.

Case Study 2: An Egg Farm on the Suffolk/Essex Border

I was travelling to see a friend in Lavenham for the weekend and stopped at the pub near Bures for lunch. I got talking to one of the locals there, and we ended up talking about dowsing and healing. I gave him a pair of rods, and I got him walking up and down the bar asking for a 'yes' and a 'no' response. It was all working well, when his wife joined us. They were having lunch so I joined them. The topic of conversation moved on to geopathic stress which, to my surprise, they had both heard of. They had an organic egg farm just down the road, and they treated their flock homeopathically. They would send a bag of feathers to a company called Crossgate Bioenergetics for testing and then, depending on the results, treat them holistically with natural remedies. You could have knocked me down with a feather.

The machine that they do the testing with is similar to a MORA or VEGA bio-resonance machine, which I described earlier in this book. It has the ability to show you if you are affected by geopathic stress, as well as many other ailments. I was shown the checklist that Crossgate uses, and was staggered at the complexity and range of problems that they were able to diagnose – and the remedies that they could supply.

I was invited to look at the two sheds where the hens were housed at night. They were free range during the day, and I was amazed at how they responded to the farmer as he walked in. The noise level started to rise – it was a lovely clucking noise. Here were happy hens. He mentioned that they were not at their best, and they weren't laying as many eggs as they should be. I wondered if there was a problem other than geopathic stress and started to dowse. Something was missing here, but I wasn't sure what. I said that I would dowse when I got home, and that I would ring him with my thoughts later in the week.

I sat down quietly with the plan and mapped out the water courses under the two barns, as well as the earth energy lines and any other detrimental areas that I could find. There wasn't much, but the water was problematical and it needed to be moved. There were energy spirals in both barns, but none showed up as detrimental to the chickens.

That led me onto my next question,

Do chickens like energy spirals?

Yes. (I was surprised)

Are energy spirals detrimental to chickens?

No.

If I can encourage more spirals to form would that help the laying process?

Yes.

Would there be any detrimental side effects on the chickens?

No.

Is it possible to enhance the spirals that are in the barns and to bring others in?

Yes.

I telephoned the farmer and told him what I had found; that chickens like energy spirals, and was it OK if I brought a few more in? He sounded slightly confused, but said 'yes' – and that he would report back to me in a couple of weeks with the results, if any.

When the call came, I was astonished. 'This is the best flock that I have ever had, laying like good uns they are. Never had eggs like it before – whatever you did, it worked, well done.' The laying kept going; I made a follow-up call some months later, and he was still very pleased with his flock.

Chickens love spirals! Job done.

I normally use an orange pen to detail spirals on my plan.

Dowsing Diagnosis Questions for Energy Spirals

1. Are there any detrimental spirals affecting the house?

2. How many?

3. Where are they?

4. How detrimental are they?

5. Which direction do they rotate?

6. Are they spinning upwards or downwards?

7. Do they have a masculine or feminine energy?

8. How far either side are the detrimental effects felt?

9. Can you harmonize all the detrimental spirals?

16. Sink Holes

Sink holes are a recent addition to my checklist. I view these sink holes rather like black holes in the universe. In most cases they are small, sometimes only 3 inches in diameter, and they allow both beneficial and detrimental energies to drain into them, and then to slip into another dimension – the etheric realm.

If you are standing above, or close to, one of these sink holes, they can suck the life force from you – that is, from the auric field that surrounds you. This will, in time, adversely affect the immune system. The short-term effect will, as the family in my next case study felt, be general tiredness. This will then become apathy, and so on. Dowse to see if you have one in your home. If you get a 'yes' response, ask the rods to show you where it is – you would be very unlucky to have two. Once a sink hole has been identified, it will need plugging.

Case Study 1: The Stevens Family, Near Harrogate

Even after I had carried out healing on their home, the Stevens family were still feeling fatigued. They were all sleeping well, but something was missing. I dowsed to see whether I had come across this phenomenon before – and I got a resounding 'no'.

I often ask this question when I dowse: 'When dowsing for the benefit of the family, will I come across anything that I have not seen before?' If the answer comes out 'yes', then meditation will soon follow, to see if I can gain some insight into what it might be. This happened to be the case with this particular family, and I therefore needed to find out what this extra problem was, as it needed to be healed for their benefit.

I dowsed to see if it was earth energy related, and I got a slight movement. Then I asked if it was a natural phenomenon and got a 'yes'.

At that stage I saw a picture of a hole, and I dowsed to see if indeed that is what it was – and I immediately received a 'yes' response.

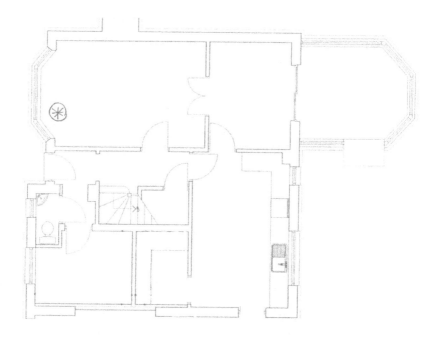

Figure 21. Sink Holes

So I asked:

Is a sink hole always detrimental?

Yes.

How big is this hole; are we talking in inches?

Yes.

I started counting, got to three and the pendulum indicated 'yes'. It appeared to be a three-inch diameter hole, bigger than a plug hole in your bath.

Does it resemble a plug hole?

Yes.

Can energy drain or get sucked into it?

Yes.

Both?

Yes.

Does it allow both beneficial and detrimental energy to drain away?

Yes.

So, if I was standing over one of these areas, would I start to feel tired?

Yes.

Well, that was the answer to the family's problems; now I needed to solve it for them.

As I mentioned a little earlier, the physical world can give you clues as to how to heal in the spiritual world. What do you do if water is draining out of your bath? Put a plug in it – the solution was a simple as that. I will discuss this in more detail in the healing section, later on.

I normally show sink holes with a red * on my plans.

Dowsing Diagnosis Questions for Sink Holes

1. Are there any sink holes in the house?

2. How many?

3. Where are they?

4. How detrimental are they to you and your family?

5. Can they be sealed for all time?

6. Do you need to do anything before sealing the sink hole?

7. Will you, or your family, start to feel better once the hole is sealed?

17. Karmic Problems

Definition from the *Collins English Dictionary:*

Karma n **1** *Hinduism, Buddhism.* the principle of retributive justice determining a person's state of life, and the state of his reincarnations as the effect of his past deeds. **2** destiny or fate.

So these are problems that follow you from life to life, through various incarnations. These are mistakes that you have made in a past life or lives. I say lives, because sometimes we don't learn the first time and have to repeat the assignment in our next incarnation, in order to clear the debt, or to a learn a particular lesson. I believe that karma follows us from lifetime to lifetime, until we are able to clear the debts that we have built up. You may be reliving this life in order to correct a past mistake. It's a good idea to identify if you are.

I do believe in fate and destiny, but I also believe that both can be given a hefty size-nine boot up the backside to help them on their way. Never think that your life is totally mapped out for you. We do have free will here on the planet, and it is your responsibility to use it wisely.

So, where do we start?

First, dowse to see if you have a karmic debt or debts. If the answer is 'yes', then you need to identify which lifetime or lifetimes are responsible. You'll need to find a date, what the problem actually is that led to the debt and whether it can be cleared this lifetime. Easy!

The questions need to be phrased like this (and don't forget to write the answers down as you go):

Do I have a karmic debt?

Do I have more than one?

Can I identify in which lifetime it started?

Are we counting in hundreds of years or thousands?

Please forget what the historians tell us, as we have been on this planet a lot longer than they realize. Dowse how long our particular civilization has been on the planet, then how many other civilizations there have been – and over what time period. You will be amazed by the answers.

If the answer is 'hundreds', then start to count from 100 upwards, until the rods move, indicating a particular century. Then, count in tens to get the decade, and then from one to ten to get the exact year. This is where the history lessons come in handy, or the internet. Look up the year, and see what was happening in the world.

Was I living in Europe at the time?

If 'no', then ask about the Americas, Asia, Africa, etc., until the rods move.

Was I male or female? We do switch between the sexes.

Was I a person of ill repute? I don't like to use the word 'bad', but please feel free to do so.

Did I make a stupid mistake – or was it premeditated?

Did I make the same mistake in other lives?

Did I hurt someone mentally?

Did I hurt someone physically?

Did I kill someone?

If 'no', then go through other acts of violence, such as robbery – you might have been a highwayman or a thief.

Can I learn the lesson in this life, to stop the pattern repeating?

Can I heal the karmic debt this life? Hopefully you will get a 'yes' for that question.

I will show you how to carry out this karmic clearing in a very simple way later on, in the healing section of the book. The most important thing is to learn from what you have discovered; to change your life accordingly, so as not to carry the karmic debt forward to your next incarnation.

Case Study 1: Caroline from London

I used to attend a healing group, several years ago, in Surrey. Caroline's mother, Sandy, used to attend regularly. Caroline was, and still is, a professional photographer, who had done a lot of freelance work for a number of spiritual magazines. Sandy had mentioned to her about my geopathic stress work, and Caroline said that it might be of interest to one of the magazines she worked for. She talked to one of the editors and, sure enough, they wanted to publish an article. It needed to have a human angle, so it was decided that I would do a healing on Caroline's flat in London.

The floor plan came through. I carried out the dowsing work, and then the healing. The resulting article came out in *Spirit and Destiny* in 2008, under the title 'Healing Your Home'. There were some interesting discoveries made and healed, but at that stage I didn't look at or dowse for karmic problems, as I wasn't really looking beyond the effects of earth energies and human emotions on families.

Several weeks after the article came out, and during another meeting, Sandy asked for healing to be sent to Caroline, who had recently sprained her ankle. This was duly done and, at the end, I asked what had happened.

'She is always up and down step ladders, getting the right angle for a shot. Whether she wasn't concentrating on her way down and tripped at the bottom, I don't know, but she sprains her ankles so often that I have lost count. She must have a weakness of some sort.'

I got home and dowsed, asking was there a problem that could be solved. 'Yes', came the response.

Is it a weakness in the ankles that is causing the problem?

Yes.

Is this hereditary?

No.

Is the weakness from earlier injuries?

No.

Is it a past life or karmic injury?

Yes.

Can it be solved in this lifetime?

Yes.

How many lifetimes ago was the first injury, including this life?

Three.

Can you give me a date please?

1648

From my antiques-dealing days, I knew that during the mid-1600s the English Civil War was taking place. So, the first question had to be 'Was Caroline a Roundhead or Cavalier?' She was a Cavalier, which was interesting as my family had been staunch Royalists during the conflict.

Was Caroline male or female?

Male.

Was she/he a foot soldier or cavalryman?

Cavalryman.

By now, I had started to get pictures coming into my head, rather like an old movie. I saw Caroline charging down on a small band of Parliamentarians, mounted on a white horse with sword drawn. A pikeman turned and thrust his pike (a spear approximately ten feet long) into Caroline's side, knocking her off the horse. She/he lay badly winded and also wounded. As the group approached her/him, they did something that took me totally by surprise. They didn't kill her/him, but instead cut off both feet. I have tried to research this maiming via the internet and books, but can find no record of it. However, what better way can you think of to stop a person from ever riding a horse into battle again, without actually killing them?

So this was the start of Caroline's karmic problems – and the weakening of her ankles was the debt to be carried forward.

The next life saw her living in the mid-1800s as a young farmer's daughter. I felt this was an idyllic life for her, but it was all about to change. It was late summer, and a busy time of year. A group of men were in the fields harvesting the crops, and they were using scythes to cut the corn. None of them had seen a little girl come into the field, bringing a surprise lunch for her father. Due to her height she could hardly be seen as she ran excitedly through the uncut part of the field towards her father. He saw her at the last moment. However, he could not stop the swing of his scythe, but managed to divert the thrust, catching her Achilles tendons, and slicing through them. Not as serious as having your feet cut off, but equally as debilitating. The karmic debt was still waiting to be fully repaid.

So the injuries to the ankle area were carrying on through time. However, it was getting less severe – and in this life it had manifested itself as a weakness in her ankles, which were subject to spraining. Each previous life must have seen some form of attrition, as the debt was lessening.

Caroline and I worked on the solution to her karmic problems, which necessitated her going back over her past lives and replaying each of the scenes described. This has not only helped to strengthen her ankles, but enabled her to move into her next life without this debt being carried forward.

Case Study 2: Mary from Cambridge

I was initially approached by Mary to work on her home and family.

During the course of my dowsing, I found out that she had a karmic debt from her last life here on earth.

I telephoned her and asked if she was afraid of the water.

'Absolutely terrified,' she said. 'I can't swim, and I have never wanted to.' She added, 'Both my children can swim, but I have never gone to the swimming pool with them, as I would have been paralysed with fear and worried about them drowning. I never told you about my fear of water, so how did you know?'

I explained how dowsing works, and that I get given key words sometimes. Her fear of water came through, loud and strong.

This is what had happened in her last life, to give her the dread of water – and a karmic debt. Mary was born a male, and lived as a fisherman on the north-east coast of England. She/he knew the waters well, and lived on instinct – able to 'smell the weather'. She/he knew when a storm was coming, and when not to venture out to sea. But she/he was a man that knew his own mind, to the point of being stubborn and prone never to listen to advice. She/he always knew best.

It had been raining for many days, and the river was high up the banks – not threatening to burst, but enough to warn people that a flood was likely if the downpour continued. Well, continue raining it did, and people on the banks of the river near the coast were put on flood alert. They were told to evacuate the immediate area, just in case an unnaturally high tide was experienced. Mary knew better, and refused to listen, 'knowing' that the tide would be normal – and that the flood just wouldn't happen.

Sadly, this time she/he got it badly wrong, and the waters kept rising over the banks and started to flood the land. The tide came in, and it was worse than expected. A boat came past and offered help, but Mary felt that the water would soon subside and refused it. The water came through the front door and still Mary refused help; the family went up onto the roof of the house to escape the rising tide. Mary still refused help; again 'knowing' that the water would stop rising, and that they would be safe. The last thing that Mary saw, before drowning herself, is the reproachful stare of her/his wife and young daughter, who were being swept away to their deaths in the angry waters.

She/he had had ample time in which to be rescued; none of the family had to die in that lifetime, but she/he knew best. So, in this lifetime, not only did Mary have to allow her children to swim, she also needed to listen to advice – and now she had the opportunity to heal the karmic debt, through me.

Sadly, Mary could not bring herself to carry out the necessary healing, at least not at that time. She kept seeing the eyes of her late wife and daughter, as they were being carried away by the swollen river. This vision haunted her; she could not get beyond it. She did manage, however, to get to watch her children play in the local swimming pool. She is not as dogmatic as she used to be, and does listen to advice from others. I hope that one day she can work her way through the healing.

Dowsing Diagnosis Questions for Karmic Problems

1. Do you or any members of the family have a karmic problem?

2. How many lives past?

3. What date?

4. Why did it happen, is there a lesson to learn?

5. Who was involved, for example other members of the family who were incarnated with you at that time?

6. Can it be resolved in this lifetime with healing?

7. Will it stop the pattern repeating?

8. Is there a lesson to be learned this lifetime?

18. Human Conflict or Emotional Energy Areas

I believe that many of the problems associated with geopathic stress come from human emotions – stuck detrimental energy from the past that has been left to haunt the future.

These detrimental areas can be started by a simple argument, a negative thought or stress or illness, and they are similar to disturbance lines. However, they are more like patches of energy remaining where they are caused, for example in the home or at the workplace.

There are houses in most towns and villages that regularly come on to the market – the so-called 'divorce house'. The current owners are splitting up, as the previous owners did before them and the ones before that – and so on. This repeating pattern is surprisingly very common, and difficult to break – that is, unless you know about stuck energies and house healing.

We are energetic beings and we are therefore continually generating energy. Some of it is good and some not so good. How often have you walked into someone's house and felt that it was calm and peaceful – a happy house? It just feels comfortable and homely, and you could easily curl up on the settee and go to sleep. Now, on the other side of the coin, how many times have you walked into a house and shivered? It happened to me many times during my estate agency days and, so often, they were the houses that didn't sell easily. It is well known that the decision to buy a house is made within the first few minutes of stepping inside the front door. Your subconscious picks up on 'bad vibes', as well as good ones, and if the owners have just had a filthy row, then the first thought is to turn and run.

The atmosphere that is generated during an argument is tangible. You know when a couple have just had words, as it leaves an uncomfortable feeling in the air. Can you imagine a house that has had numerous couples living there and then splitting up? All the arguments, the raw emotion, the hurt, the let downs and worry about how it will affect the children? This emotional energy has to go somewhere, and the bricks and mortar will soak it up like a sponge.

The ground, too, will bear the scarring, as does furniture and other items such as jewellery (see the next chapter, Power Artefacts).

So, as one divorcing couple moves out, another poor unsuspecting couple moves in. Gradually, the detrimental energy left behind will start to affect them. Eventually, unless they get the house healed, these harmful energies will start to adversely affect every family that moves into the house, potentially leading to yet more divorces.

Now then, there is always the exception to the rule and not all the population will be affected. Some people are 'bullet-proof', and nothing will get through to them. They are so thick-skinned that detrimental energy patterns will just bounce off them. It doesn't mean that they lack sensitivity, just that detrimental energies do not affect them.

Each house is unique – as is any office or workplace, restaurant, pub, supermarket or shop. Each will have a distinct energy pattern associated with it. If the energies there are good (beneficial) for work, rest or play then that's perfect. However, what happens when they are not? For instance, do you feel unnaturally tired, listless or drained of energy when at work? It could just be a build-up of stuck emotionally charged energy that is dragging you down – dowse to see if you are being affected by past detrimental emotions.

Wherever we are, and wherever we go, we leave an imprint of ourselves behind, whether on chairs, tables or coffee cups. We can't help it; it's just what we do as human beings. If the last person that sat on the chair you have just occupied was a depressive, how is that going to make you feel? It is very possible that you will pick up on the dark energies left behind, and start to feel quite despondent. It is good to get into the habit of space-clearing before you enter somewhere and also after you leave. Don't forget that your energy pattern will not be compatible with anyone else's – although we have adapted to live with others.

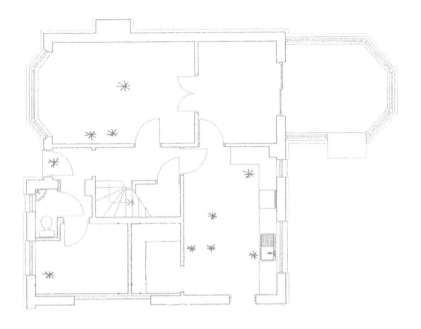

Figure 22. Signs of Human Conflict

You need to now be very aware of how your thoughts and actions affect others – not just face to face, but energetically too. Think of how many emotional energy areas you might have created over the years; dowse for them, as they will need healing. Some poor soul might just be affected by an emotional outburst that you left behind some thirty years ago, or more.

The same can be said for accident blackspots. Little did I know when purchasing my first Sat Nav system, that it would be useful as an earth-healing tool. I mainly bought it for the OS maps that it came loaded with, as I do a lot of mountain walking in Scotland. It could also help me navigate on roads so, to get used to it, I would put in a postcode locally and see if it could direct me by the shortest route. I was impressed and, just for fun, I would use it on longer journeys.

One day, I was driving towards Glastonbury and suddenly a voice from the Sat Nav said, 'Accident blackspot ahead,' and it started beeping. The beeping increased in volume, until I had passed the spot. It didn't look like anything much and I couldn't really see why it had been notified as such. Then, I got thinking that some poor person or persons had suffered an injury there, and I wondered whether they had left an emotional imprint? I turned around and stopped at the location indicated by the female voice. I got my rods out and dowsed. Sure enough, someone had been injured there – several deaths too. So the questions started to roll:

Are there any spirits here that have not gone to the light?

Yes.

How many?

Five.

Am I allowed to send them to the light?

Yes.

Has a detrimental imprint been left here?

Yes.

Is that partly responsible for the other accidents?

Yes.

Am I allowed to clear the energies here?

Yes.

If I do so will it stop the accidents happening here?

Yes.

Do I need to know what caused this to happen?

No.

So, whenever the young lady now announces an accident blackspot, I carry out a healing, normally whilst driving – I don't stop at each place any more, as I don't want to cause an accident. The outcome is another little part of the countryside healed. I bet Road Angel or TomTom never thought of that as an offshoot of their product.

Road rage also leaves detrimental areas – in the car as well as on the spot. Try to remain calm and to send the person that has just cut you up unconditional love. If you find that difficult, take a tip from my mentor Andy Roberts – I asked him how I could send unconditional love to a Traffic Warden who had given me a parking ticket in Guildford, earlier in the day. He said, 'Send unconditional love to the world, don't individualize it, the traffic warden will get his share.' Thanks, Andy. I was having a major problem with the whole unconditional love bit, but there is always a solution to a problem; you just have to look for it.

Case Study 1: A Troubled House in Surrey

This house was an estate agent's dream, a large detached double-fronted Edwardian villa with five bedrooms, three reception rooms, kitchen, a separate breakfast room, garage and a large rear garden – it had it all.

When I first went to value the house, it needed a little updating. On the surface it was a very saleable property. However, once you scratched the surface, it was far from perfect. The current owner was going through a very nasty divorce, and the previous owners had done the same. I didn't delve any further at the time, but I subsequently found out a great deal more about the history of the house. It was what I refer to now as a 'divorce house', an unhappy home that needs clearing of bad energy. In other words, it was full of detrimental human emotions. I had no real idea about stuck energy, or the effect it can have on people, at that stage in my life. If I had, then I probably could have saved at least two marriages.

The house had been on the market with another agent, but the sale had recently fallen through, due to a chain having collapsed. I knew, as soon as I walked through the door, that I had a buyer who was perfect, sitting in rented accommodation. Once back in the office, I contacted them and I arranged a viewing to take place the next day. The prospective buyers saw the house and fell in love with it straight away. The only problem was, unbeknownst to me, they had made an offer on a house two days earlier, and were waiting for an answer. Two days later they telephoned me to say that they wanted the house; they offered a price for a quick sale, and my clients accepted. The sale went through relatively easily, apart from a few hiccups due to the divorce, but they were soon sorted out and the house sale was completed.

I met the new owners several weeks later in the High Street. They and their baby daughter seemed blissfully happy with the house, and with life in general. Three years later, almost on the anniversary of their completion day, I received a telephone call asking me to come and value the house with a view to selling it. I arrived and, over a cup of coffee, Carol explained to me that the marriage had ended – and the house had to be sold. 'Why the marriage has broken up is a mystery,' she explained. 'We were so perfect together and loved the house so much – and then it was all over.' There was no one else involved. It had just been a gradual decline in feelings for each other and then, all of a sudden, the love just disappeared. I remember Carol saying, 'It was as though the love and happiness were sucked from us.' She continued, 'Neither of us really knows what happened, but we are sure that we don't want to be together anymore.'

The house did have a cold feeling about it, but I put it down to lack of heating. I didn't know then that the energies in a house could find a weakness in a person or family and exploit it.

We put the house on the market and again it sold quickly – this time, to a lady with two young daughters, who was moving into the area and wanted a spacious older-style house in a village location. Carol had found an empty house locally, and her ex-husband was renting in London. So, two months later, the house had a new owner.

Three years later, again almost on the anniversary of the moving date, we received a telephone call to go and value the house. 'Not again,' was the comment from Neil in the office. Neither of us could believe what had just happened. Neil Berry had worked with me for many years; he had been responsible for finding the last buyer and had struck up a good relationship with her during the buying process, so I asked him to come with me. When we arrived, we couldn't believe what we saw. The house was a mess, the lady was in a terrible state and her daughter was trying to placate her. The house energies had struck again – however, this time the owner's weakness was alcohol, not lack of love.

The house had been decorated since I had last seen it and the kitchen replaced. It was in very good order. However, the rooms were in a shambles – it just felt unloved and unwanted. Neil and I both hoped that we could persuade the lady to stay, but she was adamant that she was going to move; she hated the house and couldn't wait to go. The eldest daughter had the responsibility of looking after her mother, and you could see the strain on her face – it was getting too much for her.

Neil and I valued the house and put it on the market once again. It sold very quickly to a lovely couple with two children, who were moving into the village from some distance away. Shortly after this, I sold my company, but stayed living locally. I got to know the new owners some twelve months later, through a mutual friend. I told them that I had just started working with geopathic stress, and that I was healing houses of past problems. I explained that their property was an ideal candidate for this work, and briefly described the history. They did look rather sceptical, but were open-minded people – and they agreed to me healing the house.

To my knowledge, they are still there, some ten years later. I hope that I have managed to resolve and stop the repeating patterns. The past human emotions were cleared away, as were the earth energy problems, to leave the house in peace, balance and harmony for the family – for them to live with the energies that they have created, and not be haunted by anything that had been created in the past.

General Cases of Human Emotional Energy

When I first started dowsing houses, I would note down all the areas where detrimental human emotions were found. Now, this is fine if you only have five or six areas, but when you get to twenty and upwards, it can get a little tedious working out what happened, when and by whom. I now lump all the negativity together with a combined minus effect, and then clear it away.

Here are some of my findings from the early days:

201

Case Study 2: A House in Hitchin

When dowsing the floor plan of the house, I picked up seven individual areas in the kitchen, all set in the corner of the room. I asked my client what happened there, and she answered, 'That is where my husband always stands when he gets back from the office and has a ten-minute rant about his day and how bad it has been.' It came out at a combined -6: he must have had some bad days there.

Case Study 3: A House in Croydon

I picked up a detrimental area by the front door, at -5, and also one just outside the front of the house, at -6. I dowsed that both were acts of violence. My client told me that her son and a friend had started arguing about something in the hall. The friend had turned around, punched and then kicked her son. The lad ran for the front door, got it open, but was caught just outside by the son. Another fight started and blood was spilt. They have since made up, but the emotional energy was still there and needed healing – otherwise it could have started to influence whoever stood on those places in the future.

Case Study 4: A House in Dursley

When dowsing this particular property, I found a detrimental energy area in the living room, right next to a settee. This was pure emotion, and very deep. I kept picking up an illness and worry. When talking with my client, he told me that was where the telephone point was, and where his wife sat whilst talking to her mother. Her father, apparently, had been very ill recently, close to death at one stage, and this was where she sat and listened to the prognosis every night. Her angst and worries had left an imprint on the settee and the telephone – both needed working on.

Case Study 5: An Inn near Great Missenden

This was a real eye-opener for me. On the face of it, public houses and inns should be places where you go to enjoy yourselves. However, there are so many reasons why people drink, and the more that they do, the more their emotions are heightened. This obviously leads to a lot of dark energies being left behind in a seemingly innocent place. Be aware of what you might be walking into.

I was asked by the owner to do a healing on his country pub. It was situated down a long no-through road close to Chequers – an idyllic setting. However, it was full of spirits, the ghostly ones as well as the alcoholic type – twenty-two all told – together with several water veins and energy spirals. I also found ten areas of detrimental emotional energy that needed healing.

One of the areas I found dowsed at -10, and was situated in the top floor bedroom of the inn. Now, -10 on the scale is murder or suicide. So the couple must have had a terrible argument, with murderous tendencies being brought to the surface. I picked up both mental and physical emotions, so a few punches or slaps must have been traded. I spoke to the landlord and asked him if he remembered anything unusual about two of his guests, sometime in the last six months. 'Well, because I sleep in the annexe I didn't hear anything, but I do remember a couple who sat at the breakfast table with a huge black cloud around them. I didn't want to approach, as they looked so angry that I felt that one of them might snap and start a fight. Their bedroom was in a mess, but nothing was broken. They didn't stay the second night and drove off.'

That must have been them. I cleared the inn of all the detrimental problems that I found, and did so regularly after that, until the landlord decided to close the pub and re-develop it.

Case Study 6: A House near Peterborough

My client and her husband had split up about eight years ago, but she stayed on at the house with her son. Her ex moved out, and was living in a nearby village. He would regularly walk into the house unannounced, as he felt that it was still his property. This obviously upset Pat, as she was trying to get on with her life, and she didn't want her ex turning up at all hours.

There is much you can do with barriers of light to ward off ex-husbands, psychic attack and the like. I carried that out but, during the course of the dowse, I picked up a particularly bad emotional area in a small room upstairs. When I dowse, I normally scan the floor plan onto my computer and take off all the information that a client has included. I don't want to be led, and I don't want it to look as though I have drawn in a line, say across a bed, purely to justify my work.

As this room was off the main bedroom, it was clearly an en-suite bathroom, but no fittings were shown. The various emotional areas found were along one wall. I telephoned Pat and asked her where her bath was situated. 'Along the back wall,' she replied, exactly where I had found the emotional areas. Pat said that she does her thinking when she lies in the bath, and this enables her to offload the problems of the day, including those with her ex. The trouble is, these energies have to go somewhere, and they had soaked into her bath, started to heighten, and then to deepen her concerns, worries and moods. She said that she had started to feel so cross in the bath recently that it was having a negative effect on her, rather than a positive, relaxing one. A healing was carried out, and the bathing experience returned to being one of pleasure not pain.

If you only have a few emotional energy areas in your home then you can mark them individually with a red circle on the plan however if you have more than say ten areas then I would suggest only marking those above -5.

Dowsing Diagnosis Questions for Emotional Energy

1. Does your home have any emotional energy areas?

2. How many?

3. Where are they?

4. How detrimental are they?

5. Are they inherited?

6. What caused them?

7. When were they caused?

8. Can they be healed?

9. Will there be another layer to heal later on?

10. Do you need to find a way to stop them happening?

11. Does leading a spiritual life reduce detrimental emotions?

19. Power Artefacts

These are items full of detrimental thought patterns and angst, found within the home or workplace. They can radiate bad energies, causing irritability and illness, spreading disharmony amongst family and friends.

It can be a simple table or chair, an ornament, jewellery box or table lamp. Often these objects are made by people working in poor conditions and being paid very little. Their 'bad energy thoughts' will transfer into whatever they are making. Power objects are centres of negativity. Can you imagine, for instance, sitting in a sweat shop in the Far East making yet another teddy bear for the European market – then, at the end of the week, getting only a few rupees? I cannot think for a minute that you would be happy. Frustrated? Yes. Resentful? Yes. Have a dislike for the teddy bear? Definitely. Does this make for a happy toy? I don't think so.

Inherited heirlooms can and often will be power artefacts, bringing detrimental energies from past generations to affect us in the present. A chair that has seen generations of misery can only hold bad feelings. A mirror that has been owned by a person not happy with their looks can easily reflect detrimental thought patterns. Even modern items of furniture can be cause for concern. If a person lifting, say, a chest of drawers slips and drops it on his foot, the anger has to go somewhere, and it is more than likely the chest will be the target of his ire.

Old dining tables can often be a source of stored-up detrimental energy, with several generations of children having sat around the table in a formal way – having to endure endless comments from their judgmental elders. 'Sit up straight,' 'Don't eat with your mouth open,' 'Hold your knife and fork properly,' 'Why aren't you working harder at school?' and so on. You cannot blame any child from fleeing the table at high speed to avoid the interrogation. The longer the detrimental comments are made, the more the table and chairs will soak up the negativity. Gradually, these objects will become so powerfully charged that they can start to influence those gathered around the table. As soon as you sit down you will begin to feel irritable, picking up on past energies, and start making snide comments – until the whole table is in uproar for no apparent reason.

Wooden carvings, ornaments and gifts brought back from our holidays abroad can also be affected. There was a classic case of a lady client who bought an old totem carving from a street seller in Africa. The whole of her family thought that it was ugly, but she loved it, and she hung it in her study when she returned from the trip. Within a few days she started feeling faint, and she developed a bad headache that just would not go away. 'I feel as though something is inside my head and I am experiencing strange thoughts, I am not myself,' she told me on the telephone. 'I also feel as though something is watching me all the time; it's beginning to freak me out.' Now, this conversation took place about six weeks after her return from Africa. She had seen a doctor who prescribed tranquilizers, as he felt that her symptoms were stress-related (she did have a demanding job in the City), and he was considering a brain scan as the headache would just not go away.

She had searched the internet and had come across my website, read the 'entities' page (though I now call them attachments), and felt that the symptoms mentioned closely matched hers. 'Now this might sound crazy but . . .' went the start of the telephone conversation. I listened, and then asked her to send a floor plan of the house, so that I could concentrate on where or what the problem might be.

I always psychically protect myself in the morning, and reinforce this before I start work. It doesn't stop your sensitivity and keeps you safe. Today was different, however; no sooner had I started dowsing the plan, than I felt a clamminess creeping up my arms. It was a very unpleasant feeling. I paused and asked that 'triple protection' be given to me whilst working and this stopped the feeling in its tracks. There was a powerful negative energy point in the house, and I needed to find it. As my hand hovered over the study, I knew that that was where the dark energy was emanating from. I put a mark on the plan, indicating that the problem area was on the far wall of the study – a carving or mask of some sort, I felt. I telephoned my client immediately, and asked what was there. She told me about the totem carving that she had bought and asked, 'Do you think that's the problem?' Then she added, 'Of course it is, but why didn't I think of

208

that, it seems so obvious now.'

I dowsed further, and I found that the totem had been carved by a local Shaman in Africa, many years beforehand, and it ended up somehow in the hands of a street seller. A Shaman would have known about the energies in the totem, and been able to deal with them; a western woman who had just bought it to hang on her study wall, wouldn't. A spirit had inhabited the totem, and it needed to be moved back to where it came from. I asked if it was to be sent to the light, but was told 'no'. It was obviously needed back in Africa, so I helped it to go. My client's headaches stopped almost immediately, and her life returned to normal. She still has the totem carving on her wall and now even the family like it – now that it has been cleared.

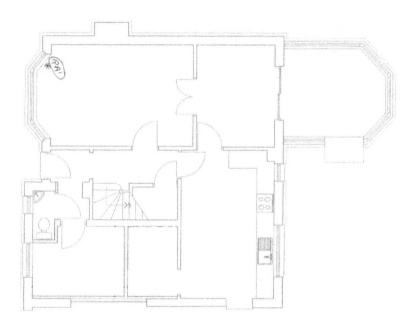

Figure 23. Power Artefacts

Whenever you go to the shops and bring back items that you have bought, take delivery of new furniture, books, etc., always spend time healing them of any past energies that they might have picked up. It is a good habit to get into, as these artefacts – however beautiful they may be – can have a detrimental effect on you. However, once identified and cleansed, they can take pride of place within the family.

Case Study 1: Tim's Table

If you have seen my DVD, 'Intuition – Your Hidden Treasure', you will know the story of Tim's dining room table. However, I would like to repeat the story here for those of you that haven't.

During the course of filming the DVD, we wanted to include a short piece on 'power artefacts', those innocent items in your home that can spread melancholy or have detrimental human emotions attached. I had dowsed Tim and Nicky's house, and I knew that the dining room table had problems attached. It wasn't until the filming started that I discovered what they were. We wanted the session to be spontaneous – and so it turned out to be.

The table dates from the late-William-IV/early-Victorian period and is made of mahogany. They had bought it, together with a sideboard, from a local antique shop in Tunbridge Wells some years before. They had never thought that it might have any detrimental energies attached.

I first dowsed for a date for the detrimental energies – between 1940 and 1944. This gave me a place to start.

How detrimental is this table to the current family?

-8

Was it to do with the war?

Yes.

Had the family lost anyone during the war?

No.

Was it to do with emotion and worry?

Yes.

The fact that the Germans might actually win the war?

Yes.

Were the family in fear of their lives?

Yes.

Did the family live in London?

Yes.

The questions went on, and eventually I found that the detrimental energies had started to attach at the beginning of the war, from the fear and anxiety the whole family felt, whilst sheltering under the table during German bombing raids.

I did a healing on the table, and the sideboard, restoring both to their former glory. I also did a past healing on the family concerned.

Case Study 2: A CD in York

Most of you have heard the expression 'the customer is always right'. Well, during one conversation with a client I was told, in no uncertain terms, that I was wrong when I found a power artefact on a windowsill in her study. She was adamant that all the windowsills were kept clear in the house.

Let me explain the circumstances. I dowsed a house in York, and found the power artefact; furthermore it felt like a black and white photograph, and it had a detrimental charge of -5. I do sometimes find that a residue has been left by an earlier article, but mostly they are current problems.

I emailed the report and floor plan to my client, and I received a telephone call from her shortly afterwards. 'It all looks very interesting, and I am glad that you have found all the energy and water lines that affect the house. Now I know why we have all felt unwell since we moved here.' She continued, 'However, where you have indicated a power artefact on the sill in my study is wrong. There is definitely nothing there. I don't allow things to be left on windowsills, especially in my study.'

I felt adamant that the object was still there. I dowsed again, whilst talking on the telephone, and then confounded her further by saying that the subject of the photograph was a man. She was equally adamant, and said that she didn't even own a black and white photograph. 'I am not at home tonight as I am working away, but I will have a look and call you once I get back.'

The next telephone call came with an apology, 'I am so sorry to have doubted your findings, but at the time I couldn't think of anything that the artefact might have been. Even when I walked into my study, nothing was visible on the windowsill. I had to look over my desk – and then I saw it. I had been to a MBS (Mind, Body and Spirit) show last weekend and I bought a DVD. I did have second thoughts before buying it, but it looked interesting. When I got it home, I got a funny feeling about it – something wasn't right. I took the DVD out of the case and put it on the windowsill to be thrown away. On the disc was a black and white photograph – and it was of a man.'

The DVD obviously hadn't been filmed with the best of intentions, and it was giving off detrimental vibrations. My client's subconscious had picked up on this, and that was why she had hesitated before buying it. Some people in the MBS world are in it purely to make money from a willing but unsuspecting public. Dowse before you buy – not only will it save you a lot of money in the long run, it will also point you in the best direction for your further education.

Case Study 3: Caroline's Tray

This particular problem came to light during the writing of the article that appeared in *Spirit and Destiny* magazine, and once again it features Caroline, the professional photographer.

During the course of dowsing her apartment for problems, I came across a power artefact in her living room. I marked it down as a table, and it was giving off a detrimental reading of -7, and was therefore quite powerful. On talking to Caroline, she said, 'I have only just moved into the apartment, and I have very little furniture there; I don't own a table either.' I was mystified, as there was clearly, to me, something there that was giving off noxious energies. I checked again, as it might have been residue from the previous owner. No, it was

212

definitely still in the apartment.

I received a telephone call a few days later from Caroline saying, 'I know what the table is. I got back to the apartment last night, cooked myself some pasta and started watching the television. I became aware that I was sitting cross-legged on the floor, exactly where you had put the cross marking the location of the power artefact. It wasn't a table as such,' she explained, 'I have got into the bad habit of eating my food off a tray and, once finished, I would often leave the tray on the floor until I needed it again.'

Dowsing is quite literal. Sometimes, you need to dig a little deeper to get the power artefact exactly right. The questions that I asked here were:

Does this object get used most days?

Yes. – asking the question this way eliminates ornaments and trinkets.

Does it have a flat top?

Yes.

Can you eat from it?

Yes.

Is it made from wood?

Yes.

I had pictured in my mind a flat surface that people ate their food from, and I had naturally assumed that it was a table. However, I should have delved further by asking:

Is it a table?

No.

Does it have legs to support it?

No. (That would probably have got a 'yes' in this case)

Then your imagination would be needed to work out what it might be.

The tray had been brought back as a present from Israel. It had been made on a kibbutz, and had seemingly taken on the deep emotions and worries that surrounded the country at that time. I carried out a healing on the tray, and asked that the people who have handled it in the past receive healing too.

Case Study 4: Stuart's Ring

I met Stuart when he attended two courses that David Lockwood and I were tutoring at The Sanctuary of Healing near Blackburn – and I liked him instantly. Stuart was just starting out on his 'spiritual journey' and he was like a sponge, soaking up everything that David and I threw at him. Even when the course finished, he was there with so many questions – a perfect student.

Several years later, I ran a one-to-one Geopathic Stress Practitioners course for Stuart. He came to my home, just outside Avebury, late one Friday afternoon. Although I enjoy cooking, we decided that a visit to The Black Horse, just next door, would be a good idea. I could sit and outline the course in detail, and prepare the way for an early start. During our talk, I noticed that Stuart kept fiddling with a ring on his finger. After an hour, I asked him where he got the ring from. 'It belonged to my late mother, why?' I told him that he had been unconsciously playing with it, turning it round and round. 'I haven't had it back long, as I had to get it enlarged after Mum had passed away, and perhaps I am not used to wearing it yet.' His mother had not been well, and her passing had been a blessing at the end. Her suffering, however, had been passed into the ring that Stuart was now wearing.

'Have you dowsed it for detrimental energies?' I asked.

'No, I never thought about it,' he replied.

'Go on then – here, borrow my pendulum.' I always carry one in my pocket; you never know when you might need one.

Stuart dowsed, and sure enough the ring was affected by detrimental emotional energy (-4). It was a genuine power artefact, and needed healing. We sat by the bar and carried out a short ceremony to heal the ring. The locals were quite used to me by now, and took no notice.

Stuart still wears the ring in his mother's memory, however, it is now okay for him to do so. Before it was healed, his subconscious was telling him to take it off.

Case Study 5: Puffins and the Gas Company

This is a recent case for me, and one that makes me smile every time I think of it. I was approached by a delightful lady after she had attended a two-hour workshop that I was tutoring at the first *Paradigm Shift* magazine roadshow in Guildford, Surrey. She felt that her house needed dowsing for geopathic stress, and she hoped that this would help with a few problems they were experiencing.

During the dowsing work, I picked up what felt like a power artefact and noted down its location in the study. Here is what I put in the report:

-3 in detrimental effect.

A small oil painting hanging on the wall to the left of the desk in the study. It feels as though it is a painting of two figures sitting by or standing by a lake. It has picked up detrimental energies over the years and needs clearing.

The two figures turned out to be puffins and the lake was, in fact, the sea. I asked about the history of the painting and my client laughed, then explained. The place where the painting now hung was, up until recently, her husband's rogue's corner. They'd had, for some time, problems with their local gas company, who were convinced that my client ran a company which owed them a large sum of money. In fact, both my client and her husband were retired and had never been involved with this company. However, the gas company knew better and the bills kept on coming. It didn't matter how many times my client telephoned and explained the situation, the bills were becoming more and more threatening.

So, the husband began to research the gas company. He put together a list of officials, his 'hit list'. Every time they received another missive from the gas company, he would telephone a name from the list, and he gradually started to work his way up to the top man. The bills did stop eventually, the misunderstanding was cleared up and an apology received. The animosity that the husband felt for the gas board soaked into the photographs, then into the wall, to later affect the painting.

Healing was given to the painting, the wall and to the gas company officials.

When marking power artefacts on the plan I would normally use a green *.

Dowsing Diagnosis Questions for Power Artefacts

1. Are there any power artefacts in the house?

2. How many?

3. Where are they?

4. Why did they become detrimentally charged?

5. When did they become detrimentally charged?

6. How detrimental are these power artefacts to the family?

7. Can they be healed?

20. Technopathic Stress

Many of us will suffer from the detrimental effects of man-made energies. Whether it is an underground or overhead electric cable, power lines, a mobile telephone mast, tetra mast, general household wiring or Wi-Fi. Even a gas or water main can cause health problems. Electro-smog is here to stay.

I believe that over the years we do, slowly, build up immunity to these electrical energies. However, just as we are about to get there, along comes something else to confound the issue. There has been much controversy over the years regarding the use and building of overhead power lines, the large pylons that stretch across the countryside. If you walk underneath one you can feel the air crackle around you; hold one end of a fluorescent tube above your head and see what it does. Can you imagine living underneath one permanently? It cannot be good for your health.

Along come microwave ovens – heralded as a major boon to cookery, supposedly giving us more leisure time. They certainly are quick but how healthy are they? During my various dowsing courses I demonstrate how detrimental these things actually are to our health, whether cooking or on standby. When microwaved, food is 'nuked'. If you were to heat milk to boiling point in a microwave oven, it loses at least 60% of its vitamin content. You may argue that you are at least getting 40% goodness from it, but what is wrong with 100%?

Then there are mobile telephones. There is so much information and disinformation reported in the press on the detrimental effects of the mobile or cell phone. I would point you in the direction of www.powerwatch.org.net, a website that provides a great deal of up-to-date information and published papers on the effects of the mobile telephone on our health.

I know that when I use a mobile telephone for just a few minutes, my ear starts burning and my head feels fuzzy. Now I may be just one of the two thirds of people who are sensitive to the ill effects of the microwave radiation generated by the mobile, but two thirds of the world population is a huge number. I have since learned that we can harmonize the energies coming from a mobile so that they become beneficial. However, do try to limit your exposure time and use your mobile wisely.

Then we have Wi-Fi. In 2008, Godalming in Surrey became one of the first towns in the country to provide free wireless internet access; this was a double whammy for the people there, as it was also the first town in the world to have a public power supply, introducing electromagnetic fields into people's homes and the start of technopathic stress.

I have spoken to many people about the side effects of Wi-Fi; these include headaches, lethargy, mild depression and sleeplessness. Try switching your unit off at night before going to bed or, better still, switch it on only when you need it. Sure, you might get some Wi-Fi leaking into your home from your neighbours, but it should be diluted, as it has to come through walls to get to you.

Research has indicated that radio frequency radiation can cause changes in cognitive function, bring about molecular changes in cells, damage chromosomes, decrease short-term memory and induce cancer. For further information on EMF's view these sites:

- www.tetrawatch.net

- www.powerwatch.org.net

- www.sitefinder.orcom.org.uk

- www.revolt.net

- www.microwavenews.com

Another bugbear of mine is low-energy light bulbs (the cheaper variety), and I advise all my clients not to use them. Replace them with the normal 'old-fashioned' bulbs whilst they are still available. I don't want to get into conspiracy theories, but as soon as a government starts to give you something for free, it is time to wonder why and start researching the product.

They came to my attention some years back, when talking to a homeopathic vet who lived in Hampshire. She noticed that a high number of owners were bringing their cats and dogs to her, suffering from epilepsy. There seemed to be a spate of them, all of a sudden, and she started looking for a link. The animals came from a wide area, so it wasn't a localized problem. She looked at the food; there were a few matches, but not enough to account for all the fits. She started visiting the pet owners' homes; the only common denominator was low-energy light bulbs. She asked for them to be removed for a month to see what would happen. Guess what? The epileptic fits stopped, completely – the UV light obviously had a profound effect on them.

Now, if animals are affected that way, what happens to us humans? Many of us are trying to be kind to the planet, but sadly the larger manufacturers and the governments aren't. They just seem to be interested in increasing their profits by introducing the word 'green' to many of their products, enticing us, the public, to buy more of their goods, irrespective of whether they are good for the planet or not. These low-energy bulbs also contain a high level of mercury, and they should be disposed of in a special container at a recycling plant – certainly not in your normal dustbin. If you accidentally break one in your home, the government recommends wearing protective gloves and a protective mask to clear it up. Put the pieces of the bulb into a sturdy box, and seal it with tape. Then take it to a waste disposal site and hand it to a contractor there. A little different from an old-school light bulb.

None of us wants mercury around the house. It is toxic and known to cause damage to brain, kidneys and lungs if we are exposed to a large amount of it – or a small amount over a longer period. We also don't want it put in the earth, where it could leach out into a watercourse – and then back into our homes.

Alternatives are beginning to emerge, and Halogen or LED's seem to be the way forward. Perhaps the more expensive daylight-type bulb (www.emfields.org) is an option. Neither emits UV light, and they are still cheap to run, due to their low voltage.

I feel that the harmful effects of EMFs (Electro-Magnetic Fields) can be lessened by intent, although the ASA (Advertising Standard Authority) would disagree. We are electro-magnetic beings, and healing is also electro-magnetic, so why can't we affect man-made electro-magnetic fields? I believe that we can harmonize them to work with us, rather than against us. However, currently no machine could either prove or disprove this theory – unless you use dowsing rods or a pendulum – or, of course, the power of prayer, which is such a powerful tool.

Just think, every time you use your mobile phone, it could fill you with beneficial, not detrimental, energies. You can also harmonize, by intent, the water supply coming into your home. The list is endless.

Case Study 1: A house near Huntingdon, Cambridgeshire

Mum, Dad and two sons (15 and 13) lived in a detached property on the edge of town; the family were at loggerheads much of the time, had sleepless nights and the house was always in disarray. Mrs Walker wanted the family to be happy and felt that clearing the 'horrible energies' there would help solve their problems.

However one of their main problems came from an unlikely source, a detrimental technopathic stress issue at -8.

Does this affect the whole family?

Yes.

Does it affect them equally?

No.

Are the parents affected more than their children?

No.

So the two sons were bearing the brunt of whatever it was in the house that I had found.

Is it causing them not to sleep and therefore making them irritable?

Yes.

Are we looking at computers and mobile phones?

The rod twitched slightly showing that I was on the right track.

Does the house have Wi-Fi?

Yes.

Is this the main cause of the boys' problems?

Yes.

There was a lot of general earth energy and human emotional problems associated with the house but they hadn't highlighted the reasons for sleepless nights, which was caused by the Wi-Fi.

I telephoned Mrs Walker and asked about the Wi-Fi, 'Yes' she said 'We had it installed six months ago and now thinking back that was when the boys' problem started.' I suggested that she switch it off at night and see what happened. Peace was restored, 'All I could hear all night was the snoring.' She told me the next day.

There are wonderful little boxes available that use the electric wiring in your home to bring broadband into the rooms where you use your computer, laptop or game console, the ones that I use are called Devolo and are available online or in many electronic stores. They are great as you have a device that allows you to switch your wireless box off and still have internet access throughout your home.

Case Study 2: A family in Guildford, Surrey

I received a telephone call from a concerned Mother whose son, Jon, had constant buzzing in his ears; he said it sounded as though he had a bee's nest in his head. She had taken him to the Doctors but they couldn't find anything wrong. 'It's driving him crazy' she said, 'Can you do anything to help?'

I immediately thought of a psychic attack but on dowsing the question got a no response. I had to dig deeper and again found that the problem

223

was man-made.

I called her back later on that day and told her to switch off the cordless telephone and see what happens. 'How did you know that I have a cordless telephone?' she asked. I then explained how dowsing works, that I had purely asked the question and got a yes response from the rods.

She did as she was asked but didn't say anything to the family. After about twenty minutes a little voice piped up.

'Mum.'

'Yes, Jon?'

'My head isn't buzzing anymore.'

'That's good darling, finish you tea and see how you feel then.'

She then went and turned the telephone on to see what would happen.

'Mum the bees are back!'

She switched the plug off and the buzzing disappeared. She left the telephone off that night and Jon didn't complain again. The next day, she threw out the DECT phones and bought a low radiation system, once installed, Jon had no further problems. It turned out that Jon was a sensitive lad and the effect of the radiation from the DECT phones registered as a massive -9.

Dowsing Diagnosis Questions for Technopathic Stress

1. Do you have detrimental technopathic stress in the house?

2. Where does it come from?

3. How detrimental is it to the family?

4. Should the Wi-Fi be turned off at night?

5. Should you change the low-energy light bulbs?

6. Can it all be healed by intent?

7. Can these energies all be harmonized to work for the good of the family?

8. Does an amethyst crystal help with the EMFs from a computer?

9. Is the microwave detrimental to our health?

10. How detrimental is the food once cooked in the microwave?

11. Should you use it at all?

21. Guardian of the Site/Spirit of Place

Humans vibrate at a certain level, as do crystals. In fact, everything that we have around us is vibrating, including the devic realms – those unseen beings that help life to survive on this planet, keeping us all in balance. I say unseen, though there are those that do see nature spirits, Guardians of a site and spirits of place. I am not one of them, but I do feel them when they are close.

I feel that a Guardian is more of a spiritual being, and that a spirit of place is more devic. I.e. of the earth.

Guardian of the Site

The best way to experience a Guardian is to go to a sacred site; take Avebury, for example. The stones are an ideal place to 'feel' the energies of one of these beautiful beings. It is not there purely to protect the area, but also to impart information to those who are prepared to listen and communicate. Always ask permission before you enter a sacred site; you wouldn't dream of walking into a stranger's house without knocking on the door first – it's the same at Avebury, Stonehenge, et al. Confirm with the Guardian that it's OK to proceed, before you enter the hallowed grounds.

I find the best place to be with the Guardian at Avebury is the south-east corner of the site. There, you will find two large trees with a complex visible root structure beneath them. Sit there quietly with your eyes closed – and just 'be'. Clear your mind, as much as you can, anyway, and see if anything 'comes through'. This could be in the form of a voice, or of an imagined thought that seems to come from nowhere. They communicate in many different ways, and you can ask for this to be in a way that you might recognize.

When house healing, I always like to communicate with the Guardian, if there is one present. However, not all homes have one. You might find a Guardian or spirit of the house, but they are different to a main Guardian of place, who is a far more powerful being. I will always communicate with them whilst carrying out my healing work on the house. I purely ask, out loud or in my head, to communicate with the Guardian. Either I wait for a verbal 'yes', or I watch a dowsing rod move to confirm that I can; it really is as easy as that.

I like to check on whether they are happy or not. If they are not happy, then I try to find a solution to what ails them. They can be disgruntled for many reasons, for example, when new homes are built on their patch, humans are not keeping their gardens in order, trees are being cut down, there is a general disrespect of the countryside, and so forth. I try to explain why this has happened, that we as humans use and abuse the land, and that we also need new homes to live in. You can normally placate them.

Imagine an earth with no humans – the words peace, tranquility, harmony and balance all come to mind. Then look at the world now; no wonder the Guardians get upset. They have been here for millennia, and are concerned about the people and buildings that have appeared over that time.

Spirit of Place

Spirit of place (sometimes called Genius Loci) is much the same, but slightly different. They, too, can be found at sacred sites, however, in human terms, they are the general managers. The Guardian is the CEO – and elementals, who we will look at later, are the workers.

Holy wells or sacred springs, for example, Swallowhead Spring opposite Silbury Hill, close to West Kennet long barrow, are the perfect places to experience the spirit of place. They can often have a calm beauty about them when the Guardian is more grandiose and extreme (in modern language). They can bring a sense of peace and tranquility, when you 'tune' in to them. They are very pastoral, being of the country, and are helping manage and preserve the sanctity of their sacred place. Being 'middle management' they are always busy, keeping peace with the Guardian and ensuring that the elves, trolls, sylphs and undines are doing what they are supposed to be doing – looking after the flora and fauna about them.

Sadly we, as humans, like to leave our mark when we visit a holy site and Swallowhead is no exception. Often, the central tree is covered with cloth and notes, as a remembrance of a lost soul or a spoken wish that needs to be further enhanced by leaving a trinket. They are known as 'Clootie trees' in Scotland. A 'Clootie' or 'Cloot' being a strip of cloth or ribbon dipped in holy water, and offered to the tree spirit or the spirit of place. It is thought to represent an ailment; as the rag disintegrates, the ailment is supposed to disappear too. A lovely idea which goes back hundreds if not thousands of years. Whilst cotton and natural fibres rot, nylon, etc. doesn't – and I am sure that neither the tree nor the spirit of place find it amusing. Please, only leave a memory there, nothing else.

So, when you are at a sacred site, holy well or spring, try and communicate with the devas. If you don't feel too self-conscious, talk to them out loud or, if you prefer, say it in your head. I try and explain modern life to them; how we, as humans, are affected by stress and work, etc. With Guardians, I like to tell them that our homes and gardens are important to us, and that we are very similar to them – Guardians of our own small patch of the countryside. It seems to help.

Case Study 1: My early days dowsing at a sacred site

I decided many years ago to visit the Avebury area and do some earth healing (I was young and naïve). I picked on the West Kennet long barrow as the ideal place to go to clear the energies there. I didn't know about Guardians and Spirits of Place in those days. I didn't ask for permission before I barged into, what was tantamount to being, the Guardians' home and started to clear the detrimental energies I found there.

It felt like there was a large weight on my head, but I ignored it. I continued dowsing and as I did, more and more pressure was exerted. Before I knew it, I was on my knees and unable to stand. I crawled out, thankfully no one was around at that time, and sat on one of the large stones at the entrance hoping and praying that I hadn't got a brain tumour (that was my first thought). As the pain and heaviness started to lift, I heard a low laugh. I looked around, but no one ever appeared. I then wondered if I had heard the laugh at all or was it my imagination.

I walked slowly back to the car, exhausted and bewildered. It wasn't until a few years later that I learned there were Guardians at most sacred sites and that it is a good idea to ask their permission before entering. I dowsed whether the Guardian was responsible for my headache that day and got a resounding 'yes'.

Lesson learned.

Case Study 2. Unhappy Guardian delays house sale

I was approached some years back by a gentleman who was trying, unsuccessfully, to sell his house. It had been on the market, a buoyant market, for about a year. He was beside himself as he wanted to move to be nearer his son, some 150 miles away in Wales.

He would see would-be buyers drive up to his house and then drive away again. He'd had three viewings in the early days, since then nothing. His estate agent was mystified, the house was now looking excellent value but no takers.

David called me out of sheer curiosity, he had heard about me from a friend who had recommended me after I worked on his house. The first question was:

'Can you help me sell my house?'

I always keep a pendulum or dowsing rod near the telephone for just such an occasion. It gave me a positive response so I told him that I could. I am never quite sure how, until the floor plan arrives.

David had been in the house for some 18 years having bought it as a project. It was unkempt when he bought it and the gardens were a jungle. From the photographs that he sent me he had transformed the place, it was now a beautifully decorated property with delightful gardens and that, as it turned out, was the problem.

During my dowsing of his floor plans I found some earth energy problems. There was also some detrimental human emotion, but not enough to put buyers off. Then I got to the question of whether there was a Guardian or spirit of place in situ. The Guardian came through big and strong, it certainly wasn't at all happy, a -9 not happy.

It turned out that the Guardian did not want David to leave; it was convinced that the next owner would allow the house to fall into disrepair and let the gardens become overgrown. The Guardian loved the gardens and didn't what anything to change. As buyers stopped outside the house, he used similar techniques that I had come across at West Kennet all those years before; he made them feel uncomfortable and chased them away.

I tuned in and communicated with the Guardian; I pleaded David's case and eventually got its agreement to let him move on with his life. The compromise being that David would sell to someone who was a gardener, or at least loved gardening, ensuring the continuation of his good work. A whole queue of people then came to visit the house and a buyer was found, a charming couple who fell in love with the garden and they promised David that his good work would continue.

David told me that he spoke to the Guardian on the day of his departure and asked it to help the new couple settle in. He didn't get an answer but my pendulum told me that the Guardian would.

Dowsing Diagnosis Questions for Site Guardians

1. Do you have a Guardian of the site?

2. Do you have a spirit of place?

3. Do you have a spirit of the home?

4. Is each one happy?

5. If not, how detrimental are they to you and the family?

6. Are they detrimental to the pets?

7. Can they be placated by intent or actions?

8. What do you need to do to make them happy, i.e. plant a tree, etc.?

9. Should you talk with them regularly whilst in the garden?

10. How long have they been there?

22. Place Memory

These can be termed areas of conflict or trauma; something so upsetting has taken place here that it has left an indelible mark deep in the ground. Yes, it is caused by human emotion and suffering, but this goes far deeper, leaving the land scarred for hundreds, if not thousands, of years.

They are often the result of large battles, great agony, or anguish (either human or animal), and they tend to appear as fixed areas. They are often found within a home or workplace, and they don't move.

They can cause many problems for the client and family, including nightmares (if sleeping above or within the affected area), mood swings and arguments, temper tantrums in infants, broken sleeping patterns and night sweats.

Your own subconscious will pick up on these areas and it will try to warn you in various ways. When people involuntarily shiver, they will often joke that 'someone has just walked over my grave'. Actually, you might just have walked over someone else's resting place. The sudden onset of a headache can be a warning sign, as can butterflies in the stomach or the solar plexus chakra point. Learn to listen to your body; be aware of what it is doing and try to find out why. Try dowsing the problem.

If I find a place memory problem when dowsing a floor plan, it is a good idea to ascertain what date it occurred, and then to find out why the detrimental energy was left there. By understanding the cause, it will help in the healing process. Look for the discarnate soul that might be connected to the place memory. They will need to be dealt with first, before you carry out any further healing to the area.

The two World Wars added massively to the problems, as have all the conflicts in the world since. I was in Tibet several years ago, and I personally experienced some of the detrimental energy left over from the Chinese invasion – and of the atrocities that they carried out. Tibet in the 1950s was not the land of milk and honey that many people envisage; Shangri-La it was not. However, it was moving slowly into the twentieth century, after years of being 'out of bounds' to foreigners. It did not deserve what the Chinese refer to as a 'cultural revolution' (I prefer 'cultural destruction'), the murder of Buddhist monks and nuns, the desecration and sacking of the temples, the torture and killing of ordinary Tibetan people. It was an appalling period of both Chinese and Tibetan history.

Along with my Bhai (Brother, in Nepalese) Subash Tamang, we travelled across the Tibetan plateau, heading for Mount Kailash and Lake Manasarovar. We were going to perform the Kora, a circumambulation of Kailash, the holiest mountain in the world for many Asian faiths. We passed through many small towns to reach this 'holy grail', and each one had been touched by the Chinese – visually with drab grey concrete buildings and spiritually with hate, jealousy, avarice and the suffering of the local people. Seeing the reality from ground level is far more sobering than reading books or watching news reports on television. It is a stark reminder of the savagery of people. It is sobering to consider how any country can be driven to attempt to wipe an entire nation of its traditional beliefs. The towns are very sombre and during our stops for food and fuel, I experienced many upsetting feelings that I would now call a reaction to place memory.

One in particular was very poignant. We stopped at a small village called Payana for the night. It was made up of a number of single-storey houses, built by the Chinese to house the nomads, a few places to eat (you can't call them restaurants) and a number of guest houses. On the face of it, it was a pleasant enough place, if you ignored the piles of rubbish everywhere. It felt dark and uninviting, and I would have been happier if we had driven on and slept elsewhere. When I tried to explain this, Subash, our driver, Temba, and our guide, Pinjsoc, didn't realize that I meant the quality of the energies, not the quality of bedrooms. The problem with the Tibet Plateau is the lack of villages – the next one was five or six hours away, and anyway, it would have been no better.

I was psychically protecting myself each day and then again at night, but that didn't help on this night. Don't forget that this was and still is a highly spiritual country. Imagine what energies are present when a

Buddhist monk starts to chant, multiply that by several hundred as other monks chant, then by two thousand years, and you should start to get an impression of how high the vibrations are there. You can almost taste them; they are that strong. So, despite the vibrations being positive, it was a spiritual overload and most days I had a headache; partially it was the altitude, as the Plateau is around 14,500 feet above sea level, however, the energies there are so very strong that they seemed to penetrate my psychic protection – so much so that I contacted Andy Roberts from my mobile telephone to ask his advice. He gave me a mantra to chant, which helped.

On entering my bedroom, I was suddenly struck by utter sadness and melancholy. I have never felt so alone and vulnerable as I did that night. I started to meditate, and then asked questions as to why I felt the way I did.

Has harm to another human being happened here?

Yes.

Did that person or persons die here?

Yes.

Were they tortured?

No.

Imprisoned here?

Yes.

How many people were here?

Five.

Did they all die here in the village?

Yes.

How long were they locked up here?

Three days.

Were they then killed?

Yes.

Did any one of them die in this room?

Yes.

Male or female?

Male.

How old was that male?

Twenty-one years old.

Have they all gone to the light?

No.

How many need moving on?

Two.

How detrimental is this place memory to me?

-8

So there I was, in the most stunning countryside imaginable, sitting in a room that had seen one man die and a further four imprisoned and awaiting their death, at a massive -8 in detrimental effect to me. Three of them had gone to the light, however, two had remained behind for some reason. I asked if I could move them through, and I got a positive response. During the short soul rescue ceremony, I felt their anguish; I don't normally feel anything so this was very poignant to me. I then set about healing the room, the furniture and anything else that I could think of. It did help to improve the feeling in that room. I did a further healing before I went to bed, and again before we left in the morning. During the final healing, I was aware that the room smelled of lotus flowers – and I took it that I had done a good job.

I did a lot of soul rescue whilst in Tibet, and also place memory healing. Once you start this type of work, there is never a dull moment.

It is always good to dowse and to find out how to fix and heal the problem. This might involve a soul release, earth healing, room healing or people healing and it will depend very much on the cause.

Depending on how deep the problem is, you may need to carry out further healings. Other layers might exist; dowse again in a week or so to check if further healing work is needed – and carry it out.

Case Study 1: House in Bolton for Sale

I was approached during my early days of house healing by a lady living in Bolton, Lancashire, who asked if I could do something to help her sell the family house. She had read an article that I had been asked to write for *Kindred Spirit* magazine entitled 'Property Dowsing'. In it, I explained about stuck energies, geopathic stress, spirits and other unforeseen problems that might stop a house selling. Her home had been on the market for a year; lots of cars would stop outside, look – and then drive away again – not one person had viewed it. The price had been reduced several times, and the house was now looking very good value for money. They had bought a plot of land, and their new house was just about ready to move into – they were getting desperate to sell the old house.

A friend had lent her the magazine, and said that they had nothing to lose by talking to me and seeing if I could help. She was sceptical about the whole spiritual aspect of what I did, but was happy to give it a go. We talked about fees, and she started to back away from the whole idea. 'My husband would never agree to that amount,' she said. I didn't think that it was a huge amount, but the whole charging procedure for healing is a minefield. I said, 'Look, I'll tell you what we can do. You pay me half now, and then when a buyer is found, and this will be within a six-week period, you can pay me the other half.' We had ourselves a deal, and I waited for the floor plan to arrive.

Don't forget that their house had been on the market for just over twelve months, and not one person had viewed it – talk about putting your money where your mouth is. Still, I was convinced that I could do it.

The floor plan arrived, with half the fee as agreed, and it showed a good-sized three-bedroom family house, in a well-thought-of road on the outskirts of Bolton. As I carry out my initial dowse, I make rough notes, and I add further details later on as I go deeper into meditation. There was nothing obvious as to why the house hadn't sold – until I reached the question of 'Place Memory' and found the following:

> **This detrimental area has been here since the battle of 1510 and centres, more or less, on your house. It is approximately 800 yards in radius.**

I asked the following questions to make sure that I was on the right track:

Is this why the house hasn't sold?

Yes.

If I heal this area will the house start to attract viewers?

Yes.

Is it people's subconscious stopping them viewing the house?

Yes.

So I started to delve further:

How many people died in the battle?

Eight.

How many of them were buried here?

Three.

Were many more injured?

238

Yes.

How many more were injured during the battle?

Nineteen.

Did any of them die of their wounds afterwards?

Yes.

How many died?

Nine.

Have they all gone to the light?

Yes.

So I just need to do a healing on the land, clearing the place memory?

Yes.

It had probably been more of a local skirmish, but people had died there and had left a permanent reminder to haunt future generations of house sellers and buyers. Death, suffering, greed and hate had been part of making this detrimental area – God's love and light were needed to heal the scars.

Because the detrimental effects had spread into the road, when would-be buyers stopped their cars to look at the outside, their subconscious mind picked up on the death and bloodletting that had occurred hundreds of years beforehand, and it warned them off. I sent off the report, discussed my findings with my client – and waited.

Three weeks later I received a telephone call saying, 'Guess what? We are moving out in three days' time to our new house; we have found a buyer. The lady is renting our house for six months, whilst she finalizes the completion date of her home to a developer, she has already exchanged – then she buys it. Since you healed the house, we have had five people to view, all of whom loved it, but she was in the best position to buy, with cash, and wanted to move quickly, so we sold it to her. The cheque is in the post already; we are so pleased with your work and we want you to heal our new house for us too.'

The new house wasn't too bad, mainly energies left behind by the various tradesmen who had been working there – although three spirits had already taken up residence and I did find an ancient trackway running through their lounge.

Case Study 2: Hairdressing Salon in Guildford, Surrey

The telephone call began with 'My business is awful, can you help me please?' I asked what the business was, and why she felt that I might be able to help. 'It is a hairdressing salon,' she replied. 'I am in a good location; I have spent money on the inside and outside to make it look really good and nothing. No one looks in the window; they just pass me by as though I don't exist.' I asked why she thought that I could help and she replied, 'Well, friends of mine had their place Feng Shui'd recently and that worked. I just feel that something isn't right here; one of my beauty technicians is always ill and I get a headache when I stand at the reception area. Can you come and have a look please?'

Guildford was only a few miles from where I was living, so I arranged a time to visit the salon.

I knew the area well, but I did not remember seeing the salon at the address given, so I parked my car and walked towards where the salon was supposed to be. As I turned the corner, to my surprise, there it was. Actually I vaguely recognized it, but for some reason I hadn't remembered it. I had arranged to visit after closing time, as I wanted to sit and get a feel for the place, without the owner having to explain to staff and customers what I was doing there. There was a strange presence in the salon; the energy was all wrong. I stood at the reception desk and immediately felt the effects of water running beneath me. I dowsed and found several water veins, an earth energy line and a few disturbance lines, but I felt one particular area was quite malevolent. That was where the beauty technician sat; frankly it didn't surprise me that she was always ill. I sat there and immediately felt the dark energies surround me, pulling me down. It was almost as though my life force was being sucked from me. I didn't like it.

Even though it was 7pm, there were still a lot of people walking past, but the owner was right – no one actually looked in, or even acknowledged the salon. It was as though the place didn't exist. I walked outside and stood looking at the salon. It was brightly lit, both inside and out, well decorated and looked chic. The owner had done a good job on presentation. It deserved better.

I took rough measurements, and I sketched a plan once I got home. I started work immediately, mainly because I was intrigued at what I might find during the dowse. Six spirits had taken up residence here; perhaps they wanted a new hair style or needed their nails to be painted, who knows? There were three quite detrimental water veins, two earth energy lines, a ley, various energy spirals, a reversal point and an unhappy spirit of place. Then there was more to come in the form of one very detrimental place memory and a subconscious place memory.

I marked the place memory on the plan and wrote:

> **Marked with a dotted outline and exactly where the nail technician sits. This is the site of a gibbet dating back to 1098 where people were hanged; this site was used for 194 years. Very bad energies were left here and extremely detrimental to anyone sitting there.**

Two of the spirits that I found had come from this period and had been hanged from the gibbet. I dowsed their crimes and they were both quite petty; certainly not enough to be hanged for. The deaths on the gibbet left so much detrimental energy in that particular area of ground that the poor technician was picking up on them, being badly affected by them, feeling ill and having to go home to recover. I had only sat there for a few minutes and I felt the effect – even with full psychic protection. The poor girl was in the seat for several hours at a time, completely at the mercy of theses noxious energies – no wonder she hated the place. I had to carry out several healings to rid the salon of the detrimental effects of the gibbet and the residues of those that had died on it. After a few weeks, the technician's headaches stopped, and she became part of a successful team. The salon got busier, especially once the second problem was overcome.

Whilst standing outside the salon, I was aware that no one gave it a second glance, even though it was brightly lit and almost right in front of them as they walked along a wide pathway to get to the car park. As I started to walk away, I felt as though I was travelling down a tunnel, or at least a much narrower path than I was. I got the rods out and started asking questions:

Is there a reason that people don't see the salon?

Yes.

Is it subconscious stuff?

Yes.

Can it be healed?

Yes.

Can I do the healing?

Yes.

Can I do it without finding out what the problem is?

No.

Oh well, it was worth asking.

When I walk am I travelling along a tunnel?

No.

Could it be misconstrued as a tunnel?

Yes.

Are there trees or bushes either side to give this effect?

Yes.

Was the ground banked either side of this pathway?

Yes.

Was this an original gate or pathway into Guildford?

Yes.

Was it used for several hundred years by human traffic?

Yes.

Did one of the banks run through the salon?

Yes.

Was the banking man made?

Yes.

So do people's subconscious minds still see the banking and follow the human energy pattern?

Yes.

We had found out what the problem was. A path led into ancient Guildford, and it was raised both sides and planted with thorn bushes to stop undesirables from sneaking into the town. This footpath was used for several hundred years, and the energy from that usage had been indelibly imprinted into the ground. It is well known that sheep follow set pathways from instinct, and humans were doing exactly that when walking in our ancestors' footsteps in Guildford. The salon was invisible, because a huge bank of earth ran through it – or rather a huge bank used to run through it. Although it was no longer there, people's third eyes could still see it and would naturally follow past energy patterns.

My notes said:

It appears that there was a raised ditch/hedge running along either side of the path, this goes back many of hundreds of years, and the energies are still there. This gave people a tunnel vision (or should I say it gave their subconscious a tunnel vision), their eyes would automatically follow the old energy pattern; it appeared as though the salon was not there.

Once I had found out the problem, I could do the healing. I simply had to ask that all old energy patterns from the past were wiped clean and that the salon became visible to all who passed. It worked, and within a few days people began to take notice of the salon and the appointment books began to fill up. People would often come in and ask how long the salon had been there; they had never noticed it as they had walked past.

Case Study 3: A Large Department Store in London

This was an interesting case; one where I found that the internet confirmed my dowsing. A lady telephoned me one day and asked if I could do some work for her. I replied that as long as it was legal, the answer would be yes, what does she have in mind?

'Well,' she said, 'I work in a large department store in London, and the floor that I work on is having problems with a ghost. Do you think that can you help?'

'I am sure that I can,' I replied, and she then went on to explain the problems that they were having. Actually, it was a problem that affected one particular lady – the head of the department. One minute she would be fine and the next a strange look would appear on her face and her character would change – she would become another person. I asked if there was a pattern to it. She thought about it, and said that yes there was.

'It's when she moves into the other side of the building, she comes back and she is different for about ten minutes. I am sure that a ghost is affecting her.'

She drew me a rough floor plan and sent it. I started working on it and, although I did find a couple of spirits, and asked them to go to the light, it was something quite different that was affecting this lady. I found that halfway along the office there was a detrimental energy area, a negative place memory, and her subconscious mind was picking up on that. I dowsed further and noted the following:

I also found a blanket of negative energy here, and I marked it with a dashed purple line on the plan. The centre of this area would be found in the room to the right of where you sit. It dates back 67 years ago (1940), when I get the impression that a bomb hit the building, setting part of it on fire. I don't get the feeling that anyone was killed though. It was just a very negative act.

I went on the internet to look at the history of the building, to find out whether it had, indeed, been hit by a bomb in the Second World War. It had. I was overjoyed that what I had found dowsing had just been verified by historical facts. A bomb had partially destroyed a corner of the building, and then a fire had broken out. Luckily, the London Fire Brigade were on the scene quickly and the flames were put out before too much damage was done. However, the detrimental thoughts behind this act, like the planning of the raid, the making of the bomb and the bomber's thoughts as he targeted London were still there in that rebuilt part of the store. The lady in question was obviously sensitive to these energies, and had picked up on them as she walked from one part of the office to the other.

I did a healing on the department, and I asked that the lady be helped in any way possible. I felt that she should be given healing, as there was no reason why she should bear the brunt of what happened many years ago. It seems that my prayers were granted, and she was affected no more. The department suddenly became a calm place to work; no more mood swings were apparent and my client was happy with the outcome. Whether their business improved or not I don't know.

When finding a problem area on your plan I normally draw a ring around the area using a purple pen.

Dowsing Diagnosis Questions for Place Memories

1. Is there a detrimental place memory within your home?

2. How many?

3. Are there any in the grounds of your house?

4. Where are they?

5. How detrimental are they?

6. When do they date from, AD or BC?

7. What century?

8. Why did they occur?

9. Can they be healed?

10. Check for lost souls, move them on before you start the healing.

11. Are there various layers to heal?

12. Any subconscious layers to heal?

23. Elementals

The true workers of the world. These wonderful beings toil away for the good of the planet, keeping us, the flora and the fauna healthy. They are unseen by most, but their names will be familiar, as they have been part of our folklore for generations.

They are named after the four elements: Earth (gnomes), Water (undines), Wind (sylphs), and Fire (salamanders), and they are aligned to the cardinal points of a compass.

They are generally happy creatures, and they are content to spend their time in the great outdoors doing what they do naturally – dedicating themselves to care for the animal and plant life here on earth.

They are not the sharpest tools in the woodshed, and they can easily get trapped in your home, garage or garden shed. If you are outside in the garden with your children – perhaps you working and them playing – then the elementals will be all around you. They love people enjoying themselves, especially children, and also you working alongside them, helping to tend the garden. They can easily get carried away with this euphoria and follow you into your home, garage or shed – then your troubles begin. They can easily become trapped and, in their confusion, find it difficult to escape. Even if you had a red exit sign at the door, they probably wouldn't follow it.

Now, being trapped in a strange place is going to be upsetting for anyone, especially if you have spent the whole of your life outdoors. The interior of a house will be completely alien, and all the nooks and crannies will just cause further confusion – panic and chaos will ensue.

So you now have four, five or more elemental spirits trapped in your home, charging around trying to get out. In human terms, it would be rather like informing a group of eight-year-old boys that you are going out for two hours and asking them to behave while you are gone. What state would your house be in by the time you got back? Well, much the same happens with trapped nature spirits.

They normally show that they are upset by causing certain problems in your home, including electrical and plumbing faults, acrid smells like stale tobacco or off meat, unusual noises such as tinkling in the pipes, flickering of lights, etc. They can also be responsible for whirling and clicking noises in rooms, as well as giving the house a melancholy feel.

They can also spread a feeling of nameless restlessness in people, making you feel ill at ease in your own home.

When they are trapped in your home, they are always detrimental and need to be moved outside. Back in their own domain, they will, once again, be happy toiling in the garden. Some, however, can be quite spiteful, and your pets can suffer at their hands. They will spend their time chasing cats and dogs around the garden, not giving them a moment's peace, blocking them from getting back into the house. Cats and dogs can become quite traumatized.

Dowse to see whether you have any trapped in your home, garage or shed. Ask if they are detrimental to you and the family. They can also be separated into 'beneficial' and 'non-beneficial' for your garden. Once found they need to be moved on, diplomatically and thoughtfully, as they have feelings just like us – although they are quicker to lose their temper, and can be quite bellicose. Keep the good ones and move them back into your garden; the others need to be moved to a nearby hill or field.

They are true nature spirits, and they have as much right to be here as us – in truth, probably more so. It is our encroachment on their domain that puts us in conflict with them. Talk with them when outside; ask for their help when planting and gardening. They and the plant life will listen and respond. Happy elementals mean a beautiful and bountiful garden. The people at Findhorn understand and work with this devic realm – with some startling results.

Earth Spirits

Gnomes are the devic beings that control and ensure the stability of planet Earth. They are born with the ancient wisdom and knowledge of past generations of earth workers; they help ground plants, through encouraging strong roots.

They have no tolerance for anyone that harms Mother Earth and will actively fight to protect the planet; they are the Home Guard if you like, staying at home to ensure the safety of the countryside.

They are of the North and concern themselves with the products and treasures of Mother Nature. They commonly live beneath rocks, within the soil, or around the roots of trees and bushes. If you sit quietly and look, you might be lucky enough to see one, especially if you ask.

They will help you in the garden, but only if they feel you are worthy. Be considerate towards the plants, shrubs, birds and bees in your garden, and they will assist you greatly. Try connecting with them when you are outside; seek their guidance when planting a bulb or a shrub and ask for it to grow strong and healthy and see what happens.

They normally dress in green or russet brown clothes, blending in with their surroundings.

Water Spirits

These are known as Undines, and they are of the West. They inhabit streams, ponds, waterfalls, seas, sacred springs and wells; they are one of the most beautiful of the nature spirits, both graceful and elegant.

They control the water, the life blood of our planet. They direct the flow of the rivers, the tides of the seas and the courses of water down mountainsides. When you consider how much water there is on this planet, these nature spirits lead a busy yet fruitful life.

They are normally dressed in greens and light blues to blend into their background. They are considered very compassionate; however, as with Gnomes and other spirits, they can get very upset should anyone take advantage of Mother Earth.

If you have a pond in your garden, call upon the Undines to care for it and its inhabitants, the fish, frogs, water beetles, etc.

Air or Wind Spirits

For those of us that walk or climb mountains, sylphs or air elementals should need no introduction. Often, as I reach the summit, I feel exhilarated, and my body seems to vibrate at a higher level. You feel alive and aware of . . . well, I suppose of how small a cog you are in the large machine of life.

Even when you climb or walk alone, when you reach the peak of a mountain you never are alone – someone or something is always with you. That something is a sylph, an elegant, beautiful air spirit that has guided and looked after you during your climb, then welcomed you to the top. The wind blowing through your hair on a seemingly still day; a feather dropping in front of you or a leaf floating by are all signs of a sylph.

The sylphs are of the East, and are not only responsible for controlling the air, providing us with a breathable atmosphere, but also for our inspiration when we create. They help our mental attitude, allowing our minds to fly.

They are ethereal beings, and they have delicate gossamer wings, rather like a lacewing, when they hatch. They try to keep our air clean, a hard job these days, and apparently they don't like people who smoke because they smell funny and they don't look like normal human beings. Smoking distorts our appearance somehow, and sylphs get confused.

Fire Spirits

Salamanders control the element of fire, and this goes hand in glove with one of our most primeval senses, survival. Fire is essential for our warmth and wellbeing; a world without fire would be unthinkable.

The salamander is from the South, the direction of the sun at the hottest time of the day, and through this, our bodies are kept warm. The fire elementals work through our bloodstream and liver, keeping our life force pumping around our bodies. Our emotions are also controlled by the fire spirits; someone who is very emotional can be called 'hot-headed' for instance.

They are the strongest of the elementals and also the most primitive. The kundalini in yoga is the releasing of our internal fire, the serpent that rises up the spine to our head, producing a spiritual awakening within us.

We could not survive without being surrounded by these four groups of important beings. When I first started on my spiritual path, I discounted so much along the way as 'New Age speak'. Gradually, through trial, error and experience, I have come to realize that, unlike scientists who 'have to see before they can believe', you 'have to believe before you can see'.

Elemental beings are now part of my life. I believe and sometimes see them – mainly as shadows, as they do vibrate at a lower level than us. They are there to help us, we just need to ask. Be still, and try to be aware of what is going on around you. Sit, look and listen – you could be very surprised by what happens.

Case Study 1: Minster Road in Godalming, Surrey

One of my first direct encounters with elementals came when I had just moved into a house in the Busbridge area of Godalming. I decided that I would use a bedroom at the back of the house as my dowsing room. I set up my desk, chair and computer, ready to start work. Suddenly I was aware of an awful smell in the room.

Almost at the same time my youngest son, Charles, popped his head around the door and said 'Phoarr what is that horrible smell?'

'Don't look at me, I didn't do it!'

'Well if you didn't who did?'

Now, that was a good question and I started asking questions of my pendulum.

Did someone or something cause that unpleasant smell?

Yes.

Was it human?

No.

Was it caused by an elemental?

Yes.

How many are there in here?

Six.

Were they all responsible for the smell?

No.

Did just one of them cause it?

Yes.

Was it a way of showing displeasure at me using the bedroom?

Yes.

Does the elemental feel that the bedroom is his domain now?

Yes.

So in its mind I am trespassing?

Yes.

The house had been unoccupied for over a month before Charles and I moved in, and the elementals must have been having a real good time in the empty place; it must have been party central, as I eventually found twenty-two in residence. Twenty-one of them I moved very easily into the back garden. One, however – the smelly one – didn't want to go. It was happy in living in the back bedroom, and it made its protest known by generating even worse smells every time I suggested it went back into the garden.

There had to be a way of getting rid of this Gnome, for that is what he was, and his appalling smells. Being nice wasn't working, I had to get sneaky.

Do Gnomes like flowers?

Yes.

Does this one have a favourite?

Yes.

At this stage I walked downstairs and asked the pendulum,

Was the flower in the back garden?

No.

So it was in the front garden – and I went out through the door.

Is it to the left hand side?

Yes.

When my finger points at it, please indicate a yes response.

I pointed my finger at the front door and started moving it in a clockwise direction. The pendulum moved, and I was looking at a beautiful passion flower in full bloom. 'Got him,' I thought.

Could I tempt him out of the house to look at this?

Yes.

So, I went back upstairs, picked up a cordless telephone and pretended to dial.

'I have the most beautiful passion flower in the garden; I have never seen a bloom like it, quite stunning.' I felt that I had done enough to get his attention, but I hoped that I hadn't 'over-egged it'.

'I know what I'll do; I'll go and take a photograph of it, then email it to you.' On my way downstairs I surreptitiously dowsed to see if he was following me – 'yes' he was. I imagined his excitement at seeing his favourite flower; the anticipation must have been tremendous as I felt him charge past me as I opened the front door.

'Look at that, isn't it beautiful,' I told him, pointing at the passion flower. 'I now ask you to dedicate yourself to its wellbeing; tend and care for the plant. See that it grows big and strong.'

I then quickly nipped back into the house and shut the door, before the Gnome changed its mind. The smells stopped, and the passion flower kept on blooming. He was a happy Gnome; I also used to leave little bits of chocolate for him when I remembered.

Case Study 2: Garden Pond and its Precious Family

This involves a garden pond, some very expensive Koi carp and a missing water spirit.

I was just about to start working on a client's house when he called to say that he was having trouble with his new fish pond in the garden. Actually, he was having trouble with the fish in the fish pond.

I had successfully worked on his last home and, after moving to a larger property two years later, he wanted me once again to clear the energies and to harmonize his new house. He had been a collector of Koi carp for many years, and one of the main reasons for moving was to have a larger pond for his fish.

The house needed a lot of work, as the last owners must have led a rather turbulent lifestyle. It had been on the market for about six months, which was unusual for a house of its size, and although a lot of people had viewed it they had not had any offers. My client had sold his own house very quickly and for a good price. He put in a low offer which, to his amazement, was accepted – and two months later he and his family moved in.

I received the telephone call to say that they had exchanged and were moving in seven days. Could I work on the house before they moved in, as the atmosphere was awful – 'very dark and uninviting' were the words he used. I explained that unless the current owners agreed for me to heal the energies in the house, I could do nothing until after they had moved out. They were oblivious to the muddled energies in their house, and it wasn't my place to change that for them.

We agreed that it would wait until completion day, and that he would call me as soon as the vendors had moved out. He didn't want to enter the house with the energies as they stood, so I would remove the three spirits and various other human-manifested life forms that were there, and I would work on the earth energies, etc., the next day. My telephone rang at 14.30 to say that they had gone, and I went to work whilst they waited outside for the green light from me. What the removal men thought, I really don't know. My client did explain to them what was happening, and they didn't bat an eyelid. I called fifteen minutes later to give them the all clear – and they moved in.

The next day I did what I had to do for them, and my client reported that the atmosphere in the house felt so much better. The children had an undisturbed night's sleep, and they all felt very much at home.

All was well until I received a telephone call about four weeks later saying, 'My fish are dying – is there anything that you can do to help?' I dowsed and got a 'yes' response.

'Yes, apparently I can,' I replied, 'But I don't yet know how, I need to sit and ponder this one.' He explained that he had just finished building a large fish pond in his garden. The company that he employed had planted it with the correct vegetation and made sure that the filtration system was all in order; he had then taken delivery of ten large Koi carp. They seemed very happy for a few days and then, one after the other, they started dying. He called the company who built the pond, and they came back and tested the water. They could not find any reason for the fish to die, hence his telephone call to me.

So I sat and dowsed the problem:

Is there a problem with the pond?

Yes.

Is the problem due to the construction of the pond?

No.

Is there a problem with the cleanliness of the water?

No.

Have the dead fish been injured by a heron?

No.

Were the fish healthy when they arrived?

Yes.

If I don't solve the problem will all the other fish die?

Yes.

No pressure there, then.

Is the pond in the wrong place?

No.

Does it have anything to do with earth energy lines?

No.

Is it a man-made problem?

No.

Is the problem related to what I do?

Yes.

Is it a spirit problem?

Yes.

Does it have anything to do with elemental spirits?

Yes.

Has building the pond upset them?

No.

Is something missing?

Yes.

Does the pond need its own spirit guardian?

Yes.

An Undine?

Yes.

Can I ask for one to dedicate itself to the pond, fish, other wildlife and vegetation?

Yes.

I gave a huge sigh of relief; you never know where the questions will take you and how long it might take. So, all I needed to do was ask for an Undine to become a guardian or protector of the garden pond. This was carried out by conducting a small ceremony on site.

The fish stopped dying; the pond started to flourish and, once my client was sure that harmony had been restored, he purchased some more fish to fully stock the pond. I can't claim to heal all ponds of their problems, but was happy that I could there.

Case Study 3: Larry the Cat in Gloucestershire

This case involves my good friends Kate (the animal communicator), Jools, Nathan and their cat, Larry. Their home appeared earlier in the book – it has been quite a saga working on the problems found there as the bungalow is built on an ancient site and the layers are very deep.

In recent weeks we have been speaking, as Larry, their cat, had a few problems and went missing. He is a home-loving cat and loves his pineapple igloo (don't ask), he is sensitive, but also quite adventurous and does often roam the neighbourhood; however, he loves his food and home comforts.

I received a call from Jools who was worried about Larry, who had been gone for a day, and she asked for my help. She had gone around the neighbourhood calling his name but there was no sign of him. I asked for a photograph and sent it to Kate. The first thing that she saw was the colour green and she felt Larry's discomfort. He had picked up an attachment which Kate described as yucky and quite nasty.

Larry had picked up a lawn elemental and it had attached itself to him, hence the green colour; it was very detrimental and quite spiteful. He had been acting a little skittish when in the garden and it was now obvious why. He had been taunted by this elemental for some reason and it had then attached itself to Larry, who decided enough was enough and left. Unfortunately, the lawn spirit went with him.

Removal was simple enough and within half an hour Larry reappeared, much to the relief of Jools and Nathan. He looked a little bedraggled but otherwise healthy, and within a few minutes of eating he was asleep in the living room, in his igloo.

Dowsing Diagnosis Questions for Elementals

1. Are there any trapped elementals in your home, garage, outbuildings and cars?

2. How many?

3. What kind of elementals are they?

4. How detrimental are they?

5. Are they attached to anyone (human or animal)?

6. Is it OK to move them into the garden?

7. Should they be moved further away?

8. If in the garden, will they be detrimental to your pets?

9. Are there any detrimental elementals in the garden that need relocating?

10. Should you talk to them whilst in the garden before you start work, cutting the grass, etc.?

11. Are there any further issues, caused by the elementals, that need to be dealt with?

24. Tree Spirits

Most large and majestic trees will undoubtedly have their own spirit attached. They are there for the wellbeing of the tree, and for all the wildlife it supports. They are similar to elementals – in that they can work with or against us.

They are there to nurture the young sapling when it is first planted; they can be attached to the seedling itself as it leaves its mother tree to start a new life, or they can simply move from one tree to another at will. As the tree grows, the spirit will ensure that it has the correct nutrients, and that sunlight is absorbed via the leaves to bring strength. Tree spirits are also wonderful healers; just lean up against an ancient oak and feel its energy.

If you are going to be doing any pruning work in the garden, please inform the tree spirits, elementals and the shrubs of your plans. Plants and trees, just like humans, have an aura surrounding them and this can be easily damaged. Telling the tree what you are doing will help it. Living next door to Allyson and Me must be interesting, as we are always outside talking with the trees and shrubs. I always tell them why I am about to start pruning: to ensure new growth, that they are overhanging the road or they look a bit scraggly.

Please also be careful when chopping down trees in the garden as they might have a tree spirit attached. A displaced tree spirit is not good to have in the house. They, like elementals, can cause all sorts of problems. Check when you bring in logs to burn on your open fire; make sure that the final one hasn't got a tree spirit attached. They can move from log to log until there are no more to move to, then they will be in your home.

Dowsing your home regularly will determine if you have a displaced tree spirit there or not. They can be attached to a new table or chairs; a child's wooden toy can easily be affected, as can a carving – or even the timber framing in a house.

If you find a tree spirit in your home, they will need to be moved out of the house – preferably to another tree or shrub – but, please be diplomatic. Always ask where they want to go to.

Case Study 1: Tree Spirit and Elementals in Lancashire

The 'powers that be' are great teachers. Just when you thought that you had everything under control, they will throw you a curveball that will lead to much head scratching. Often the answer is logical and staring you in the face – but you just cannot see it for whatever reason. Don't forget to use the experience that you have gained in the physical world, when dealing with problems in the spiritual world.

A recent case got me thinking. I was working with a couple in Lancashire; the wife felt that she was being affected by spirits, and the symptoms were getting worse. I worked on the floor plan and found various earth energies and emotional problems that were easily sorted out. The site of their home was once a sacred place, and there were a number of detrimental layers to clear over several weeks. The spirits in the house had been moved on and all the energies had been cleared, but there was still an underlying problem that kept re-appearing. It was an elemental problem; the smells gave that away – they ranged from mild tobacco to acrid and sickly. I worked with them, as I normally do, and the house would improve for a day or so, but then the smells would return – not so strong, but always there in the background.

Whatever I was doing was working; however, something was niggling in the back of my mind. I couldn't work out what it was, until a follow-up telephone call with my client revealed that he had cut down a large tree a year or so beforehand – and he asked me if that could have caused any problems. I dowsed and realized it was a displaced tree spirit. The elementals had kept returning, because they wanted to draw my attention to the homeless tree spirit. It seems obvious now, however, at the time I couldn't see it. A short ceremony later, the tree spirit was moved from the house to another tree, and the elementals – and the smells – went away.

Here are some general questions to ask. They will help your garden thrive, and keeping the spirits happy will pay dividends.

- Do trees and shrubs have an aura?

- Does talking to them help when about to prune?

- Do they have a tree spirit attached?

- If 'yes', should I ask its permission before I start pruning?

- Should I tell the tree or shrub what I am about to do?

- Is it a good time to prune?

- If no, when is a good time?

Case Study 2: A House near Bures, Suffolk

Whilst carrying out a healing on this house, I came across a power artefact in my client's living room. It dowsed as a -10, so I knew it was very powerful, and would be able to influence anyone in a detrimental way if they sat or stood close to it.

I couldn't get a clear picture of it in my mind. It was made of wood, but didn't dowse as a table, although it was about the same height. It had a flat top, but it wasn't wooden like the rest of the item, and it didn't have any legs either. It was located in the centre of their room, where a low table would normally be, but it just didn't feel like a normal table. I dowsed that it not only had a tree spirit attached to it, but it was also a power artefact. You don't always find that this is the case, but please do check.

The tree spirit was from an oak tree, which had been cut down to make furniture. The tree spirit was quite happy to dwell with the seasoning timber, but got quite upset when they started cutting it up. It had moved from timber to timber, finally ending up at my client's house, firmly attached – to something I couldn't identify I carried out a distant healing on the 'something', moving the tree spirit to a nearby wood, where it attached itself to a beautiful oak tree that was devoid of a spirit. I also cleared the 'something' of the detrimental energies that had built up, and the house became calm.

I visited the house several weeks later, as I was visiting a friend in Sudbury, and I took the opportunity to call in and see how my clients were getting on with the healed house. They seemed very happy; reported that the house was much cosier than before and that it felt more like home. I was offered a cup of coffee and taken into the living room. There, right in front of me, was the 'something' – sat in the centre of the room with my cup placed on it. It was a low table, however not like one that I had ever seen before. It was made from solid baulks of oak timber, to my client's own design, stacked on the floor with a sheet of glass placed on top. I thought that it was wonderful, and said so.

'Well, there is a story behind that,' said Bill. 'It isn't exactly what I wanted – and the carpenter and I have fallen out over the design. I really don't like it, and it makes me cross every time I see it.'

So, there we had the reason behind the detrimental energies attached to the table. The frustration that Bill felt in not having the table exactly as he pictured it had soaked into the very timbers that it was made from – and it had started spreading its detrimental influence over the family, including Bill, making him even more cross.

Dowsing Diagnosis Questions for Tree Spirits

1. Is there a misplaced tree spirit in your house?

2. Is there a misplaced tree spirit in your garden?

3. What kind of tree spirit is it i.e. oak, spruce, elm, yew, etc.?

4. Where it is?

5. How detrimental is it?

6. Can you help?

7. Would dedicating it to a specific tree help?

8. Is there a tree in the garden that is suitable (if not go to the next question)?

9. If I purchase a new tree, and plant it in the garden, then dedicate it to the displaced spirit, will that appease them?

25. Animal Spirits

Just as human beings get stuck on the earth plane, so can animals. They may be unaware that they are dead, perhaps as the result of an accident, or have stayed due to the sadness of their owners.

Pets are a major part of a family, and their passing can have a profound effect on adults and children alike. Dogs, for instance, are constant companions; they are always there and happy, in most cases, to give unconditional love to everyone. Cats are the same, but can often be 'out on the prowl' and rather more independent.

When any pet or animal dies they, as humans do, get their chance to move into the light. However, this process can be interrupted, and their souls will become earthbound and they become animal spirits.

The willingness to stay and comfort their grieving owner is one reason that they may stay. If a bitch died whilst giving birth to her pups, she may stay on to care for her litter. A cat, having been run over, might have died so suddenly that it doesn't realize it is no longer alive. Cows, pigs and sheep are not exceptions.

Your old family pet from years past may still be with you. You might have inherited someone else's pet when moving to a new house. The cat might still be sleeping in an airing cupboard, where it has for the past forty years. An animal spirit might have been attracted to the 'vibes' of a particular family member, following that person around and affecting them with detrimental energy.

All spirits that have not gone to the light have a detrimental energy about them – it cannot be helped. It is the same with humans that have passed over; they need to go to the light to continue their evolution. If they don't, their soul cannot progress.

Once a soul (human or animal) has passed to the light, I believe that it can then come and visit us whenever it wants. There are many stories of owners seeing their favourite dog sitting at the bottom of their bed just before they pass over themselves; ready to guide them into the light. Cats are well known for their healing qualities when alive, and this is the same when they visit us from the light. Again, there are stories of cats healing their owners of various illnesses, even though they have been dead for years.

Dowse to see if you have an animal spirit in your house or garden. You will need to ascertain why they are here and also what they want. Check first to see if they have gone to the light, as they may need sending on if not. Then check to see if they are there to say hello to a certain member or members of the family, to provide healing or maybe even a warning.

Animals have feelings, so please be empathetic. Talk to them and comfort them; they may be very confused and lost. Send them healing too.

Case Study 1: Alfie, my Border Collie

'A legend in his own lunchtime,' as my old friend, Max, used to say. Alfie was the classic border collie, sharp as a tack, neurotic and great fun to be with. He was, to me, the perfect dog and the boys and I had such adventures with him. His early passing was so sad.

He knew everything, or appeared to. If he didn't, he certainly would never let on. He was like a shadow and was rarely away from my side until we went on a hike – and then he was off, free as a bird, running to and fro, stopping only to check on my whereabouts. Once he knew where I was, he would set off again. His intelligent brown eyes never missed a thing – whether it was a bird flying by, or seeing an attractive female who might be persuaded to rub his stomach. He was, to put it mildly, a tart.

I had a special whistle, something to do with the shape of my teeth I think, and he would react to it immediately, coming back whenever I wanted him to. My boys were also trained to the whistle, as was Allyson. This unique noise came in very handy when we were climbing mountains. They would stop what they were doing straightaway, and look at what I wanted them to do – normally to stop them falling over a ledge.

He'd had a swelling on his side for some time, but the vet said that it was nothing to worry about. Alfie didn't seem bothered by it, so we let it pass. Sadly it was too late to help him when, several months later, the vet mentioned the 'C' word. It had spread so quickly, there was no hope. The decision was made to put him to sleep as he didn't deserve to suffer, and frankly it would have been impossible for such an active dog to get any enjoyment from living a sedentary life.

The telephone call came to say that Alfie was dead. The funny thing was, that at that moment, he was by my side, or more accurately, his spirit was by my side. He was looking up at me with those deep brown eyes. He had come to say goodbye. I stroked him, and told him to go and follow the light. As he ran off I gave my whistle one last time; he stopped, turned to look at me and then went. I admit that my eyes ran with tears; even sitting here typing I feel very emotional. I am looking forward to reacquainting myself with Alfie; when I too, go to the light.

Case Study 2: Buster the Dog

I was shopping in Waitrose when my mobile rang.

'Do you believe in ghosts?' said the female voice.

'Yes, I certainly do,' I replied.

'Good', she said, 'That makes the conversation easier.'

There I was, in the middle of the frozen food section, talking about lost souls – who said that life was boring?

'My name is Ann, and I am having problems with my son who keeps waking up in the middle of the night. He gets very upset and won't go back to sleep.'

'So, where does the ghost come into this?' I asked.

'Well, he wakes up and starts shouting at Buster, the dog, telling him to stop pulling at his bedclothes.'

'So where does the ghost come into this, exactly?' I asked again.

'Buster, he's the ghost, he died three months ago and my son keeps seeing him.'

The penny dropped. Buster was the discarnate soul. 'How often does he see him?' I asked.

'Most nights, and sometimes during the day. Evenings tend to be the worst time though,' Ann said.

I asked how Buster had died.

'We had to put him to sleep; it was so sad, the family were hysterical. They all worshipped him, but my son was his favourite. They were inseparable when Buster was alive.'

By this time, I was getting funny looks from the manager of the store as I was sitting on the floor, trying to take some notes on the back of my shopping list. I apologized to Ann and said that I would call her back from the car. It also gave me a chance to tune in to Buster, and to find out why he was still there.

When I rang Ann back, I told her that Buster was indeed still with us, and that he would need moving into the light. He had stayed because of his concern for the family. They had been so distraught at his passing that he decided not to go to the light, but to stay with the family.

My heart went out to Buster, such a dedicated dog, who put the family's needs before his own. He only wanted to play with the boy, who sadly did not understand the concept of life and death – and only saw Buster as a nuisance, especially when he woke him up in the middle of the night.

There are many people who are visited by their dead pets, often bringing them solace and healing. Now, this is all well and good when the pet has actually gone to the light, and they then return of their own accord. However, Buster's spirit or soul hadn't gone on, and he was giving off a detrimental (sorrowful) energy, which was further affecting the son.

Ann asked if I could send Buster to the light, and I agreed to do so straight away. After a few words and a short ceremony, he went willingly. I had explained to him why he should go, and that he could come back to visit the family whenever he wanted. They saw him a few weeks later, charging across the lawn towards the postman.

Dowsing Diagnosis Questions for Animal Spirits

1. Do you have a displaced animal spirit in your home?

2. How many?

3. What are they?

4. How detrimental are they?

5. Are any of them past family pets?

6. Are you allowed to move them to the light?

7. Will they go willingly?

8. Do they need someone to help them go across?

26. Spirit Lines

These are lines that spirits will use to travel around the globe; they are rather like our footpaths, but much longer. These 'ghost highways' allow freedom of movement to hundreds, if not thousands, of lost souls around our planet. You would be unlucky to find one running through your home, but it can happen.

Sensitive people, seers, children and family pets will be able to pick up on the movement of these spirits, and will be aware of them passing through the house. Obviously, this can be very disrupting and upsetting. How often have you seen a baby's eyes follow something in the room that you can't see, or hear a family pet bark at nothing? This can be a single lost soul moving around, a resident guardian or a spirit line allowing many discarnate beings to pass through your kitchen or living room.

Because we are building more and more houses, the chances are that one will be built over a spirit line. The first one that I came upon during my dowsing work had me quite perplexed.

I had found three spirits in the house. My client was very sensitive and could not only sense their presence, but could see them too. She wanted her uninvited house guests to be moved on, and I did so; they were quite happy to go. The next day I received a call to say, 'They are back.' I dowsed, and found that yes, there were further lost souls in the house, but not the same ones. I moved them on, and all was peaceful for a few days. Then the same thing happened – this time, four more arrived. I moved them on and then started to wonder why it was happening.

Are there layers of spirits to move on?

No.

Are they the same spirits returning time and time again?

No.

273

Will the spirits keep coming?

Yes.

All I could picture in my mind was a long queue of ghosts, standing patiently and waiting for their turn to walk into, or through, my client's house.

So I asked that exact question and got a 'yes'.

Is it some sort of spirit line?

Yes.

Is this quite normal?

Yes.

Is my client just unlucky to be living on one?

Yes.

Am I allowed to clear the complete line of spirits?

Yes.

Can I then divert the line away from the house and all other houses that it affects, as appropriate?

Yes.

So I did just that and over 300 spirits went to the light that day. The line was healed, and then diverted. The client hasn't been disturbed again since.

I don't find that these lines are harmful, although they can be quite distressing for people. They can sometimes have a detrimental charge attached; it really does depend on what has happened on the line to make it so. I am normally picking up on past human emotion.

Case Study 1: A Cottage in Witley, Surrey

I was valuing a beautiful period cottage in a small village on the outskirts of Godalming, when the couple recounted this story; the ability to dowse the past or, in other words, to dowse backwards in time, can provide you with the answer today when, at the time, you didn't fully appreciate what was happening. The couple had been there about three years, and it was time for a move.

I do remember a chill running down my spine, but in those days anything to do with ghosts scared me. I didn't understand the whole process then, but I do now. To use a modern term, I am very chilled out about it.

It began with the lady soaking in the bath (the story, not the valuation). The couple had only just moved into their two-bedroom cottage and Beth had decided, that night, to have a good, hot soak. The door had been left open, so that she and Garry could continue talking. Garry came in with a glass of wine and left it on the side of the bath, walked out and shut the door. The next thing they heard was the sound of the bathroom door being kicked and punched. It suddenly flew open and crashed into the wall. The glass of wine was picked up and smashed on the floor. Beth stood up and screamed; water spilled over the edge of the bath onto the floor and then, within a few seconds, everything returned to normal.

They stood there looking at each other, both a little stunned, then they burst out laughing. Beth did say that it was probably bordering on hysteria, rather than 'wasn't that funny?' They decided to leave the bathroom door open for a few days, so they could settle into the cottage. They did not want to have a repeat of the episode until they were prepared. They wanted to find out why it had happened, but in a controlled way.

Two weeks later, they decided that they would try again but this time Beth would not be in the bath. As she put it, 'I didn't want to scare away the ghost, if that is what it is, with the sight of me standing there stark naked and screaming.' They stood outside the bathroom, pulled the door to and waited for banging to start – nothing happened. Still they waited and nothing moved. Eventually they got fed up and started cooking a meal for the evening. The bathroom was on the ground floor of the cottage and had been a later extension, probably in the 1970s, and a small hall separated it from the kitchen. They had been so absorbed in preparing the meal that they had forgotten about their experiment. All of a sudden the bathroom door was almost torn off its hinges, as it was thrown open to smash against the wall. Garry dropped food all over the floor and Beth screamed. They were both aware of 'something' passing between them. This helped them, they said, as they then knew that they were dealing with a ghost. They sat down and worked out that the times of the occurrence coincided – about 6.45 in the evening. So, they shut the door at 6.40 the next night and, sure enough, the door was kicked open within five minutes.

They decided to investigate why this was happening. If the door was left open, they didn't have a problem, but every time they shut it the door was forcibly opened. They telephoned the previous owner who, they said, sounded a little sheepish when asked about the ghost – and he admitted that it was one of the reasons they had moved. Their research involved photocopying old maps of the village, to see how it was originally laid out, in an effort to find a logical reason behind their spirit problem.

The Star in Witley is a grade-II-listed inn, and has been the hub of the village for centuries. There are several local footpaths that lead in its direction even today. However, in the past, there was another one that has disappeared under a housing development and their formal gardens – one that went past Beth and Garry's cottage, straight to the pub.

The spirits did not like their path being blocked, especially when it was keeping them from their regular early evening drinking session at the pub. One of the spirits, there were four, started using the pub several hundred years ago, and had encouraged other 'locals' to stay and drink with him, rather than go to the light. I had been in the pub one evening with friends, and had taken several photographs there. An orb showed up in one of them, right by the bar. I dowsed it a few years back, and it appeared to be one of the lost souls.

I didn't know about spirit paths at that time, or the fact that we are able to help spirits to continue their interrupted journey to the light. I have, since those estate agency days, learned a great deal about the afterlife and I did ask if I was allowed to help them move on. I received a 'yes' from my pendulum. I conducted a short ceremony, and off they went without a glance backwards. The pub lost four of its regular drinkers that day, but I bet that they hadn't paid for a pint in years.

I like to finish clearing a spirit line by asking that it be diverted from people's houses, and to run unobstructed through gardens and pathways instead. They are free of spirits, but can be used at any time by others in the future. I have never been back to the cottage since; I often wonder if the owners or house feel any different.

Beth and Gary successfully moved house, and ended up buying another cottage through my company. The lady owner there had recently passed away, having been in the house for most of her life; the house needed a lot of work to modernize it but they did a beautiful job. The old lady stayed on in spirit, not wanting to leave what she considered 'her home'; she was, however, very benign and became an integral part of the family.

(It is funny what you suddenly remember when typing. I had forgotten about the old lady until I started to write this case study. I have just asked her if she is ready to go to the light and received a 'yes' from her. I have now spoken to her and, after a short ceremony, she has gone to the light; she is now at peace with her family.)

Case Study 2: A House near Huntingdon

This is what I typed, when writing the report for my client at the time. She was having a number of problems in the house; the spirit path was actually in the garden, but the influence was felt in the house.

-10 in detrimental effect. This is where the spooky stuff comes in. An ancient (500 BC) spirit or funeral path runs through your grounds, that was used by Druids to carry the dead to their resting place. Locals felt that it was the way to the underworld, and that it was sacred and holy ground. It still has those energies attached, and the human subconscious still feels them. This funeral path needs deconsecrating, the energies cleansing and the path diverting.

This was an interesting house to dowse – and the spirit path was just one of the spirit problems that the couple faced. Neither of them particularly liked being out in the garden, especially at night. Jane was certainly the more sensitive, and she felt tired and drained most of the time. That was the reason that she contacted me.

During my dowsing I asked the question, 'Will I find something unusual here?'

'Yes' came the response. It is a question that I always ask; it adds to the suspense of the dowse. I had come across spirit lines before, but none as detrimental as this one, with as many spirits using it regularly.

Yes, it had been used as a funeral path and yes, it had been used for many hundreds of years, but to have such a detrimental charge was unusual. The negativity had obviously built up over time, and was now affecting hundreds of people up and down the eastern counties – including Suffolk and Cambridgeshire. It would need to be cleared of spirits, healed and then diverted energetically from all the properties that it affected.

The first thing that I dowsed for was the number of spirits using the path. I asked if it was in the tens or hundreds, and got hundreds. I started counting from 100 and reached 500, when the pendulum indicated that I had reached the right figure. I then needed to find out how many over that figure there were. The next question was: 'In tens, how many more spirits are there using this line?' Ten? No response. Twenty? No response. Thirty? No response. Forty? No response. Fifty? This time I got a 'yes' movement of the pendulum. Then I had to dowse the final single figures – one, two, and got a 'yes'. There were 552 spirits that hadn't gone to the light, and at one time or another they were walking through my client's garden.

I asked if it was appropriate to send them all to the light, and I got a 'yes' response. I conducted the soul rescue/spirit release ceremony, and then dowsed to see if they had all gone – but I got a 'no' response. Five hundred and eight had gone through; the rest had stayed behind for some reason – and I had to find out why.

Was there a specific reason why most went and some stayed behind?

Yes.

Was one of the spirits holding the others back?

Yes.

If I move that one spirit on can the others go?

Yes.

Had that lead spirit done harm to the others whilst alive?

Yes.

Is it a male?

Yes.

Does he feel guilty, and is he afraid of retribution?

Yes.

Was he a figure of authority whilst alive?

Yes.

Is the problem anything to do with a school?

No.

Does it relate to a church or religion?

No.

Armed forces?

Yes.

Army?

No.

Royal Navy?

Yes.

Was he the captain of a ship?'

Yes.

Does this pertain to the Second World War?

Yes.

Did he and his colleagues die in battle?

Yes.

Does he want to make certain that all his men get to the light?

Yes.

Did he fear that if they went through with the masses that some might get left behind?

Yes.

Can I now move them through?

Yes.

I conducted the special ceremony for the captain and his crew; they all went through this time – the brave captain went last.

I checked to make sure that the line was clear, and I got a positive response. I carried out a general healing, and then asked if I could divert the spirit line from all the houses and buildings that it affected – and I received another 'yes'.

When I find a spirit line I normally mark it with a purple line.

Dowsing Diagnosis Questions for Spirit Lines

1. Is there a spirit line affecting your home?

2. How many are there?

3. How detrimental is it?

4. How many spirits use it?

5. How long is it?

6. How long has it been in existence?

7. Can all the spirits be moved into the light?

8. Will they all go at the same time (if not then find out when you can do the clearing)?

9. Is the line now fully healed?

27. Chakra Balancing or Blockages

Please read the chapter about chakras for a full description of what they are, what they do and why they can be out of balance or blocked.

I like to make sure that my clients are in good shape, as far as their chakras are concerned, as we need them to be working at their optimum to ensure best health. It is easy to find out if any of them need attention, purely by asking the question.

I like to find out which, if any, of their chakras are out of balance or blocked. They can sometimes be corrected by taking a specific flower remedy. However, they might also need more in-depth healing, and this process will be explained in Part 3: How to Heal.

Check out what colours you naturally wear; they can give you an early warning sign that a particular chakra is out of balance, or just about to become unbalanced. A chakra that is out of balance can say a lot about how you feel, and what mood you are in.

Also, dowse to see if they are all spinning correctly – that they are turning in the right direction and at their optimum performance. Don't forget to dowse the chakra at the back, as well as the one on the front.

I would use the following questioning to ascertain which chakra is out of balance or blocked etc.

Are any chakras out of balance?

Yes.

How many?

Two.

Is it the base chakra?

No.

Sacral chakra?

No.

Then the Solar Plexus and so on until you have found the affected pair.

You can use the same technique for blocked chakras and by asking the right questions you can even find out what caused the problem.

Case Study 1. Heart Chakra out of balance

During the course of dowsing one client's house I found that her husband's heart chakra was well and truly out of balance - 65% out of balance. I found out that it happened three years beforehand and involved a trauma.

When I spoke with Sally she picked up on my comment and asked if a blocked or out of balance chakra could change someone's characteristics? I told her that it could easily do so and asked her why? 'Well, three years ago Ben's mother died and he went through a very difficult time, ever since then he has been like a 'cold fish' and quite unemotional, we just want the old Ben back. He also spends so much time at work and the children rarely see him.'

I did have to clear a few attachments but they had only added slightly to Ben's emotional problems, his heart chakra was the main reason for his remoteness.

I have described how to clear and/or rebalance Chakras in the healing section of the book so I won't go through the process here. The healing work was carried out over two days and Ben's heart chakra was cleared and rebalanced. I received a telephone call from Sally a few days later saying that Ben had changed, almost overnight, he had come home early from work with a huge bunch of flowers and was now in the garden playing with the children. He put it down to finally connecting with his feminine side but Sally said that she knew better. 'I feel that he is back with us again.'

Not all people turn around that quickly, it is wonderful when they do and receiving that sort of telephone call always gives me a warm feeling in my solar plexus. Wow.

Case Study 2. Throat chakra out of balance

This case always brings a smile to my face. My client, Jen, was a single lady who told me that she was only four foot ten inches tall and that she could never say no to anyone asking for her help at work.

This lead to her having a massive work load and due to the stress that she was under she was beginning to show signs of Myalgic Encephalomyelitis (ME). We talked about how geopathic stress can wear down the immune system and that carrying out a healing of her home would certainly help but she would have to bring some changes into her work life.

She didn't like conflict and would go out of her way to avoid any situation that might lead to a disagreement. She mentioned that her boss was over six feet tall and that she felt intimidated when he stood next to her; there was a full sixteen inches difference in their heights so I wasn't surprised by her comment.

As I dowsed through my checklist I found out that her throat chakra was not only blocked but also out of balance. This fact alone would lead to someone to not be able to speak their mind and to hold back from 'telling people how it is'.

Much of the healing work that I do leads to self-empowerment; people get a belief in themselves that wasn't previously there, or perhaps had been many years ago. We all learn diplomacy; well most of us, as we get older, but sometimes this can go too far and you become the office skivvy.

I carried out the healing on Jen's house, rebalancing and clearing her throat chakra in the process. As I ask for regular feedback I received a telephone call about a week later:

'I've told them,' she said

'Who?'

'All the people at work, I told them that I wasn't their slave and that things are going to have to change.'

'Wonderful, what was their reaction?'

'They took it all on board, apologised and have organised an office reshuffle'

'What about your boss, how does he feel about what you said?'

'Well, as you know he is much taller than me so I stood on the desk and looked down on him, I told him in no uncertain terms how I felt and what was he going to do about it? I admit that I felt I had gone too far and expected him to fire me on the spot. However he burst out laughing, apologised and immediately gave me a pay rise.'

When I picture little Jen standing on a desk talking to her boss probably with her finger waggling, it always brings a smile to my face, I would have loved to have been a fly on the wall.

Chakras are very much part of our individual make-up and can easily go out of balance or become blocked. It is good to have the ability to recognise the fact that one or more need to be healed before the problem gets too deep.

Dowsing Diagnosis Questions for Chakra Balance/Blockage

1. Are any of your chakras out of balance?

2. Which ones? (Remember front and back)

3. Can a flower remedy rectify the problem?

4. If not do they need individual healing?

5. Which one or ones?

6. Can wearing a specific colour bring the chakra into balance?

7. When did this happen?

8. Are any of your chakras blocked?

9. Which ones? (Remember front and back)

10. Can a flower remedy rectify the problem?

11. If not do they need individual healing?

12. When did this happen?

28. Anything Else Running Through the Site

This is a general question that I ask when dowsing a plan of my clients' homes – you will get either a 'yes' or 'no' response. If it is 'no' then you are in luck, if 'yes' then you need to start asking lots of questions to find out what it might be. It could be anything from an ancient trackway to a funeral path or Roman/Pagan road, a ditch, a driveway, a drover's path, a tunnel . . .

First of all, you should plot the course of the problem on the house or garden plan, so that you know where it runs and how it affects the family. Then I would suggest that you try to date the problem, as this will give you somewhere tangible to start. Once this has been done, you will need to work through as many questions as you can to determine the details.

A knowledge of British history (if it is a property in this country) will be helpful, otherwise carry out some research via the internet. Check through old maps and surveys of the area, as they might help too.

Once you have found out exactly what the issue is, you will then need to work on how to heal the problems within the path, ditch or whatever, so that it is left in peace, balance and harmony for the family.

Case Study 1: A House in Cranleigh, Surrey

I had known Edward and Sarah during my estate agency years, but it wasn't until I had sold the business that they became firm friends. I was honoured to be asked to clear and heal their house of detrimental energy. As always, I asked the question, 'Am I going to find anything interesting or unusual during this dowse?' I got a 'yes' response and started dowsing. It wasn't until I reached 'Is there anything else running through the site?' that I found out what the unusual aspect was. This is what I found:

-5 in detrimental effect. An ancient road/trackway dating back to 1554. I have map dowsed this track, and it links

Brighton to Gloucester. I feel that the early track was for peasants, taking their wares to markets in Horsham and Guildford, however, due to the travel by monks, priests, etc. it became a holy route. It needs clearing and cleansing and it should then be fine.

Who would have thought that they would have an ancient trackway running through their back garden, and especially one of such importance? Because it didn't run through their home, neither Sarah nor Edward would have been affected, on a day-to-day basis, by the detrimental energies contained in the trackway. However, when they were sitting on, or working close to the line they would have been.

I found a number of spirits using the line, but it had mainly been affected by human emotions and upsets. Because the trackway was known to have monks and priests travelling along it, thieves and other unsavoury characters would lay in wait to rob and murder any poor, unfortunate soul that came along. The spirits were some of those victims, several of whom still meandered along the path, living on instinct and distant memories. Remember, when moving spirits on, please invite them to go to the light. Never use force or threaten them; ask for each of them to receive a vision of what awaits – most will go without a backward glance.

Once the spirits had gone, I cleared and healed the trackway of all the remaining detrimental energies.

Case Study 2: Stables on the Surrey/Hampshire Borders

I was called in to carry out a healing on a house, stables and land via a mutual friend, Stuart Gordon, a physiotherapist living in Liphook. Stuart had mentioned that his friend had been having problems with the horses for some time now, and felt that a healing would help. I spoke to the owner and organized a visit later the following week.

There were certainly a lot of earth energy and emotional problems in the house, stables and outbuildings. The horses were often spooked when being led into certain looseboxes, and when they were out in the fields they were regularly having minor accidents.

All in all, there was a lot of work to do, as well as the 'something unusual', which I had located running up the extreme right of the land. It was early days for me, and I wasn't as adept then as I am now at asking questions or visualizing what the problem might be. It dowsed at -5 so it was very detrimental to both people and animals. It was running beneath the ground, but it wasn't a tunnel; it wasn't a water pipe, electrical cable or a drain either. I dowsed for oil and gas and got no reaction from the rods. So, I went on site again and started dowsing. I picked up the area straight away and was standing there pondering the problem when the owner came up and said, 'Have you found the pipeline that runs up to Heathrow Airport? It supplies all the fuel for the aircraft there.' Aviation fuel is different to either oil or gas; I just hadn't expanded my mind enough to include avgas.

It had a detrimental charge coming from it. I could sense it through my feet; I started to feel a little unsteady and had to move away. No wonder the horses had problems in this particular part of the paddock. I asked if the energies could be cleared and then a barrier put around the pipeline to stop other people and animals from suffering the same effects as me. I got a 'yes' response and erected the psychic barrier.

Dowsing Diagnosis Questions for Anything Else.

1. What century does this anomaly date back to?

2. Is this BC or AD?

3. Has it contained human traffic?

4. Is it above ground or below?

5. Is it man made or natural?

6. Was it used daily, weekly, monthly, etc.?

7. Has anyone been hurt here?

8. Has anyone been killed?

9. Is there anyone buried here or close by?

10. How detrimental is this problem?

11. Can it be healed?

12. Will protection be needed from the effects in the future?

29. Fabric of the Building

This is a quick check to find out whether detrimental energies are stored within the fabric of the building, and not just earth-energy-related detriment rising through the floor of the house. It is all well and good healing the family and interior of the house; however, you do need to check that the building itself hasn't been affected by detrimental energies and whether this is part of the problem.

Avebury, for instance, is a prime example of this. If you look carefully at some of the houses in the village, you will spot a number of large stones incorporated within their external walls. They undoubtedly come from the large sarsen stones that originally made up the stone circles – a number of which were broken up in religious fervour. Now, the negativity of that act could well have seeped into these smaller stones whilst they were being broken up. The villagers were led to believe that the stone circles were associated with Devil worship, and therefore had to be demolished. They must have been fearful of retaliation, and also desperate to rid their village of this unseen evil threat. Their thoughts, fears and animosity would have soaked into the stones and they, in turn, would radiate this energy outwards to affect the occupants of the cottages that they now supported.

Looking at the fabric of a building did not occur to me in the early days and it was not a question that appeared on my checklist. I had not, at that time, come across anything like it before now.

At the beginning of the work in the next case study, I asked the following questions:

Am I going to find anything interesting or unusual during this dowse?

Yes.

Will it be something that I haven't discovered before?

Yes.

Is it man made energy?

Yes.

Did the current owner have anything to do with setting it up?

No.

Are we looking hundreds of years ago?

Yes.

Great, I do admit to liking a challenge and when something new turns up, it gets the grey matter working.

Case Study 1: Cottage on the Coast of Lancashire

I was asked to work on what looked like a beautiful cottage, set in an idyllic location overlooking the sea. Still, appearances can be deceptive, and that was the case here.

The cottage, like many houses, had general geopathic stress issues, as well as a lot of stuck emotional energy. The cottage was hundreds of years old, and had seen life in many different guises. As a result of these inherited energies, my client was feeling very lethargic and was generally unable to move forward in his life.

The dowse was fairly straightforward. Because of its location, there was only one stress line affecting the house, but there were also two energy spirals – and three old spirits that needed moving on. I carried out all the healing that I felt was necessary, and asked the pendulum if everything was now sorted – I got a 'no' response.

Is the house now clear of detrimental energy?

Yes.

Are the gardens clear?

Yes.

Have I done the healing properly?

Yes.

Do I need to do something else?

Yes.

Have I healed the outside and inside of the house correctly?

Yes.

But there is more to do?

Yes.

Do I need to work on my client further?

No.

I was a little stumped, and not sure how to continue. I had healed the outside of the house, the inside and my client. What more was there?

I telephoned my client, hoping that a conversation might shed some light on my predicament – luckily, it did. I told him what I had done; that my work wasn't finished; and that I wasn't sure how to continue. So, I asked him whether there was anything strange or unique about the cottage. 'Yes, there is,' he said. 'The stone that the cottage is constructed from originally formed part of a local monastery that was demolished during the dissolution of the Abbeys by Henry VIII.'

A light bulb must have suddenly appeared above my head. Of course, I had worked on the inside of the building and the garden, clearing them and my client of detrimental energies – but what I hadn't worked on was the fabric of the cottage. It sounds so simple sitting here typing, but that is with the gift of hindsight.

Does the fabric of the building contain detrimental energies?

Yes.

Are they to do with the demolition of the monastery?

Yes.

Have the thought patterns of the people affected the stones?

Yes.

Was there violence by the people against the priests?

Yes.

Were they vehement?

Yes.

Did anyone die?

Yes.

So the vehemence with which the people had torn down the monastery, and their dislike of the priests, had led to bloodshed. These detrimental thought patterns had been retained in the stones, and my client had unwittingly been affected by them. It was a form of cellular memory, but linked to building materials, rather than humans, this time. I worked on these patterns and, once finished, I asked,

Have I successfully carried out all the healing this time?

Yes was the response. What a relief!

Case Study 2: A Detached House near Clitheroe, Lancashire

The family were having all sorts of problems. They were constantly at each other's throats; arguments were the order of the day and a marriage split-up was being discussed. They had been a 'normal family' before they had moved into their new house about nine months previously, but since then it was as though four strangers had moved in together.

The wife was seeing a psychiatrist, and it was he who had suggested getting the house dowsed for geopathic stress. He felt that 'something' was creating the problems for the family, and that they had inherited a bad spirit, who was causing these upsets to happen. In reality, it was much simpler than that.

This time the question about the fabric of the building was included on my check list, and the pendulum indicated that there was a problem there.

How detrimental is the problem?

-8

Is this problem man made?

Yes.

Are the detrimental energies found within the building fabric?

Yes.

Are they coming from above the ground?

No.

Are they coming from below the ground?

Yes.

Are the problems coming from the foundations of the house?

Yes.

Is the concrete the problem?

No.

Do the noxious energies come from the hardcore used?

Yes.

Do the energies come from the original building?'

Yes.

A quick call to my client confirmed this fact. The original building on the site was a psychiatric hospital – a large one that had been there for many years. When it had been demolished, most of the brickwork and old cement had been used for the foundations of the new houses built on the site. Can you imagine what must have gone on in that hospital over the years – the patients' turmoil, despair, hatred, madness, cruelty and anxiety? All soaked into the very fabric of the building materials, which were now supporting a small estate of family houses.

After several healing sessions, I did manage to clear all the layers of detrimental energy underneath the house. The last I heard was that the parents were still together, and that life had returned to what it used to be.

On the plan, I would put a black circle around it and mark it FB (as in Fabric of Building).

Dowsing Diagnosis Questions for the Fabric of the Building

1. Is there anything detrimental about the fabric of the building?

2. How detrimental is it?

3. Is there more than one area affected?

4. Is it above the ground?

5. Is it below the ground?

6. Does the detrimental energy come from the earth?

7. Is it man made?

8. From when does it date?

9. Can it be healed?

10. How many layers are there?

11. Does it involve an act of violence?

12. Are any spirits involved with this energy?

30. Curses or Spells

You would be surprised by how many curses or spells have been cast over the years that are still current. A curse or spell stays until it is lifted. It may be 200 years old, or cast just a few months ago; the effect is still the same – detrimental to the person, family or house.

Contrary to popular belief, you do not have to be a witch, or to have any training in the mystic arts, to cast a spell, or to set a curse against a family or a place. A purely malevolent thought, or an expression of greed or resentment, can set off a train of events that can last for years. The words 'I hate you', said with enough intent or vehemence behind them, can be enough to have a detrimental effect on another person or family.

Be careful what you wish on your next-door neighbour, the detrimental thoughts that you send to a traffic warden or perhaps a policeman who has just stopped you for speeding; they can have an everlasting negative effect.

Sometimes, you will find that it is not you or the family that has been cursed, but the house that you live in, or even the ground that it has been built upon. So, be both specific and all-encompassing with the questions that you ask.

Spells can be very person, place or wish-specific – and they can be used for both good and bad. There are spells for jobs, love, hate, marriage, divorce, fertility, money, envy, business, revenge – the list is almost endless. Talismans are used by some to exact their revenge on others, whom they feel may have hurt or injured them in some way – or perhaps, in their eyes, need taking down a peg or two.

Sending bad luck thoughts is not good for your karma. So, when you are dowsing this particular subject, don't forget to ask whether you have, consciously or subconsciously, placed a spell or curse on anyone during your life. If you have, ask to find out if it is still current.

Case Study 1: House near Grantham, Lincolnshire

People can become very territorial when it comes to their homes and gardens. Boundary disputes are quite common and the ill-feeling that they cause is rarely forgotten. Some issues, if not resolved, can be argued about for years and years, leading to a great deal of upset. Spells and curses are often the result. It was so in this next case, as I reported to my client:

> **-5 in detrimental effect. I have found a spell that was put on the house 22 years ago. It was cast by a local lady who had a dispute with the then owners of the house. It was possibly a boundary dispute that caused much animosity.**

It was one of the first spells that I had found, and I was quite intrigued by it. They always say that spirit moves in mysterious ways, and this reminded me so much of what I used to deal with in my life as an estate agent that I had to smile. The couple had not been in the house long when they both started to feel 'under the weather'. Neither of them felt entirely 'at home', whilst in the house and a black cloud seemed to be hanging over them. I was asked if I could clear the house of past energies and spirits to enable them to settle in, and to be at peace with their new home.

It was reasonably straightforward and I found many of the normal problems associated with geopathic stress, human emotions and the like. They could be healed – although there were a few layers to clear, which I did over several weeks. When asking the question on curses and spells, the pendulum said that there was a spell. I dowsed to find that it was a quite potent -5, so then I had to find out why it had been cast.

Was it cast against my client?

No.

Was it cast against the house?

Yes.

How many years ago was it cast?

22 years.

Did the person who cast it live within the village?

Yes.

Were they neighbours?

Yes.

Are they still living there?

Yes.

Do they still bear a grudge?

Yes.

Was it placed on purpose?

No.

Can the spell be lifted?

Yes.

That will give you a good idea of the process of finding out the reasons behind a curse or a spell being cast. The important thing to find out is, can it be lifted? It the answer is 'yes', then game on!

I called my client and asked about her next-door neighbour. There was only one, and the information she received when buying the house was incomplete. These days, any dispute with your neighbours has to be legally declared, and there was mention of a boundary dispute some years back, which had been settled in court and was no longer an issue.

Sadly, it had been resolved in court to the satisfaction of the past owners, but the neighbour had not been happy with the ruling. Quite simply, the whole matter had simmered in the neighbour's head, and out of it had popped a subconscious spell that my client inherited. They had met the neighbour briefly, but she seemed very unfriendly. She seemed to glower at them whenever they saw her in the garden.

The whole dispute had kicked off when the last owners had decided to extend the house some twenty-five years earlier. Their neighbours put in an objection to the local planning department, who upheld it. A small parcel of land that belonged to the house, which the neighbours had been allowed to use as an allotment, was then taken back by the previous owners and fenced in. The plan was resubmitted with a small number of changes and passed; the extension was then built shortly afterwards – much to the neighbour's disgust.

What had gone on in her head I don't know, but a spell on the house and land was the result. The owners of the house eventually had to move due to ill health; neither of them had been well for years and, after much persuasion, their family finally got them to move closer to them. My clients then bought the house, and immediately started to feel the detrimental effects of the spell and of the animosity behind it. The problems started with a mild headache that steadily got worse. Coughs and colds led to the husband getting pneumonia. The wife was having stomach problems and painful periods – neither of which she had suffered from before.

Once the spell had been found and lifted, life started to return to normal for them both. Their health improved; the house felt like home and they even started to converse with their neighbour. My client said that they would never be the best of friends, but she was now acceptable as a neighbour.

Case Study 2: An Apartment in West London

> **-3 in detrimental effect. A curse put on the house back in the late 18th century by a man who owed the then owner of the house some money. With his hostile feelings of envy and jealousy, he put a nameless curse on the whole house.**

As I have mentioned before, most of my dowsing and healing work is done from a distance. However, when necessary, I will travel to a client's home, especially when a challenge is thrown down.

Let me explain. At an Earth Energies event I met a fellow dowser and we got taking about her apartment in London. She mentioned to me that it felt dark and unwelcoming, and she always felt unwell there. She also mentioned that several other dowsers and healers had worked on the energies there, but none had been totally successful in healing the apartment. So, I asked if I could have a go at healing the problems that she faced.

'Do you think that you could do any better than the others?' she asked – and something in the back of my head said that I could.

'Yes I can,' I continued, 'because, what I look for and heal is probably different to what has already been found.'

'Right' she said. 'I challenge you to do better – and I will know!'

The apartment overlooked a typically picturesque London square, although I didn't get a good feeling about it when I walked around the corner from the tube station – but that is another story. I felt slightly uneasy when I rang the doorbell, and I mentally increased my psychic protection before the buzzer sounded, allowing me access to the stairs up to her apartment.

Once in the flat I started to feel as though a weight was dragging me down. I sat in the living room, waiting for the coffee to brew, when Anne came in. She asked if I was feeling all right.

'Whenever I sit there', she said, 'I always feel a little odd.'

I always seem to do that – sit or stand in the most detrimental of places – and then start to feel awful. I picked up several water veins running beneath the apartments, as well as an earth energy line, two spirals, a very detrimental place memory and several other problems that would need to be dealt with. I also picked up on an old curse, dating back to the late 1700s that was still current – and was affecting all the occupants in the building.

I told Anne what I had found and I carried out a quick healing, promising to do more once I got back to the safety of my own home. The curse was an odd one, and it had certainly added to the 'heavy' feeling in the apartment. It had been brought about over money, a gambling debt, and the gentleman who was owed the money, quite rightly, wanted it repaid. The debtor didn't see why he should pay; he felt the man had far too much money anyway and certainly wouldn't miss the few pounds that he owed him. When pushed to pay, he did, but with such disgust that a curse was the result – not just on the man he owed the money to, but on the whole family and their house.

Since those days, the family had long since gone and the building had been split into apartments. The family had had a lot of bad luck, and their home had fallen into disrepair. Developers then bought and converted the Georgian building into various apartments, meaning that all the new occupants were subjected to the curse.

I lifted the curse and did a complete healing on the apartment. Anne was delighted, and she started to feel much lighter and able to move forward with various plans. And the challenge? I had surpassed all of Anne's expectations and the apartment had become her home. I received a delightful letter from her, telling me that she would always be happy to provide me with a testimonial should I need one.

Dowsing Diagnosis Questions for Curses and Spells

1. Is your family affected by a curse or spell?

2. Is the house affected by a spell/curse?

3. Is the land affected by a spell or curse?

4. If it is a spell, how many?

5. If it is a curse, how many?

6. How detrimental is it/are they to the family?

7. Were they/was it cast on purpose?

8. Was it a subconscious thought?

9. How long has it been in existence?

10. Is the person that cast it/them still living?

11. Can the spell/curse be lifted?

12. Can I send healing to the person responsible?

31. Anaesthetic Traces, Vaccinations and Heavy Metals

I like to spend some time dowsing my clients for these health problems. This is by no means an exhaustive list, so please add anything else that you wish to dowse for.

I do feel that once you remove the 'geopathic stress' problems from your home, your immune system should start doing what the immune system is good at – healing your body from within. Your auric field will start to strengthen, thereby protecting you and your body from external detrimental energies.

Anaesthetics

Modern anaesthetics are far better than those used up to the late eighties and early nineties. The side effects are shorter lived. People who would have been in hospital for weeks are now out after a few days, bright and cheerful, whereas before that they would take a long time to 'come to' and feel normal. A quick dowse is worthwhile to see if any traces are left over from operations prior to that time.

Vaccinations

A needle gets stuck in your backside almost as soon as you are born. That is just the start of a long and painful relationship with a necessary evil. I call it a necessary evil because it prevents, cures and causes us many problems. There is still much controversy over MMR, the combined measles, mumps and rubella cocktail that children are subjected to at an early age. It is as much the carrier and preservative, which contains mercury, as the drugs themselves that can cause serious side effects. It has been said that Autism, for instance, has been linked to the mercury contained in these 'shots'.

Please research the internet for more information on this topic. Don't just go like a lamb to the slaughter when it comes to injecting a foreign substance into your body. Check out the side effects first, and then see if there is any alternative. We do need mainstream allopathic medicine in our lives, although there can often be a complementary alternative that is worth considering.

With the introduction of a Hib/Meningitis C booster in September 2006, UK citizens are now receiving more vaccinations than ever. The list currently includes:

Diphtheria

Pertussis (Whooping Cough)

Meningitis C (three doses)

Polio

Mumps

Cervical cancer (girls at 12)

Flu

Tetanus

Haemophilus Influnzae type B

Pneumococcal infection

Measles

Rubella

Tuberculosis

Various boosters

Travel Vaccines (if going abroad)

Certainly not a good cocktail. Traces of mercury can be found within most, if not all, of them. Please bear in mind the World Health Organisations warnings on mercury:

Mercury is highly toxic to human health, posing a particular threat to the development of the child in utero and early in life. Elemental and methyl mercury are toxic to the central and peripheral nervous system. The in-halation of mercury vapour can produce harmful effects on the nervous, digestive and immune systems, lungs and kidneys, and may be fatal. The inorganic salts of mercury are corrosive to the skin, eyes and gastrointestinal tract, and may induce kidney toxicity if ingested.

Neurological and behavioural disorders may be observed after the inhalation, ingestion or dermal application of different mercury compounds. Symptoms include tremors, insomnia, memory loss, neuromuscular effects, headaches and cognitive and motor dysfunction. Kidney and immune effects have been reported.

Heavy Metals

Obviously, mercury is a heavy metal and links into this section. The main gruesome fivesome are (in alphabetical order):

Metal	Body Organs Affected
Aluminium	Central nervous system, kidneys, digestion system
Arsenic	Blood, kidneys, central nervous system, digestive system, skin, liver, lungs, bladder
Cadmium	Gastrointestinal system, liver, placenta, kidneys, lungs, brain, bones, central nervous system, reproductive organs
Lead	Bones, brain, kidneys, thyroid, liver, central nervous system
Mercury	Gastrointestinal tract, brain, kidneys, liver, kidney, central nervous system

Throughout our lives we are exposed, in one way or another, to all of the above metals. I remember, as a young boy, breaking open a thermometer and playing with the mercury, rolling it backwards and forwards on a metal tray with my fingers. It was fascinating to watch it reform when it had been split into smaller pieces.

Amalgam fillings, aluminium saucepans, car batteries, baking foil, underarm deodorants, tobacco smoke, pesticides, lead paint, contaminated fish, some drugs, some tattoo inks, even water – all contain traces of these metals.

Here are some of the effects produced by heavy metal build-up in your body:

- Unexplained fatigue

- Irritability

- Depression

- Mood swings

- Cold hands and feet

- Bloated stomach

- Twitching of muscles

- Insomnia

- Painful joints

It sounds just like geopathic stress, doesn't it? Just think, if you are rid of the effects of both man-made products and earth energy problems, how good you are going to feel.

Dowse the list to find out if you have a build-up of any of these potential health risks in your body. Some people, including me, have gone as far as having all the old amalgam fillings taken out of their teeth and replaced with modern composite resin or cement. You will probably need to find a dentist specializing in this work, so that matters are not made worse by ingesting even more mercury as your old fillings are removed.

The list below shows known elements that have been proven to help your body detoxify itself from these heavy metals. If, after you have dowsed, you are worried about the levels of heavy metals that you have found in your body, it is best to seek help from a registered homeopath. They will be able to offer advice and guidance, through nutrition and homeopathic remedies.

Metals	Known Detoxifying Elements
Aluminium	calcium, magnesium, iron, manganese, vitamin B complex, vitamin C
Arsenic	vitamin C, alpha-lipoic acid
Cadmium	zinc, iron, vitamin C
Lead	calcium, iron, zinc, vitamin C
Mercury	selenium, chlorella, vitamin C

I consult Janet Lewis, who is based near Caterham in Surrey, when a client needs specialist help. Her contact details can be found at the end of the book. She has successfully treated several of my clients over the years, and I have received excellent feedback from them.

There are also a number of Ayurvedic ways to treat the build-up of heavy metals in your body, including foot patches.

Filtering your drinking water will help. Either use a jug stored in the fridge, or fit a full filtration system on your mains water supply. You can even buy kettles with a built-in filter. Your tea and coffee will taste better, I assure you.

Dowsing Diagnosis Questions for Anaesthetics/Vaccinations

1. Does your body have any detrimental anaesthetic traces?

2. How detrimental is it?

3. Can it be cleared or healed?

4. Any detrimental traces of a vaccination?

5. How detrimental is it/are they?

6. What vaccination was it?

7. What age were you when you had the vaccination?

8. Is mercury the problem?

9. Can the problem be cleared or healed?

10. How long will it take?

11. Do you need to seek out a specialist to help?

12. What kind of specialist?

13. Will you feel better once this problem is clear or healed?

14. Do you have a problem with heavy metal levels in your body?

15. Which heavy metal or metals is/are responsible?

16. At what age did this exposure occur?

17. How did it happen? Diet, work, etc.

18. How detrimental is it?

19. Can it be cleared?

20. Do you need to seek out a specialist for help?

21. What type of specialist?

22. How long will it take?

23. Will you feel better after the treatment?

24. Is it beneficial for you to filter your drinking water?

25. If you don't, how detrimental is the water?

26. How detrimental is fluoride to you and the family?

32. Anything Else to be Considered Regarding Your Health

This is a very wide-open topic with many different routes that can be followed. I would suggest during your early dowsing that you stick to just a few rudimentary questions and build on them as you become more experienced.

You could start with dowsing your vitamin and mineral levels, finding out if you or your family need to take a course of vitamin C or multi-vitamin tablets for a number of weeks to help boost the immune system. Dowse the lists below for what you might need:

VITAMINS	MINERALS
A	Calcium
Thiamine B_1	Chloride
Riboflavin B_2	Chromium
Niacin B_3	Copper
Pantothenic acid B_5	Iodine
Pyridoxine B_6	Iron
Folic acid B_9	Magnesium
Cobalamin B_{12}	Phosphorus
C	Potassium
D	Selenium
D3 Cholecalciferol	Sodium
E	Zinc
K2	

Do check on the internet for recommended dosages as the UK has different guidelines to the USA.

Or perhaps you might need to take a flower remedy to help balance your body whilst healing is being carried out.

You can use dowsing to find out whether a back pain necessitates a visit to an osteopath or physiotherapist and then dowse a list of local practitioners to find out the best one for the treatment.

Dowse whether or not a healing session with a Reiki practitioner would be of benefit to you or the family, you could add Bowen, massage, aromatherapy, Aura-Somer, colour therapy, and spiritual healer to the list, and see what answers come.

I will often recommend Bach Flower remedies or similar during the few weeks after I have worked on a client's house to clear the geopathic stress; it can help to balance the family whilst the energies are changing and settling. I have a print-out with all the Bach remedies on six pages with four rows and two columns on each page. I ask what particular remedy is suitable for a particular member of the family, what page number, which column and then which row. I normally write the information as 4-2-3 and look up the resulting remedy. In this case it would be Scleranthus, good for those who find it hard to make a decision. I then dowse how many drops are needed, taken in a tumbler of water, whether to take them in the morning or just before bed and the duration.

The walls of your stomach allow the absorption of the remedies to happen much quicker and more efficiently than putting them directly on your tongue, so it is far better to take the drops in a tumbler full of water and sip it.

Don't just stop at Bach, there are so many more to choose from. I have listed just a few below (dowse the list for the best range for you):

1. Baileys Flower Essences

2. Alaskan Essences

3. Australian Bush Flower Essences

4. Findhorn Flower Essences

5. Wild Animal Essences

6. Gem Essences

N.B. This is not meant to replace the qualified practitioner but you will be surprised at how accurate dowsing can be in picking up on many of the characteristics of the person you are asking for. However, please be aware that many of the remedies contain a small amount of alcohol and therefore may not be suitable to anyone with an alcohol intolerance.

Dowsing Diagnosis Questions for Treatments/Therapies

1. Would you benefit from a therapy? Which one?

2. How many weeks would you need to go?

3. Who is the best person to see?

4. Are you short of any vitamins?

5. Which ones?

6. Would a course of, say vitamin D3, benefit you?

7. How long should you take them for?

8. Which brand is best for you?

9. Are you short of minerals?

10. Which ones?

11. Would a course be of benefit?

12. How long do you need take them for?

13. Do you need a particular essence?

14. Which make is best for you at this time?

15. Which essence do you need?

16. How long do you need it for?

17. When do you need to take it? (am or pm)

18. How many drops do you need?

19. Will it help your energy levels?

33. Human Interference Lines

These are rare, and I have only found them twice in all the years that I have been dowsing and healing. They do exist, however.

They are human-created disruption lines, set up mentally and mechanically to affect other people in a detrimental way – rather like white noise, but with no sound attached. The energies that they produce interfere with our brain patterns. Rather than sending and receiving clear impulses to and from the body, they become scrambled and are not easy to interpret. You may experience buzzing in your ears, headaches and balance problems; you may also feel rather nervy and restless.

These intent lines disrupt our lives. They spread melancholy and negative thoughts, leading to disturbed sleep patterns and irritability.

Case Study 1: A House near Brighton, East Sussex

Do you remember the all-important question to ask before you start dowsing? 'Am I going to find anything interesting or unusual, etc.?' Well, I asked and got a 'yes' response, so I was on the alert for what it might be all the way through this particular house. I had got to the end of my checklist and nothing unusual had appeared, so I asked if it was something that I hadn't come across before and I got 'Yes'. I started to dowse over the plan, asking to be shown the direction or place of this new detrimental aspect. The rod moved, showing me the angle of the line, and it ran straight through the house and out the other side. It dowsed at -6 in detrimental effect on the family, so I needed to find out what it was, how it was caused and how to heal it.

Is it some form of energy line?

Yes.

Is it from the earth?

No.

Human created?

Yes.

Has it been created on purpose?

Yes.

Was it created to be detrimental to humans?

Yes.

Is that its express purpose?

Yes.

Are they set up by human intent? I got a slight movement meaning that I was on the right track, but needed to dig deeper.

Can they be set up in various ways?

Yes.

Is human intent one of them?

Yes.

Can a machine produce similar results?

Yes.

Is this a machine-produced line?

Yes.

How long is the line, in miles, do I count in tens?

No.

Hundreds?

Yes.

I counted, and reached 500 then 20 then 8 = 528 miles.

I got out my atlas and started to dowse, the line went over the channel and into central France where it stopped. I then dowsed five similar lines coming from this location. It seemed as though someone down there was up to no good.

A machine was transmitting a disruptive energy pattern that travelled straight through my client's house and, of course, many others on its journey. I needed to ask further questions to get to the bottom of why these lines were there.

Is the line meant to be malicious?

No.

Do the people who built it know what it is doing?

Yes.

Do they care?

No.

Is it a by-product of something that they are working on?

Yes.

Can I do any healing work on this line?

Yes.

Can I block the energies coming from it?

Yes.

Am I allowed to do this?

Yes.

Will it benefit my client?

Yes.

So I set to work, trying to find a way to clear and heal the line, and also to block the outpourings of detrimental energy that it was producing. Much of this work combines practical as well as spiritual knowledge – never forget that what we learn whilst we grow up can come in very handy later on.

I had spoken to my clients about the line, and asked them if they or their two children had suffered from buzzing in the ears, imbalance or irritability (I know from experience that having children can lead to a certain amount of irritability, but this feeling is very different). Their eldest daughter had a history of ear problems, which resulted in frequent visits to the doctor to get them checked. Her ears had been syringed several times and grommets had been fitted about six months before, but nothing had worked, and she complained most days. I was very interested to see if we could sort this problem out for her.

After the healing had taken place, the house and the family took some time to settle down and I received feedback each week for about two months – fine-tuning the healing as we went along. I didn't mention the daughter's problem for a couple of weeks. When I did, her mother said, 'Do you know, she hasn't mentioned them since you carried out the work.' She continued, 'I will find out, and next time we talk, I will let you know.' About a week later, she called to say that her daughter was feeling fine, and that her ears weren't giving her any trouble at all.

So, job done. I feel that her ear problems were twofold; one was undoubtedly the interference line and the other a large energy spiral found beneath her bed. I had worked on both and achieved the right result.

Dowsing Diagnosis Questions for Interference Lines

1. Is your home affected by an interference line?

2. How many?

3. Is it/are they detrimental to you and the family?

4. How detrimental is it?

5. Is it created by human intent?

6. Is it the result of a machine?

7. How does it affect you and the family?

8. How long is the line?

9. Where does it come from?

10. Has it been set up on purpose?

11. Can it be healed or blocked? Which one?

34. Psychic Attack

This form of attack is quite common. Unless you are aware of what it is and how it can affect you, you will be none the wiser.

If you feel, when working through this section, that you are out of your depth or unable to deal with what you have found please contact me via the telephone number on my website www.dowsingspirits.co.uk and I will try to help you.

A psychic attack is instantly detrimental to the person who is being targeted. It normally means that someone in your life is sending you harmful thoughts, leading to a vicious headache, unclear thoughts and generally feeling unwell. It could be a colleague at work, an ex-girlfriend or wife, or even someone that does not like the way you look; consciously or subconsciously wishing you harm or feeling resentful towards you.

To demonstrate the reverse: sit and clear your mind of thoughts and worries. Then, concentrate hard on one person; picture their face in your mind; think of their name and hold them in your thoughts for two minutes. Then, mentally ask them to call you on the telephone and wait to see what happens. Invariably, you will receive that call. If it doesn't work first time, a bit like riding a bike, practice will make perfect, so try it again for three minutes. It will certainly save you money on your telephone bill.

So, you can now make things happen in a positive way. Just imagine sitting there thinking bad thoughts about someone for three minutes. How do you think that person will start to feel? It is rather like mentally stabbing somebody, except that rather than using a knife, you just focus your thoughts instead. Headaches are quite normal, but the heart can also be targeted, and pain and/or palpitations will then be felt.

It is therefore so important to psychically protect yourself at all times of the day and night. If you feel a headache coming on, dowse to see if you are under psychic attack. It may be that you are only dehydrated, but you never know. Once you are aware of this phenomenon, and how it feels, you will always walk with a bubble of light surrounding you – keeping safely inside it.

Case Study 1: Wedding Day Blues – Andy and Anna

No, it isn't the latest song release by a blues band, it's a true story and the events are very, very real.

Your wedding day is supposed to be one of the happiest days of your life. However, this turned out to be a painful experience for one of the party – the bride. Had I known what was going on, I could have done something about it, but sadly I didn't receive the telephone call until the day was almost over.

I had worked closely with Andy for several years on various spiritual projects and I had got to know him well. He had been successfully cleared of attachments, etc., but he hadn't put two and two together until it was too late.

It involved an ex-girlfriend of Andy's. Their relationship had finished almost a year before he met his future wife. His ex had never met the new girlfriend, but knew of her through a business association. She made it plain that she did not approve and started to spread disharmony with underhand comments and hurtful gossip. Andy's new girlfriend often complained of sharp, sudden pains in her head, but dismissed them as 'just one of those things'.

Despite these subversive goings-on, the relationship blossomed and an engagement was announced. News spread and emails started to be received from the ex-girlfriend, some of them quite vicious – saying that the marriage would never work. As the wedding day approached Anna was getting headaches more frequently. Unfortunately, they were dismissed as wedding stress. Andy never thought to mention them to me, even though he had suffered a similar fate some two years before.

I received a telephone call from Andy at about four o'clock in the afternoon, saying that Anna had gone down with a migraine, and could I send some healing? I agreed and, having wished him well, sat down quietly to work on his new bride. She had picked up a couple of small attachments, but something told me to delve further into the problem.

A quick way to find out in which direction to go is to run your finger down the checklist, whilst asking your pendulum to show you where the main problem is to be found. I had almost got to the end, when the pendulum gave a positive swing. The area of concern was psychic attack, and it came in as a -8 in detrimental effect on Anna, so I wasn't surprised at the severity of her headache. I cleared the attachments and I worked on the psychic attack, sending Anna extra psychic protection that should keep her safe and well. Half an hour later, Andy called me back and said that Anna was now up and about feeling like her old self again; I told him what I had found. He muttered something like, 'Oh, my God.', and then recited the above story.

His ex had obviously been sending out detrimental thought patterns for months and months, hence the headaches. On the wedding day, she must have made a special effort, focusing all the spite that she could muster directly towards Anna, hoping to spoil the party. She almost did, but thankfully Andy made the call to me, and the situation was rectified. I asked him and Anna to send unconditional love back to his ex; it is not good to fight fire with fire, better to dampen the flames with light and love.

The power of intent is so misunderstood. Good thoughts produce some wonderful healing. However, bad thoughts can really screw up people's health. Keep your thoughts positive, and send unconditional love to all whenever you remember.

Case Study 2: A Successful Business Couple

This is a classic recipe for psychic attack, especially if you add the fact that they were both retiring from their own business with a good bonus. Their son was about to take over as MD. Envy, in the form of resentment, jealousy and concern came into play in this particular case.

I was asked to carry out a healing on their home, for health reasons. They had both been feeling a little under the weather recently, and had started to visit doctors on a semi-regular basis for check-ups, scans and blood tests. Retirement was looming and, although they were both looking forward to the day, they had reservations and these were manifesting themselves in many different ways, mainly physical.

As the retirement day approached, both of them started to suffer from splitting headaches. Sue was also finding it difficult to sleep, and John couldn't settle at home or work. They searched the internet and came across my website, and called me to see if I could help. The floor plan duly arrived, and I started working on it. There were a number of earth energy and emotional issues to deal with, as well as a few power artefacts, some chakra balancing and general aura clearing. When I asked about psychic attack, the rod swung so violently that it span around. Normally, I only get a slight twitch, so this was going to be a severe case.

I asked how detrimental the psychic attack was, and got -9. I asked if it was affecting them both, and received a 'yes' response. I then went on to find out that it was a particular lady at their workplace, who was very worried about the changes that were going to happen once the couple retired. She resented the fact they were retiring and she wasn't, and also the money that they were receiving as a retirement bonus.

I spoke to my clients, and they were very upset by what I had found. They couldn't think who the woman was that was responsible for these detrimental thought patterns. They'd had a stable and loyal workforce for years; people rarely left their employ; all the members of staff seemed delighted at the news of their retirement, and they had received some wonderful letters and cards from them. However, there was one lady there who wasn't happy, and my clients wanted to find out who it was, so that they could rectify the situation.

I worked on combating the psychic attack, using mirrors and bubbles of light. Sue's headaches lessened, and then stopped after a few days. She began to sleep better, and John began to relax at home, feeling more like his old self.

I dowsed a list of employees, and I provided them with the name of the lady who I felt was responsible. They approached her on a different matter. During the conversation, it came out that she was worried about them going and how the restructuring of the company would affect her own employment. She broke down and cried, such was her relief; she could finally unburden her fears and concerns. Sue and John put her mind at rest, and told her that her job was guaranteed until she finally retired in four years' time – with a good bonus.

Case Study 3: Me

I had just moved into a farmhouse in Cherhill. On our first day in the house, the oil-fired boiler malfunctioned. Luckily, we discovered the blaze in time and saved the house from burning down. I was then interviewed by a reporter from the local paper about the fire, and an article appeared with my name attached, listing my occupation as a 'healer'.

About ten days afterwards, I received an envelope addressed to me, written in spidery handwriting. As I opened it, I felt as if someone had hit me over the head with a baseball bat – not that I have actually been hit over the head with a baseball bat, but I'm sure that if I was it would have felt very similar. I had to sit down before I fainted; thankfully I had the presence of mind to put a bubble of white light around the note, and the pain subsided. I then made myself a cup of tea, spiritual tea of course, and got my head together to combat whatever this note contained.

I remember increasing my level of protection before opening the envelope again. She, I am sure that it was a she, even though the note was anonymous, made it clear that a healer wasn't welcome in the village, and that the 'dark' would win through. I can't remember the exact words now; however, she did mention that a group of people would be sending me negative thoughts, and that I had better watch out.

My first thoughts were that this was a joke, then I remembered the pain. I had never received a hate note before, and I have not had one since. My second thought was, 'Right back at ya – with love and light.' I placed the note in holy water, from Lake Mansarovar in Tibet, for a few days. Then I put it underneath a huge citrine crystal that I own, before finally burning it and flushing it down the toilet. All the time I was sending her and the group thoughts of light and love, wrapping them all in a bubble of light and keeping them out of harm's way.

I never have had a headache like that since. It was an important lesson for me to learn, and hopefully you will learn from my experience too. Make sure that your home is fully protected at all times, and that the mail is blessed as it comes through the post box, even the bills . . . especially the bills.

Dowsing Diagnosis Questions for Psychic Attack

1. Are you under psychic attack?

2. How detrimental is it to you or your family?

3. Can you prevent it from happening?

4. Do you know the person involved?

5. Is it a family member?

6. Is it a friend?

7. Is it a work colleague?

8. What age are they?

9. What colour hair do they have (natural or dyed)?

10. What is the motivation for the psychic attack? (Money, envy, etc.)

11. Have you been under psychic attack in the past?

12. When did this happen?

13. Who was responsible? Use questions 4 – 8.

14. Can you carry out a healing?

15. Can you send healing to the person responsible?

16. Will sending healing help that person?

35. Parasites

Many people have parasites living in their body; most won't even know that they are there. They enter our body through contaminated food, water or handling household pets and not washing your hands. They live in your intestines and can be responsible for giving you flu-like symptoms, lack of energy, bloated stomach, tiredness, nausea, etc.

The reason that I include them here is that many of my clients can have mild flu-like symptoms after I have worked on them. I believe that, in some cases, parasites could be to blame. With healing, you are bringing about changes within a person's body and tiredness can often be a symptom of those beneficial energies starting to take effect. Parasites can live in a human body for years, lying undetected; you will never know that they are there until your energy patterns start to change. The parasites will sense the change, and will begin to get uncomfortable.

Therefore, I now always ask that all detrimental parasites, and their harmful effects, are cleared away during a healing session.

There are many websites giving detailed information on parasites, and on their effects on humans. If you feel that you want to go further than just asking for a healing and clearing to take place, please ask a qualified homeopath or nutritionist for help. They will be able to recommend a treatment to help flush any parasite out of your body.

Dowsing Diagnosis Questions for Parasites

1. Do you have any detrimental parasites in your body?

2. How detrimental are they?

3. How long have you had them for?

4. Did they come from contaminated food?

5. Did they come from contaminated water?

6. Did you get them from one of your pets?

7. Can they be removed through healing?

8. Should you see a specialist to clear them?

9. A homeopath, nutritionist or doctor?

10. Will you feel better once they are cleared from your system?

36. Energizing/Healing Rays

This was something that I introduced early in 2011, after meditation. I am still not totally sure what it all means, but I trust what 'upstairs' gives me, and once I get the information I must start working with it.

The concept of the rainbow serpent has been around for thousands of years, and is part of many cultures. I do believe that earth energy lines contain all the colours of the rainbow, and more. Our eyes still only see a limited range of colours, seven generally; however, this is beginning to change. Infrared and ultraviolet can now be seen by some, especially mystics and those whose energies vibrate at a higher level. Perhaps our ancestors also had this gift, although I feel that we are still growing into our brains, rather than losing the abilities that we once had.

Colours play an important part in our lives – what to wear to work, what colour to decorate a room, the colour of your car, hair, nails, shoes, handbag, tie, etc. – the list is endless. Where would we be if the world was purely black and white? Although I guess it would make buying clothes easier.

What is your favourite colour and has it changed over the years as you have matured (notice that I use 'matured' rather than 'grown up')? For instance, it is felt that your clothes should enhance the colour of your eyes; it is no good wearing blue if you have green eyes, and vice versa.

Therapists have been using colours for many years. However, this is a new way of using coloured rays to help in the healing process. I make sure that your pranic light (the light or energy that enters via your crown chakra) is healthy and that all the colours necessary for your wellbeing are present. If one is missing, then it gets replaced. In fact, the colour, or colours, may only need strengthening and it is preferable to do this individually.

I also dowse to see whether your body needs bathing in a particular coloured ray, and if so, for how long. I normally arrange a time for my client to sit quietly, and then send the beam of colour to them for the stipulated time – although it is not always necessary to do this, as distant healing works whatever the person is doing. However, people will derive benefit from sitting still for ten to twenty minutes whilst the colour healing is being carried out.

I haven't included any case studies here as this is only a small part of the overall healing experience and I would view this aspect as a bolt-on to the main body of healing that is generally carried out. Some of my clients have felt warmth as the colours are sent to them at a pre-arranged time and some can either see or feel the colour as it is being transmitted to them.

I will sometimes send the colour by intent several days after the main healing has been carried out so that the body has a chance to 'take it all in' and not feel as if it has been hit by a truck. I generally dowse to see when is the best time to send the healing rays.

Dowsing Diagnosis Questions Energizing/Healing Rays

1. Are you missing any colours that are important to you?

2. Which ones?

3. Can they be restored?

4. Can you do this using healing?

5. How long do you need to do this for?

6. Do any of the colours need strengthening?

7. Which ones?

8. How long do you need to do this healing for?

9. Would you benefit from sitting in a coloured beam?

10. Which colour or colours?

11. How long for?

12. Is there a colour that you need to wear today?

13. Will this help in the healing process?

37. Beneficial Areas to Sit, Heal or Meditate

This is the final question that I ask. Don't forget that everything I have described up to this point is looking to find and clear detrimental energies from you, the family, house, garden, etc.; this is the only time that I ask to be shown anything beneficial. Frankly, once the bad stuff has been cleared, the beneficial areas can only get better.

These beneficial areas can be called 'Energy Coordinating Points' as several beneficial lines cross here and intensify the energies benefiting the depth of the healing or the state of meditation.

Not all houses will have one of these 'special' areas, but if you have one in your home, you must start using it, as they are wonderful for contemplation, meditation, healing and inspirational purposes. The energy produced will benefit you and your family in many different ways. However, I wouldn't suggest sleeping in the area for hours on end – although a short nap would be fine.

Carrying out any form of healing, massage or manipulation within these areas will aid not only your client but also you. The energies are special and will allow you to work in deeper and more intuitive ways.

Case Study 1: A House near Orpington, Kent

House plans come in all shapes and sizes – from hand-drawn sketches to detailed architect's drawings. You never know what you will get, until it arrives through your door. In this case, it was a set of estate agent's details, with a floor plan attached, showing only the basic layout of the new house. No units were shown in the kitchen or bathroom; the builders were obviously leaving their options open.

I found various earth energy lines, spirals, water veins and three spirits within Carol's house, which I worked on and cleared. She was lucky to have a beneficial area. However, it wasn't in her living room, kitchen or bedroom, but in her bathroom. I did dowse several times to make sure that I had the correct location, and I got the bathroom every time.

Now, the problem was that the plan didn't show the location of the fittings within the room, so I hoped that it was in the same position as the bath. That way, Carol could benefit from healing, or meditate whilst lying in a hot tub. Sadly, it turned out to be the location of the WC. Obviously, a great place for contemplation.

If you are lucky to find one of these areas in your home use a light blue * to mark on plan.

Dowsing Diagnosis Questions for Beneficial Areas

1. Do you have any beneficial areas in your house?

2. How many?

3. Where is it/are they?

4. Is it/are they beneficial for the whole family?

5. Is it/are they good for you to sit in for healing purposes?

6. Can you carry out healing from the area/s?

7. Is there a particularly good time to use the area/s?

8. Can you enhance the energies in the area/s?

9. How can you do this? Further meditation, etc.

Part 3

How to Heal

Introduction

I sit here thinking about how I should start this important part of the book. In some ways, it is so simple, but in others it's so hard. This is what I have come to do naturally – so naturally that I rarely think about what I am doing. It just happens and, as the months and years go by, it is happening quicker and quicker.

We all have the healing ability within us; we are born with this gift. However, as we go through the school system, this natural talent starts to disappear. By the time we reach our teenage years, ego has taken over and we are out to conquer the world – I was, anyway! Our 20s and 30s should be a time of growth, both mentally and physically. The 40s are a time to consolidate what you have learned in the physical world, enabling you to move towards the spiritual. I feel that the so-called 'male menopause' is just the body and mind's way of saying, 'Okay, now we start to look at what life is actually all about; the real training is just about to begin.' Sadly, this is distorted by modern thinking and the media. It becomes a time of worry, with concerns over libido and manliness. Embrace maturity, it is what we should all do best. It is a good time to start to heal your inner self, and then you can begin to heal others – it is a natural advancement.

I believe this is very similar for women too, the menopause is often looked at as the ending of femininity, but that is so far from the truth it is laughable. Yes, the hormones in the feminine body are changing but so what? Do you really want babies at 50, 60 or perhaps 70? Start to look at different forms of healing. Work on yourself, as inner healing is so important to begin with, and then develop that to work on friends and family. Menopause for both men and woman can mean a fresh start to life, you have the time to begin again, to develop the intuition that you were born with and that you left behind during your 20s, 30s, 40s and possibly 50s.

We all have the healing capability but rarely do we give it the time and dedication that it deserves.

Since Andy's prophetic words, telling me that I could become a healer, I have worked on hundreds of families and their homes. I have tried to verify my healing work, asking for feedback – both good and bad – from friends and clients. Some cases have been frustrating, very testing, elongated and educational, before I was satisfied that the job was done. Never give up, and don't forget to ask the 'Highest of the High' and his legions of Archangels for help; they are never far away.

If you need help in clarifying what you have found or feel out of your depth at any stage, please contact me via the telephone number on my website www.dowsingspirits.co.uk.

I would like to repeat that it is important that the healing of your home and family is all done in one session, carrying this work out a little bit at a time is not the most beneficial way to work.

By all means, take your time on diagnosing the problem areas in your home, as it will take you time to begin with. Once you have mastered the dowsing rods and/or pendulum and learn how to ask the right questions etc., you should get quicker and quicker.

The energies that you will be dealing with may have been around for many years and they need to be shown respect, especially when it comes to dealing with spirits and elemental beings.

Keep in mind that you need to be healthy and of sound mind and body, before you carry out this work and in-depth healing on others.

There are machines on the market that claim to eradicate the effects of geopathic stress and I often get asked the questions: 'Do they work?' or 'Are they any good?' My comment on this is that I feel many of the problems that come under the general heading of 'geopathic stress' need to be shown respect or be properly identified and acknowledged, before they can be healed, especially when it involves the spirit realm.

I also believe that machines are only as good as the people that program them (either with software or intent), if they do not know about 'toxic lines', for example, how can a mechanical device clear or heal that particular problem or ailment?

Some people love gadgets and can identify with them far better than having someone heal the problems with intent. It really does depend on your viewpoint.

Tuning In Before Healing

Before I start any dowsing or healing sessions, I will say a prayer or mantra. I find most times that the Lord's Prayer is perfect for the occasion

It has been with me since I was a child, and I know the words off by heart. I know that it has been re-written into modern-day speak, but the good old-fashioned words work best for me. I don't do religion per se; this is just my way of opening the office door in the morning, or of hanging up a sign to say that I am now open for business. It shows my intention to contact the healing realms, asking them for help, and to pick up the dowsing rods or pendulum.

The Holy Trinity of Healing

I have adapted the Lord's Prayer to suit my modern healing methods as follows:

Our Father who art in Heaven, our Mother who is on Earth and our Life Giving Sun, hallowed be they names, thy kingdom come, thy will be done, on earth as it is in heaven. Give us this day our daily bread, and forgive us our trespasses, as we forgive those who trespass against us, and lead us not into temptation, but deliver us from evil. For thine is the kingdom, the power and the glory, for ever and ever. Amen.

I feel it is very important not only to use the healing energy from above but to combine it with healing white light from Mother Earth and the life giving Sun, meeting and melding within the powerhouse of the body, (the Solar Plexus Chakra) and then sending it out to the family that I am working on or anyone that needs it.

I always protect myself psychically by using the coloured layers that you read about on page 39. I light a candle, and will often meditate, and then 'tune in' to the energy of the universe.

My tuning in mantra is as follows:

To the Highest of the High, Mother Earth and our Life Giving Sun: please combine and use me today as your healing instrument here on planet Earth. I ask that my healing is of the highest standard and working for the higher good of the people and animals concerned. I would like to enlist the help of five Archangels: Michael, Gabriel, Sammuel, Azriel and Feriel; all other appropriate Archangels and Angels that need to be here; all appropriate spirits; my spirit guides, protectors and healing guides.

After that mouthful, I am ready to start. I know that I have an army of the light behind me, to protect me in my work and provide all the healing that I ask for – all for the good of us humans down here on Earth. Feel free to adjust the above mantra for your own beliefs.

I sometimes have 'spiritual music' playing quietly in the background; it can help you concentrate by drowning out any noise that might disturb you whilst you are in healing mode. All healers have their own unique way of working; none are better that any other. You just need to concentrate on the task in hand, using the following techniques to clear the house and family of all the problems that you have found.

I have the floor plan and a report in front of me, and start working through it progressively, looking at each of the questions that I have dowsed, and healing them in turn. Don't rush. It is important that you take your time on each section and visualize all that is given to you below. I have held nothing back; these are my tools of my trade, they work for me and I know that – if your intent is right – they will work for you too. This healing process works whether you are on site or a thousand miles away.

I will often speak my requests out loud. I used to get some funny looks from Charles, my youngest, but he got used to it eventually. You can use pure thought if you like, but to me the spoken word has more meaning, as does the movement of hands and arms whilst I carry out the healing.

WHEN CARRYING OUT THE HEALING MAKE SURE THAT YOU HAVE PROTECTED YOURSELF PSYCHICALLY USING THE METHOD ON PAGE 39.

Working Through the List

After you carry out a healing/clearing, always dowse to find out whether you have been successful. It may be that you need to carry out a second healing or perhaps seek the help of someone else to build up enough energy to clear the problem.

1. Spirits, Ghosts, Tricky Spirits, Trapped Souls, etc.

Soul rescue should always come first. Spirits or ghosts are tuned into a home's energies; if there are any changes, they will know about them. Their reaction can be quiet violent should 'their' home be disturbed. Please show respect and move them on, before you start changing anything in the house.

Before I contact the spirits I always ask the 'Highest of the High' for a beautiful beam of light to appear in the house. A beam will carry them to 'Heaven' (for want of a better word). I ask all spirits there, and in the local area, that wish to go to the light today, to gather round. I will read through the information that I have on the spirits, and I will keep it in mind, as I move them on.

Then I ask for each of them to be shown a vision of what they will find once they get to the light, before reciting the following mantra:

Soul Rescue – Spirit Release Mantra

Ladies and gentlemen, please do not be afraid by this direct form of communication. I have been granted special dispensation to talk to you today, to help you to continue your interrupted journey into the light.

You have been shown a vision of what awaits you, once you step into the beam of light – it is far better than staying here on this grey earth plane.

It is a beautiful place to be, and many people are waiting there for you to arrive with open arms and unconditional love.

Should you wish anyone from your past to be with you now, to help guide you on your journey, just call their name and they will appear beside you to hold your hand.

There will be no retribution for anything that you have done whilst on the earth plane, or that has been done to you, as this is part of your life's plan. This will be explained to you, once you arrive.

I therefore invite you to move into the light, to be with your family, friends and loved ones once again.

Amen

After waiting a few minutes, I will ask if all the souls present have gone to the light. Then I will ask if there are any further souls that need to go to the light today. Remember the layer system; it might be that the lead spirit has now gone, freeing up others to move through. Check for a third time, to be on the safe side – do you need to move any further spirits through?

I like to send my love to those souls who have gone through, and I ask the Highest of the High to make sure that they are happy there. If you are carrying out further healing on the house, just continue down the list. If you are purely moving spirits on, ask that the house be flooded with light and love – and that any spirit residue left behind is taken away and disposed of appropriately.

2. Detrimental or Inappropriate Attachments

The removal of these nasties is the next in terms of importance. They can manipulate moods, change energies and bring on nightmares. There are two ways in which I do this. It really does depend on the time available, how strong they are, how long they have been attached and where they are within your auric field, chakra or body.

If they are below -4 on the detrimental scale, then you should be able to use the following. I call it the 'ultra-fine mesh net of light and love' method. I always enlist the help of two Archangels – Azriel and Feriel – to help.

Standard Healing and Clearing Method

Imagine the two Archangels holding this ultra-fine mesh net of light and love at the very outer edge of the person's auric field. Then, just as a trawler would do, start pulling it from the right-hand side of the auric field, through the body, and finish at the far left-hand side of the energy field. Whilst you are visualizing this recite the following:

I ask that as the ultra-fine net of light and love is being pulled through my aura and body that all detrimental attachments are cleared – taken to the light and disposed of appropriately.

Heavyweight Healing and Clearing Method

If you have a detrimental attachment that registers more than -4, and is attached to a specific chakra, within one of your auric fields or has got into your body, then something heavier is needed. I would use the following:

Either stand or sit with both feet flat on the ground, feeling that connection with Mother Earth. Imagine white light or energy coming from the Earth, and moving up through your feet and legs, passing through your base and sacral chakras and reaching your solar plexus chakra – where it is held as a glowing ball of light.

Imagine the same light but coming from above, from the Heavenly Father (God, the management or whatever you choose to call it), entering through your crown chakra and passing through your third eye (brow chakra), your throat and then your heart chakra and entering your solar plexus – where it meets and mixes with the ball of energy from Mother Earth and also the healing light from our Life Giving Sun (which enters through the front and back of your solar plexus chakra).

This gives you a spiritual connection with the Earth and the Heavens above. Then, imagine this ball of healing light exploding from a cellular level, moving through your body, cells, blood and organs, cleansing as it goes. Recite the following:

I ask that all detrimental energy and attachments, all lower animal life forms, their seeds and tentacles, all human-

manifested thought and life forms, all parasites – all ties and cords to be cut, all past trauma and emotional energy be removed.

This continues through your auric field, cleansing that completely too.

Then, when you get to the outer edge of your auric field, ask that everything that has been displaced is taken into the universe (light), and is disposed of appropriately – and that a glowing bubble of light is left protecting you.

This is the big catch-all and I will use it several times during a healing session. It is something that you should do for yourself, at least once a week, and for your family too.

3. Human-Manifested Energy Forms

In the gallery of baddies, these guys come next. Super-attachments would be an apt name for them, as they have become so powerful that they are now free forms, able to move about at will. Your pets can see them, babies too, and the shadow that you see moving out of the corner of your eye is probably one of these – although spirits can appear very similar.

Visualization is so important in this case. Again, if you prefer, speak your request out loud, it will be heard – I promise. This time, I call on the 'Highest of the High' to place a large gilt (golden and carved, I find it easier to picture) box around the house and gardens, trapping any human-manifested thought or life forms within it. The box is mirrored on the inside because if human-manifested forms see their own reflection, they get turned inside out.

So we have them trapped inside this ornate box. Now ask, or visualize, the sides, lid and floor moving in, therefore making less and less space for them to move around. Gradually, it will get so small that they can't help but see their reflection and get turned inside out. Once this happens, ask that they be taken to the light and disposed of appropriately.

Now I always believe that any detrimental energy or beings should be given a choice to go to the light voluntarily, so, as the box starts to shrink, I visualize a thin tube leading directly to the light and offer them the chance to go. It seems less cruel this way.

Once the box fits into your hand, ask that Archangel Azriel collects it and takes it to the light.

4. Lower Animal Life Forms

These should all be removed using the Heavyweight Healing and Clearing Method.

(See **2. Detrimental or Inappropriate Attachments**)

5. Black Magic

This healing very much depends on how bad the problem is. If it is between 0 and, say, -5, then flooding the problem with light and love should work – asking for all the dark energies there to be taken to the light. However, if it is -6 and above then other methods have to be used.

This method may appear strange, but bear with me – it does work. For this, you will need to work with your higher self, using him/her as an intermediary. It helps by keeping your self at arm's length – you don't want to be a target. I visualize a courtroom scene with Archangel Michael as judge and jury. The person or persons that created the problem are in the dock; the defendants, if you like, and you are the advocate. Is it a matter of you plea-bargaining for the injured, innocent party, asking the defendant to admit their guilt. Then, take away the offending energies that they left behind.

A lot of black magic problems have been caused by people not knowing what they are doing – for example, playing with a Ouija board and reciting spells from a book that they have just bought. In this case, it is normally resolved easily; the defendant pleads guilty, and Michael asks them to clear away the detrimental energies that they have created. In some cases, you might have to go to the higher court and enlist the Guv'nor (the Highest of the High) to help. Go through the same procedure, and ask that the person be found guilty and be made to clear up the dark energies that they left behind.

I know that it sounds strange, but it does work.

6. Psychic Cords

There are two methods that I generally use; one involves asking Archangel Michael to assist in the cord cutting and the other is a gentle visualization. Both work well, they are both as powerful as each other and it really just depends on what mood I'm in as to which one I use.

Archangel Michael and his Sword of Light and Truth

Once I have found out how many cords are attached, where they join and who is responsible for doing so, I ask Archangel Michael to help in severing them.

I start by visualizing the two people standing in front of Michael, one to the left and the other to the right; I see the cords and ask that they be cut with his sword. I generally ask that the cord is cut where it joins the victim, then a second cut where the cord originates from, and finally a third cut in the middle of the cords, severing them completely. Next, I ask that all the pieces be taken to the light and disposed of appropriately.

I will then visualize placing a small mirror or mirrors where the cords were joined, to stop any chance of them re-attaching.

Floating Bubble Method

I will talk my client through this process normally, however, this doesn't always need to be the case.

If the cord or cords were attached to you I would ask you to visualize yourself standing on a cliff top overlooking the sea with far-reaching views – it is a sunny day with the occasional cloud passing by. The person that has attached the cords will be in a bubble floating in front of you. Take a pair of scissors (or use your fingers in a cutting motion) and cut the cords joining the two of you together. Blow the bubble and watch it disappear slowly out of sight until finally you can see the person no more.

Then place yourself in a bubble of white light for extra protection. Be warned that the person who attached the cords may be in touch with you; they will feel the sudden loss as you cut the ties.

7. Fourth-dimensional Portals

If you have found that your house has an open portal, it will need to be closed, but first you need to send back all the beings that have come through and I call upon my nine Archangels to assist me in doing this.

I picture the Archangels with large butterfly nets and ask them to capture all the undesirable fourth-dimensional beings that have come through the open doorway and to return them to their own dimension. Once this has been done, I dowse to make sure the task has been carried out, then shut the door, turn a key in the lock and finally put a skim of light and love (spiritual plaster) over it, asking that it be sealed for all time.

8. Water Veins/Underground Streams

Now we are getting to the geomancy stage of the healing process, looking at and working on the Earth beneath our feet, helping to bring a balance to this topsy-turvy world.

Working on and healing water veins can have a remarkable effect on people, their homes and animals; you are removing the detrimental emotion, the radiation produced by the earth and any other noxious energies contained within the water.

I suggest that you work on the water veins one at a time to begin with; however, as practice makes perfect you can tackle them as a whole. I visualize each stream being flooded with love and light along the complete length, depth and breadth, asking that all detrimental energies contained in the water be removed and disposed of appropriately in the universe. Then I flood the water again with love and light, asking that it be left in peace, balance and harmony for all living things for all time.

Now comes the best part: we are going to move the water vein from running beneath your home – not only that, but all other homes that it affects, but only as appropriate. How does this happen? Simple, you just ask.

> *To the Highest of the High, I ask that this water vein be moved from running underneath my house, both energetically and physically, and all other houses that it affects, as appropriate, for it to now flow harmlessly beneath gardens, pathways and roads, to leave the stream in peace, balance and harmony for all living things for all time.*

It generally takes between twenty-four and forty-eight hours for the water vein to move from its current position to its new location. You can dowse it after one day to see how it far it has moved; this is one of the most fascinating facets of dowsing and earth healing. I never cease to get a buzz from carrying out this type of healing, knowing that I am helping countless people as the water vein is diverted. I use the words 'as appropriate' because it may be that the water needs to continue running beneath a house because the occupants, for whatever reason, still need its energy, good or bad.

Only 'them upstairs' know why.

9. Earth Energy Lines

Healing these energy lines is very similar to working on the water veins, inasmuch as you flood the entire line or ley with light and love, asking for all the detrimental and inappropriate energy contained within it to be taken to the light and disposed of appropriately.

Don't forget, if you dowse and find an earth energy line in your home, it actually travels around the entire globe, ending up back in your front room. So when I carry out the healing I imagine the whole line glowing with light and love, around the entire planet, perhaps passing through troubled countries and spreading its peaceful message. We cannot heal the whole world, but bite-sized chunks is the way forward.

Finally, I ask that the energy line be left in peace, balance and harmony for all living things for all time.

10. Toxic Lines

Again, very similar to water veins in that I ask for the lines to be flooded with light and love, with all detrimental and inappropriate energies taken away and disposed of appropriately into the light or universe.

However, I also like to send healing to the point and/or cause of the problem. If you have dowsed that it was one person responsible for setting up the line, send healing to him or her asking for forgiveness on their behalf.

Then carry out a healing on the actual problem area, dispersing the detrimental energies into the universe, leaving the line and area in peace, balance and harmony for all living things for all time. You can also ask that any residue that is left in the house be cleared away too.

11. Reversal Points

This is a case of knowledge picked up from the physical world being used in the spiritual or healing world.

To recap, a reversal point is an area that, if kept clear, is harmless. However, if covered by a chair, ornament, flower pot, etc., it will allow detrimental energies to rise in your home. The point may be outside but it would still allow or cause noxious energies to affect your house.

If you have one in your home then it will need dealing with as follows: I first ask that any detrimental energies caused by it being covered be taken away and disposed of appropriately into the universe, then I place a manhole cover of light and love over the reversal point, finally asking for it to be skimmed with light and love (spiritual plaster) and to be sealed for all time.

12. Fractured Souls

There are many different ways to restore a fractured or torn soul. I like to make all healing procedures as simple as possible and look to find the easiest and most practical way of conducting them. This, therefore, is my method of repairing a fractured or torn soul.

I believe that the Angelic realms are there to provide us with assistance, but we need to ask them to help us, as free will is still the unwritten rule here on earth and they hold back until summoned. So Archangel Michael is called for once again (I do keep him busy) to help. I ask him to repair the tear or to restore any part that might have been fractured to the person affected. I will then place a bubble of white light around the newly repaired soul, to keep it protected until it has fully repaired itself, normally two to three days.

Some people do feel different when this healing has been carried out, some don't. There are no rules when it comes to soul repair or retrieval. You should also send healing back to the time the soul tore or fractured, to the person that caused it to happen or the event.

As always, leave everything in peace, balance and harmony.

13. Stress/Disturbance Lines (Man-Made)

This is similar to the healing that we do for water and earth energy lines, in that we individually flood the lines with light and love, removing all detrimental and inappropriate energies and dispersing them into the universe. Then we send a healing light to the area where the stress line/s was/were created. If it was, say, physical abuse by a husband on his wife, then send healing to them both, asking that all detrimental energies be removed and they be left in peace, balance and harmony.

The line will disappear; if it doesn't after your first attempt, send healing again. Deep problems can be difficult to clear in one go, layers might exist, so as they rise to the surface continue to heal them until the problem has gone.

I am a great believer in the fact that the healing we carry out will only be 100% effective should the 'Highest of the High' allow it. We only channel the healing from above, and if the Heavenly Father/Mother doesn't want a person or area to be healed it won't happen. I do send healing to people without asking their permission, trusting that the Divine Spirits know what they are doing.

14. Ley Lines/Holy Lines

The healing of these lines is the same as the healing you would do for stress/disturbance lines. Make sure that you send healing to each of the sites that the ley crosses. Should someone be 'dirtying the line' on purpose, send healing to that person and/or place them in a bubble of white light that is mirrored on the inside so that their detrimental thoughts and actions are reflected back to them. Don't forget to send unconditional love to them at the same time.

15. Energy Spirals

These are mainly the result of water veins or underground streams crossing or interacting with earth energy lines. They are similar to eddies that can be seen on the surface of a stream or river when an underwater obstruction interrupts or disturbs the flow. There will be beneficial spirals or vortices in your home, but we are only worried about the detrimental ones.

They cannot or should not be moved, but their energies can be harmonized to work with us rather than against us. It is good to know all you can about them, i.e. direction of rotation and female or male aspect, as even when harmonized a feminine spiral is still good for a female to meditate within and vice versa for a male.

The healing method is as follows: Ask that the spirals be flooded with light and love, and visualize a white light moving along the direction of the rotation until the whole spiral is alight. Then ask that all the detrimental energies contained within it are taken to the light/universe and disposed of in an appropriate fashion, leaving the spiral in peace, balance and harmony for all living things for all time.

The energy spirals should still be there when you dowse again but they

363

are now giving out beneficial, not detrimental energy.

16. Sink Holes

I treat sink holes rather like reversal points, asking that a bung or plug of light and love be placed in the hole, sealing it for all time. You can also ask that any detrimental energy that has come through the hole over the years be cleared and sent to the light to be disposed of appropriately.

17. Karmic Problems

Archangel Michael is called upon for this healing; you will need to sit quietly and I suggest that for at least ten minutes you clear your mind of day-to-day dross and think about the task ahead. Soft spiritual music can sometimes help you achieve a peaceful and calm mind; you owe it to yourself to take your time as the whole experience can be quite moving. I would suggest that a box of tissues be available, just in case.

You will need to make sure that you have the whole story mapped out; from the very first time the physical/mental injury or karmic debt started to the last, probably this life. Read through the case studies again to give you a better idea on what to look for and how to ask the questions, and slowly build up the story of your past lives. It will take time but is so worthwhile. Are you the injured party or the culprit? Have you created the karmic debt or is there another guilty party? Is it someone close to you, a family member or work colleague, perhaps someone that has already passed away?

Once you are ready, take the telephone off the hook, ditch your mobile and relax.

In order to carry out the karmic healing you will need to work with your higher self, who will be your intermediary along with the other party's higher self. Archangel Michael is there to help the process move forward smoothly; he will oversee fair play.

You now need to rerun the story through your head rather like a Hollywood movie – don't worry about the colours, work in sepia

364

Using the English Civil War case study as an example, see yourself charging at the enemy troops, feel the lance pierce your side and the hurt you felt as you fell from the horse, hitting the ground and winding yourself. Feel the fear that you would have experienced as the Roundhead troops advanced towards you and the agony when they lopped off your feet.

Picture those same troopers in front of you now: apologize to them all for having given them no option but to fight; you attacked them and they defended themselves, and they had no choice in what they had to do. Then you need to ask them to apologize to you, for injuring you the way that they did. Basically, we are looking to achieve forgiveness from all parties, to move forward having put right what once went wrong.

Then carry out the same for your next reincarnation and so on until reaching this life where you will need to ascertain whether or not you have already made a similar or related mistake, perhaps to a lesser degree, that needs healing. Once all the healings have been carried out, dowse to make sure that all is well. You might need to go back and carry out a more in-depth or second healing on a particularly difficult past-life issue; maybe an ancestor could help you. Dowse which one and work with them.

Finally, ask Archangel Michael to take away all the detrimental energy that you have generated throughout this life and all past incarnations, disposing of it appropriately into the universe.

18. Human Conflict or Emotional Energy Areas

There are two ways that I use to clear these emotional areas from a house, garden, street, etc.

You can flood each area individually with light and love, sending all the detrimental energy to be disposed of in an appropriate fashion in the universe, leaving each area in peace, balance and harmony for all time.

Or you can use the ultra-fine mesh net of light and love used in the

Standard Healing and Clearing Method. Picture it being trawled through the house by Archangels Azriel and Feriel, picking up all the detrimental emotional energies found, including energetic bed patterns (we leave emotional traces on our beds when we leave it in the morning, good and bad. If, for instance, you had a bad night's sleep the same energy patterns will still be there when you get back into bed, encouraging a disturbed sleep), and then ask the Archangels to dispose of them appropriately in the universe.

If an area that you are working on has seen a murder, rape or suicide, it may be very detrimental, say -7 upwards. Do check, once you have carried out the healing, as there may be a layer system that needs further work. Dowse to see if has been completely healed or if it needs revisiting at a future date.

19. Power Artefacts

Use either the ultra-fine mesh net method or flood the artefact with light and love, etc.

Standard Healing and Clearing Method

Imagine the two Archangels holding this ultra-fine mesh net of light and love at the very outer edge of the power artefact. Then, just as a trawler would do, start pulling it from the right-hand side of the auric field of the artefact, and finish at the far left-hand side of the energy field. Whilst you are visualizing this recite the following:

> *I ask that as the ultra-fine net of light and love is being pulled through this artefact that all detrimental energies are cleared – taken to the light and disposed of appropriately.*

If a misplaced being or a spirit is found, use the Soul/Spirit Rescue Mantra, then once it is gone, clear or heal the artefact.

Ask that the artefact be left in peace, balance and harmony for the family and all other living things for all time.

20. Technopathic Stress

There are many people out there who don't believe that electro-magnetic fields can be healed, cleared or blocked through intent or prayer. Humans and animals are electro-magnetic beings who derive benefit from healing, so why can't the same be said for man-made EMFs?

I have demonstrated via kinesiology or muscle testing that intent has a profound effect on the detrimental energies produced by mobile telephones, electricity pylons, microwaves, house wiring, etc. If you place a mobile phone in a person's hand their muscles test weak, but if you bless the mobile, clearing any detrimental and inappropriate energies from it, and test again, the muscles remain strong. There is no sign of detrimental radiation coming from the mobile. This can be said for most, if not all, electrical devices – try it and see.

If you want to double up on the safety aspect, there are scientific devices available that help block or shield you from EMFs. Alasdair Philips' website www.powerwatch.org.uk is worth visiting, as is the related www.emfields.org.

I ask that all external and internal electro-magnetic energies in the home be healed and any detrimental energies to be taken away and disposed of appropriately. I then ask that everything possible is done to harmonize the remaining energies, leaving them in balance and harmony for the family and animals.

There is much research on the internet about the detrimental effect of cooking with microwave ovens, also the effect of low-energy light bulbs on humans and animals. Please try and help yourself where you can, minimize your usage of mobile phones, change to the new LED-type bulbs that give off a healthy light and cook naturally. Research is the key.

21. Guardian of the Site/Spirit of Place

When I find an unhappy Guardian or spirit of place, I simply talk to them from a distance unless I am actually at the client's house. I explain to them that our modern lifestyle is so hectic that we don't often have time to exchange niceties or just sit and tune into what they are trying to tell us. I explain to my clients that if they are going to change anything in the house or garden, they should speak to the Guardian or Spirit of place and explain it to them.

Our ancestors understood the land, they would talk to the fairies, imps and gnomes, and they would communicate with us. Try to sit and tune into the local spirit and give thanks for what they do for us – your garden will start to bloom in many different ways.

So I send healing to them in the form of a rainbow. I ask that they be flooded with this beautiful light and that any animosity felt be taken away and disposed of appropriately, that they harmonize their energies with ours and help us with our lives.

22. Place Memory

I use the ultra-fine mesh net of light and love method, trawling the net through the home or area where the place memory has been found. Generally you will find a layer system involved, although this does depend on the complexity and reason for a place memory being started. I like to check after a few days that the healing is complete; if it isn't, I use the net again, and finally I flood the affected area with light and love, leaving it in peace, balance and harmony for ever more.

23. Elementals

I ask Archangel Sammuel to help me clear the house of these trapped nature spirits by picking them all up in a butterfly net of light and love, removing them from where they are hiding – they could be in the central heating system, under floorboards, in the electrical wiring of the house, a table lamp, the attic, etc. Once he has picked them all up, I ask for them to be taken to a nearby field or park to be released. I then talk to the elementals, asking them to dedicate themselves to the flora and fauna found locally and to be at peace with their surroundings.

I also ask that all the detrimental elementals are removed from the garden and taken to the same location, as they can terrorize your pets whilst they are out in the garden. They will often lie in wait and then ambush or mug any passing cat or dog.

24. Tree Spirits

It is a good idea to check before you cut a tree or trim the branches that it doesn't have a spirit attached. They can easily become displaced and cause similar problems to elementals.

I ask the tree spirit to transfer itself to another tree that is without its own guardian and for it to dedicate itself to the happiness and wellbeing of its new home. If you haven't got a spare tree in your garden go and buy one from a local garden centre and hold a dedication ceremony, encouraging the tree spirit into your new purchase. Do check before you buy it that it hasn't got its own tree spirit already.

25. Animal Spirits

Just like lost human souls or ghosts, these are our pets that haven't gone to the light for various reasons. A cat may well have stayed behind to comfort its grieving owner, and a dog may feel that it is still its job to round up the sheep. Before you do anything else you must move them into the light.

It is very much the same as a human spirit – I talk to them and encourage them to go to the light. I also check to see if their owner has already gone and if so I would ask him or her to come and fetch them. If they haven't, then I would turn to the cat or dog's parents and ask them to come down and help in the process. Generally, animals will go straight away if allowed; it is normally only us humans that have problems.

Once they have successfully gone they can return at any time to give healing to their owners and family.

26. Spirit Lines

These are the lines or tracks used by lost souls or Spirits to move round. There can be hundreds on any one line and these spirits need moving on before you can work on diverting the track.

To heal spirit lines, begin with the Soul Rescue Mantra. You should be able to move all the ghosts on at one go, but do check, as there can often be a layer system in force.

After you have recited the mantra, dowse to see how successful you have been – have all the spirits moved on or have some remained? If any spirits have not gone they might have been held back by a controlling spirit, so dowse to see if this is the case. If it is, then you will have to find a way of encouraging the head ghost to move through to the light before he/she will let the others go. Try the mantra again and dowse to see if he or she has gone this time. Ask the question again in a few days' time, as you might have to repeat the work.

I often find when working with a group of spirits that they seem to rush for the door en masse; perhaps they encourage each other or get swept up in the excitement of it all.

Once they have all gone to the light I will ask that the line be flooded with light and love and that all detrimental energy contained within it be taken to the light and disposed of appropriately, leaving the line in peace, balance and harmony for all time.

I will then ask for the line to be diverted away from all houses and buildings that it affects, for it to run harmlessly along roads, pathways and footpaths.

27. Chakra Balancing or Blockages

You will need to find out which chakras are out of balance or blocked before you start the healing work, following the question string in part 2 will help you do this. In a practical way, I tend to view blocked chakras rather like a furred-up kettle: they have been misused and need some maintenance work, a good spiritual wash- and brush-up to restore them to normal working order.

Method One

During your dowsing you will have ascertained which chakra o chakras have been affected and I suggest that you work on them in the following way. First, check to see which way it is spinning, then picture the chakra in your mind, see it furred up, or rusty if that is easier for you. Mentally stop it spinning and turn it in the opposite direction, normally three full turns to dislodge the blockage, then start it spinning once again in the correct direction of rotation.

Now ask for the blocked chakra or chakras (there may be more than one affected) to be flooded with light and love, asking for all the 'junk' that has been dislodged be taken to the light, disposing it appropriately, leaving the chakra fully cleared, spinning for maximum health and in balance with mind, body and soul.

Method Two

You purely use your breath to clear any blockages that you may have found. Work on each chakra separately and take your time.

First, take three good deep breaths and start to relax, listening to the rhythm of your breathing. In – out, in – out, then gradually start to introduce a colour into your in-breath, let us say gold in this instance. See this golden light fill up your lungs and then as you breathe out start to let go of your problems. See all your worries, stresses and concerns disappear from your body as black blobs in the golden light. After a few minutes, start to introduce the golden light to your blocked chakra, imagining it being drawn into the chakra during the in-breath and then all the 'junk' disappearing on the out-breath. Keep this going for a few minutes and then start working on any other blocked chakras that you have found.

You can use this method as often as you like; it will help maintain the chakras in good working order.

Balancing Chakras

There are various ways to balance chakras. You can use the breath method above as regularly as you like, as it will help your general energy levels and keep you healthy. Or you can use the following:

Pendulum Method

371

If you are working on a friend or family member, you can hold the pendulum over the out-of-balance chakra and allow it to spin. However, that is difficult to do if you are working on your own chakras, especially when you reach the crown.

Firstly, you will need to dowse to find out which of your chakras is out of balance. It may be best, however, to work on them all to start with, making sure that they are all healthy. Sit comfortably with both feet on the floor and take a few deep breaths – breathing correctly is so very important – relax and be in touch with your body.

See a healing beam of light entering your body from the top of your head, moving through to your heart and splitting, then channelling through to your hands and finally into your pendulum.

Start with your base chakra, then sacral, solar plexus, heart, throat, third eye and finally your crown. Hold your pendulum above your knees, within your emotional energy field, and start it swinging in a circular motion, it doesn't matter which direction, asking for it to stop swinging when the base chakra comes into balance. The healing will automatically go to the specified chakra; you do not need to hold the pendulum above the problem area, so long as you work within the emotional auric field.

Once you have worked through the chakras, dowse to see if they are now all in balance, and ask that they all be left spinning to ensure maximum benefit, health and protection for you.

28. Anything Else Running Through the Site

Carrying out healing in this section really does depend on what you have found, and many of the techniques that you have already learned can be used. For instance:

If there is an old disused trackway or footpath it may have a number of spirits wandering along it, in which case use the Soul Rescue Mantra. The pathway may then need clearing of emotional energy, especially if violent acts have happened along it over the years. In this instance, I would use the ultra-fine mesh net of light and love (if it is on a short length), or I might flood the complete length with light and love, asking that all detrimental energies be taken to the light and disposed of appropriately, leaving it in peace, balance and harmony for all living things for all time.

If it was the site of a stone circle or some similar place of worship, then make sure that the ground has been deconsecrated and then cleared of all detrimental energies by using the net method or flooding it with light and love, etc. Layers may well exist in this instance, so again in a few weeks' time and re-address if required.

29. Fabric of the Building

Check to see where the problem or problems lie, it may be in the foundations, perhaps using rubble from a former psychiatric hospital or sacred site, or in the fabric of the building, like the pieces from a broken stone circle which were incorporated into the walls of the house as in Avebury.

I would start off with the ultra-fine mesh net of light and love, trawling it through the house, then dowse to see if that has solved the problem. Remember to ask that the net be taken into the light and disposed of appropriately.

If that hasn't fully worked then you need to focus a beam of white light on each of the problematic areas, asking that all the detrimental energies be cleared away leaving them in peace, balance and harmony for all living things for all time.

30. Curses or Spells

I always ask for guidance from my higher self when working with curses and spells to make sure that they can be lifted. In most cases I get an affirmative answer.

I ask for my higher self to work directly with Archangel Michael and the higher self of the person who cast the spell/curse. I then act as an intermediary or lawyer for the defence, plea bargaining for my client or friend that had the misfortune to have the spell put on them. You will already know why the person had cast the spell, having dowsed it earlier. It will be a one-sided conversation, so put your case forward the best way that you can and finally, ask for them to lift it. Dowse to make sure that it has gone; if it hasn't, ask why and then find another way of pleading your case.

In most cases the curse is not current and the person that cast it has passed over, so there will not be a reason for the spell to remain. If it does and you are still having problems please contact me.

Don't forget to send healing to the person that cast the spell or curse, even if they have passed over. Never fight fire with fire, always send unconditional love, as this helps to diffuse the situation rather than inflame it.

31. Anaesthetic Traces, Vaccinations or Heavy Metals

This is a difficult area to work on as most people in the developed world have had countless injections over the years, whether for diseases like measles, mumps, tetanus, etc., or in preparation for travelling abroad. One of the main carriers used in these inoculations is mercury, which itself causes many problems.

I always ask if I can clear any lingering problems or possible side effects purely by carrying out a healing. Often the answer is yes and this is done by using the ultra-fine mesh net of light and love, trawling it through the auric fields and physical body asking that:

All the detrimental effects of inoculations and anaesthetic including any mercury in the body are cleared and that all the 'junk' is taken into the light and disposed of appropriately.

Then check to see if this has been the case. It may be that you will need to do this again in a few weeks to clear all the problems. If you can't, then I would suggest going to see a good homeopath who will be able to guide you further.

The same applies to heavy metals: there are patches which are placed on your feet that are claimed to remove many of the toxins from your body, and the idea is that they draw out the poisons. I have never used them as I find that the healing process works well for me; however, look on the internet and carry out some research if you feel that is the best way forward for you.

Chlorella and Spirulina are two supplements that are used by many people to help rid the body of detrimental toxins and fight off the effects of living in the twenty-first century, clearing the effects of trace metals found in vegetables, for example. I use them both regularly. There are several books written about these new 'wonder supplements' available on the internet, like *The Chlorella Factor* by Mike Adams.

32. Anything Else to be Considered Regarding Your Health

There is no healing to be carried out in this section but if you are dowsing for yourself, try and work out what you need to move forward once the main healing has been carried out. You may find that a particular flower remedy helps balance your mind and body whilst you undergo changes brought about by the clearing/healing process, and the same applies for friends or family members.

You can dowse over a range of vitamins and supplements, working out which are best for you, for example if you are over forty years old then Vitamin D3 (Cholecalciferol) is a good general aid to your health.

You can also dowse for food intolerances and general health issues; compile your own list or download one from:

www.dowsingspirits.co.uk.

33. Human Interference Lines

I will always ask if these lines need to be healed or perhaps blocked for a length of time.

I have sometimes found them to be necessary for the person I am working on, to keep them 'on the edge', perhaps during a business deal or transaction. Once this is done, the healing work can start.

Generally it is a case of healing the lines with light and love, putting the person affected into a bubble of white light that is mirrored on the outside to reflect any detrimental energy or thoughts coming their way, which are returned to the sender with unconditional love.

That might not always be enough; it really depends on how strong the interference lines are, how long they have been there, why they were set up and by whom.

Placing your client in a pyramid (using visualisation) after the healing is done will help alleviate the buzzing and probably fully sort out the problem. If the interference comes from an ex-wife/husband/lover, or perhaps an ex-business partner, then this interference will need to be monitored closely over the next few weeks to make sure that all is clear as, rather like a psychic cord, it can start up again. Please watch for this.

34. Psychic Attack

Once you have found out the reason and the source, it is time to put a stop to the headaches or perhaps the spaced-out feeling that may have been with you for a few days or weeks.

A psychic attack can be both mental and physical in the way that it connects to you. Mental as in thought transference, and physical with cords becoming attached to certain parts of your body and/or chakras. Both methods will affect you in an adverse way, leading to mental and physical problems.

I like to find out exactly why I am being targeted, whether on purpose i.e. conscious thought, or subconsciously, as a passing thought. That way you can work on the person once you have cleared yourself.

Either way, I use the following method:

Repelling a Psychic Attack/Psychic protection:

Stand or sit, if you prefer, with both feet flat on the ground, feeling that connection with Mother Earth. Imagine white light or energy coming from the Earth and moving up through your feet and legs, passing through your base and sacral chakras and reaching your solar plexu chakra where it is held as a glowing ball of light.

Now imagine the same light but coming from above, from Heavenly Father, entering through your crown chakra and passing through your third eye (brow chakra) your throat and then heart chakra, entering your solar plexus where it meets and mixes with the ball of energy from Mother Earth and also the healing light from our Life Giving Sun (which enters through the front and back of your solar plexus chakra).

This gives you a spiritual connection with the Earth and the Heavens above. Imagine this ball of healing light expanding from cellular level, moving through your body, cells, blood, organs, etc. (Recite the following):

> *Please remove all detrimental attachments and cords including all psychic problems, whether mentally or physically attached, via cords, to my mind, body and auric fields. I also ask that this healing light move through my body, chakras and aura, cleansing them 100%, and that when the outer edge of my aura has been reached everything that has been dislodged be taken to the light and disposed of appropriately, leaving me in peace, balance and harmony.*

Then ask to be placed in a bubble of white light that is mirrored on the outside, reflecting any further detrimental thoughts and cords being sent your way, for as long as is appropriate.

Now you need to deal with the perpetrator, and this is done in a similar fashion, placing them in a bubble of white light, but this time it is mirrored on the inside to stop any detrimental thoughts from escaping. These are then sent back to the person with unconditional love. Forgiveness is important.

35. Parasites

There are remedies on the market that help to clear these meddlesome fellows. A good homeopath or naturopath can help, as can a mild positive electrical current. The late Dr Hulda Clark invented what she referred to as a zapper, a machine that gives out a mild low energy output which kills off detrimental parasites in your body; it needs to be used on a regular basis to begin with and many people have found it very beneficial. For further details visit www.huldaclark.com

I still feel that trawling an ultra-fine mesh net of light and love through the body can produce similar results and I carry out this procedure regularly on myself. Don't forget to ask that the 'junk' be taken to the light and disposed of appropriately and that your body be left in peace, balance and harmony.

36. Energizing/Healing Rays

Colours heal; they have been used for centuries in one way or another. Even as we casually glance at a rainbow we should feel uplifted by part of the miracle of life on this planet.

Sending or sitting in a beam of coloured light will bring beneficial changes not only to your life but to others too. Imagine a beam of coloured light from above, a little like the Star Trek transporter system, surrounding you and bringing you healing, love and wellness.

I dowse to ascertain the correct colour or colours either for me or to send to my client, then I sit quietly for a designated period of time (dowse it), imagining them immersed in the beam coming from above their heads. They may not feel anything at the time but they will receive the benefits.

37. Beneficial Areas to Sit, Heal or Meditate

This is the only 'positive' question that I ask. Everything else is to track and note the detrimental energies that need dealing with.

These areas are special; if you find one in your home then you have hit the jackpot. They are perfect for healing, not only for yourself, but to carry out work on clients if you are a practitioner. Place a chair or healing couch above or within the area and see if you feel any difference in how your healing works.

They are also perfect for meditational purposes. I wouldn't suggest sleeping in or above one for any great length of time; you don't want to feel that energized all the time.

Once I have finished healing a home, everywhere in the house becomes beneficial, but these areas will always remain special and are to be treasured.

Healing, meditation, contemplation or just a quiet place to chill – they are wonderful to experience.

Closing Down

This is very important to do once you have finished your healing/clearing work; just as we had an opening mantra to start the healing process we now need a closing-down one. It is akin to locking the office door once you have finished your working day.

It is a simple mantra:

> *To the Highest of the High, Mother Earth and our Life Giving Sun thank you for using me as your healing instrument here on the planet. I would ask that any doors that were expectedly or unexpectedly opened during my work be firmly closed. I would like to thank all the Archangels that have been with me, all spirits, my spirit guides and protectors, and ask that my energies return to normal working levels. Amen.*

Changes will happen after you have carried out all the healing work, some big and some small: be observant, see where they come. It might be better sleeping patterns, the house may feel lighter and warmer, family members may be less fatigued and have more energy. They may gather together and become closer, both emotionally and physically. Watch the patterns of behavior of those close to you, or the people that you might have worked on. Feedback is so important.

I suggest that you work on your own home before you attempt to work on someone else's property. I would also suggest that you might find it beneficial getting some practical advice and hands-on experience from me on one of the courses that are allied to this book. Many people have benefitted from these courses, it also helps clarify what they have found and that the healing is working correctly.

Conclusion

To me, the work that I do has been a voyage of discovery, a voyage that seemingly doesn't have an end. I have tried to put across everything that I do to help you improve your life and the lives of those around you. Most of us are affected by geopathic stress, and clearing or healing these noxious energies can only help keep us in a more healthy condition.

I will frequently revisit (by intent) my clients' houses to carry out further healing work that might be necessary. Some files will remain on my desk long after contact has ceased as I will often be called upon (spiritually) to send some healing to a particular member of their family or to move on a spirit. I never know why the files stay; I have learned not to question this anymore.

The angelic realms are there to help, but because of universal law, they have to be asked. We all have free will and they will not interfere unless we desire them to. Don't ask, 'Can you help me improve my life?' as that it not directly asking for anything, it is simply a throw away comment. If you ask, 'Can you help me?' the answer will of course be yes, but yes to what? Frame the question carefully and ask it three times. It shows intent and that you are serious in your request. Don't be afraid to start with 'I want'.

Once healing is in your life you will never have a dull or boring moment again. I never know what is going to come my way from one minute to the next: the first telephone call of the morning could be regarding a troublesome ghost, the next about fighting cats, then a question about a health-related topic. I have been fortuitous in meeting people that have helped point me in the right direction – I never knew what Andy Roberts meant at the time but now I know he was right.

I would be very interested in getting feedback from you after you have worked through the various sections of the book. I have often said to people, 'If an ex-estate agent can carry out healing of this depth then so can many of the people on this planet.'

I would also be interested in hearing from any women who have read the book and carried out the healing on their own home. I have often found that if my female clients suffer from painful or elongated periods, a re-setting or shortening can occur after my work has been carried out. The pain can be lessened or in some cases disappear completely. My wife Allyson is a prime example of this: she has never been 'regular' through most of her adult life but can now predict, with almost pinpoint accuracy, the day her period will start and the exact day it will finish. I am not sure that her suggested title of *The Period Doctor* is one that I particularly relish, but it could be the title of my next book. Please do let me know of any changes that have occurred, as it could be very important to other women.

My email address is adrian@dowsingspirits.co.uk and my current telephone number is on my website www.dowsingspirits.co.uk.

I offer a range of courses from a basic beginner's dowsing workshop to the more complex and in-depth Healing your Home I and II. If you feel that some practical knowledge would help, please contact me for dates or see my website.

Recommended Reading Material

Many of these can be ordered from The British Society of Dowsers bookshop (www.britishdowsers.org)
Those marked with an * are now out of print, you will need to scour second hand bookshops or internet to find them.

Mythos Press:
Sun and the Serpent by Hamish Miller and Paul Broadhurst

Tom Graves series of books:
Needles of Stone Revisited
The Diviner's Handbook
The Dowser's Workbooks
The Disciplines of Dowsing by Tom Graves and Liz Poraj-Wilczynska
Elements of Pendulum Dowsing
Inventing Reality

General Dowsing Reading:
Dowsing: A Path to Enlightenment by Joey Korn
Dowsing One Man's Way by Jim Scott Elliot
Pendulum: The psi Connection by Francis Hitching
Earth Radiation by Kathe Bachler
Dowsing by Robert H. Leftwich *
Dowsing for Beginners by Richard Webster
Dowsing by Naomi Ozaniec *
Complete Guide to Dowsing (Water) by George Applegate
Earth Currents by Gustav Freiherr von Pohl *
Places of Power by Paul Devereux
Points of Cosmic Energy by Blanche Merz *
Ley Lines and Earth Energies by David Cowan and Chris Arnold
The Old Straight Track by Alfred Watkins
Spirals by Geoff Ward
Dowsing in the 21st Century by Elizabeth Brown
Powerpoints by Robin Heath
Ley Lines by Danny Sullivan
The Diving Hand by Christopher Bird
The Divining Rod by Sir William Barrett and Theodore Besterman

General Reading on Earth Energies and other esoteric matters
Silbury Dawning by John Cowie
Lines on the Landscape by Nigel Pennick and Paul Devereux
The Lost Magic of Christianity by Michael Poynder
The View Beyond (Francis Bacon) 978-1-905398-22-5
The Modern Antiquarian by Julian Cope
The Megalithic European by Julian Cope
Men Amongst Mankind by Brinsley Le Poer Trench *
The Biology of Belief by Bruce Lipton
The Creation of Health by C Norman Shealy and Caroline Myss
Lost Secrets of the Sacred Ark by Laurence Gardner
Stukeley Illustrated by Neil Mortimer

Other books that have helped my spiritual development:
The Shining Ones by Christian and Barbara Joy O'Brien
The Light in Britain by Grace Cooke *
The Ancient Secret of the Flower of Life I and II by Drunvalo Melchizedek
The 72 Names of God by Yehuda Berg
Cosmic Consciousness by Richard Maurice Bucke
The Tibetan Book of Living and Dying by Sogyal Rinpoche
Autobiography of a Spiritually Incorrect Mystic by Osho
Talking to Heaven by James Van Praagh
Celt, Druid and Culdee by Isabel Hill Elder *

Other books of interest:
The Powerwatch Handbook by Alasdair and Jean Philips
The Elphite by Michelle Gordon
The Earth Angel Training Academy by Michelle Gordon
The Doorway to PAM by Michelle Gordon

If you have enjoyed this book, have any questions or feedback, you can use the contact details below. Please do leave me a review on Amazon, I really would appreciate it.

Email: adrian@dowsingspirits.co.uk
Website: www.dowsingspirits.co.uk

My website gives up-to-date information and details on workshops and dowsing courses that I am running. They are held around the country and often close to ancient or sacred sites.

They include:

Introduction to Dowsing
Dowsing for Health I and II
Earth Energies I
Dowsing for Health and Healing I, II and III
Healing Your Home I and II
Healing with Sacred Symbols

The British Society of Dowsers
01684 576969
www.britishdowsers.org

Homeopath:
Janet Lewis
01689 890754

Independent Publishing Services were provided by Michelle Gordon:
The Amethyst Angel
theamethystangel@hotmail.co.uk
theamethystangel.com

Lightning Source UK Ltd.
Milton Keynes UK
UKHW020924191120
373678UK00005B/130